Mountain Biking
Michigan

Help Us Keep This Guide Up to Date

Every effort has been made by the authors and editors to make this guide as accurate and useful as possible. However, many things can change after a guide is published—trails are rerouted, regulations change, techniques evolve, facilities come under new management, etc.

We would love to hear from you concerning your experiences with this guide and how you feel it could be improved and kept up to date. While we may not be able to respond to all comments and suggestions, we'll take them to heart and we'll also make certain to share them with the authors. Please send your comments and suggestions to the following address:

The Globe Pequot Press
Reader Response/Editorial Department
P.O. Box 480
Guilford, CT 06437

Or you may e-mail us at:

editorial@globe-pequot.com

Thanks for your input, and happy travels!

Mountain Biking
Michigan

Erin Fanning and Keith Radwanski

FALCON®

GUILFORD, CONNECTICUT
HELENA, MONTANA

AN IMPRINT OF THE GLOBE PEQUOT PRESS

Contents

NORTHWESTERN MICHIGAN:

NORTHEASTERN MICHIGAN:

EASTERN UPPER PENINSULA:

WESTERN UPPER PENINSULA: ROCKY FORESTS AND RUGGED NORTH WOODS ... 206

In memory of my father, Stan Fanning;
his courageous and joyful presence still leads me on the trails.

Acknowledgments

Spanning two years of riding and researching, this book has been a collaborative effort—from the many fat-tire enthusiasts who let us pick their brains about local trails to the land management professionals and advocacy volunteers who took the time to review the rides. We want especially to thank Don Palmer, Dave Johnson, Randy McKenzie, Jay Neff, Mike Klein, Sam Raymond, Terry Hansen, Ron Stenfors, Marianne Kronk, Courtney Borgondy, Todd Scott, Terry Kinzel, Dave Tramski, Toby Rhue, Steve Krantz, Walt Arnold, Nick Nowland, Dennis Nezich, Sandy Richardson, Jim McMillan, Lynn Yoder, Larry Kinney, Dean Sandell, Michael Vigrass, Chris Davis, Paul Gaberdiel, Joyce Angel-Ling, Norm Roller, Anne Okonek, Steve Brown, Kelly Challis, Cindy Olson, Jerry Walters, Edward Hunt, Bill Kosmider, Roland Johnson, Brent Walk, John Haffenden, William Brondyke, Don Mikel, Tony Stachowiak, Tim Collins, Paul Noyes, Fred Tyszka, and Greg Hokans for their advice, insight, and time spent looking over the rides. We also want to thank Bruce Kantor and Kurt and Sophia Radwanski for their companionship on the trails. Finally, Michigan's extensive mountain biking trail systems would not exist without the dedicated volunteers of the Michigan Mountain Biking Association and other advocacy groups across the state. Anyone who steers onto a Michigan trail owes these hardworking individuals a debt of gratitude.

Preface

HOW A TIRE COMPANY INSPIRED A MOUNTAIN BIKING GUIDEBOOK

The much-loved 1950s Firestone bicycle sits alone in the garage. Thick with five coats of paint, it is the bicycle on which Keith and his four brothers and sisters learned how to cycle. Each child picked a color for the bike—a single speed with coaster brakes—when it was his or her turn to ride it, and Keith's father diligently applied the paint. Keith's colors were blue and yellow, the University of Michigan's colors, an obvious choice for an impressionable five-year-old.

Teetering down the street, he followed in his older brothers' and sisters' tracks. He quickly graduated to a three-speed Speed King with a gear selector on the middle bar. When he wasn't tearing around the neighborhood with his buddies, the three-speed became his paper route transportation. A brief flirtation with a ten-speed left him dissatisfied because of jumping gears. He returned to the three-speed concept with the Texas Ranger. Fitted with a gasoline motor, called Chicken Power, the bike allowed him to cruise up to 15 mph.

Unlike Keith, I came to cycling relatively late in life. Sure, I had the requisite ten-speed that every kid owns, but I secretly yearned for a single-speed girl's bike with a banana seat. Yes, I was pretty uncool. Besides, I never figured out how to use all those gears, and my bike sat in the garage more than it was used.

It wasn't until my mid-twenties that I discovered the pleasure of coasting along the countryside or gearing down to climb a steep hill. Joining a bicycle club on a whim one Saturday, I was the only rider on an inexpensive mountain bike. After cranking out 20 miles, the other riders encouraged me to move on to a fast, lightweight road bike. That week I bought a sleek Italian racing model and began what I hoped would be a lifetime of cycling.

Keith introduced me to mountain biking, first on the craggy mountains of Washington State then later in his native Michigan. I was hooked, intrigued with the skinny trails and swooping downhills. With so many interests in common, Keith and I often talked about writing a book. It wasn't until we quit our jobs to travel full-time in our recreational vehicle that the dream became a reality. Combining my writing background with Keith's knowledge of Michigan's trails, we began riding the hundreds of miles that would become this book.

The mountain bikes we ride today are a vast improvement over Keith's Firestone or even my mid-eighties mountain bike. Pumped up with shock absorbers and quick shifting, they are a gearhead's delight. But mountain biking isn't about a fancy bike with a cool name; it is climbing to the top of the Gogebic Ridge and gazing out over the Ottawa National Forest as the wind ripples across red and orange leaves on a cool fall day.

Our hope is that the trails in this guidebook will give you the feeling of excitement that your first "Speed King" gave you as a kid, regardless of your cycling level. We want to share with you the magic of discovering a great ride for the first time—so dust off your mountain bike, select a ride, and get ready for a mountain biking adventure.

Welcome to Michigan

Our friend Bruce Kantor often says, "If Michigan had mountains it would be the perfect state." He might be right. Michigan offers 6.5 million acres of state and national forestland, 11,000 inland lakes, and more than 150 waterfalls and is the only state with shoreline on four of the five Great Lakes.

But it is the obvious lack of big vertical relief that made our western friends laugh when they found out Keith and I were writing a mountain biking guide to Michigan. "How can you write a mountain biking guide for a state without mountains?" they asked. My response was simple, "You have obviously never mountain biked in Michigan." What Michigan lacks in vertical relief it easily makes up for in constantly rolling hills and steep descents.

Mountain snobs need only climb to the top of Mount Lookout on the Keweenaw Peninsula and gaze out at Isle Royale National Park, 50 miles away in Lake Superior, to realize that Michigan offers a unique cycling experience. It is an experience that includes groomed singletrack trails designed specifically for mountain bikers, the third most miles of rail-trails in the United States, and access to portions of the magnificent North Country Trail, a designated National Scenic Trail.

In fact, the sheer number of possible trails to ride while researching the guidebook overwhelmed us. Early on, Keith made a list of about 250 possible trails, not including 93 rail-trails and miles and miles of ORV trails. After riding more than 100 trails and 2,000 miles, we selected the sixty-seven rides for this book. You will find something for everyone—from the seasoned veteran looking for singletrack to the vacationer looking for a few hours of diversion. Splitting the state into six regions, we discovered that there is outstanding riding throughout Michigan.

The western Upper Peninsula offers the most rugged mountain biking, with underused routes like the Gogebic Ridge Trail hosting challenging singletrack looking out over miles of dense forest. The eastern Upper Peninsula boasts one of the most breathtaking rides in Michigan on Grand Island, where sandstone cliffs provide endless views of vast Lake Superior.

Narrow singletrack twisting through hardwoods and past inland lakes can be found on the North Country Trail in northwestern Michigan. If you prefer superbly groomed singletrack, look no farther that the VASA Singletrack Trail in Traverse City. Views of Lake Huron and about 35 miles of trails are the specialty at the Black Mountain Recreation Area in northeastern Michigan, also home to the epic 80-mile High Country Pathway.

Traveling downstate to southeastern and southwestern Michigan, cyclists find miles of singletrack developed specifically for mountain bikers. The famous Potawatomi Trail attracts day riders from as far away as Toledo. The Fort Custer and Highland Recreation Areas twist and turn, creating a web of singletracks.

While riding, keep in mind that Michigan is not just a series of dirt trails but a state with a rich geologic history and an abundance of wildlife to enjoy. The following information will give you something to think about during your explorations. The best way to experience Michigan's outstanding terrain is to slow down and not let the great outdoors become a green blur as you whiz by.

MADE IN MICHIGAN

Thank the Great Ice Age for Michigan's various landforms—from the rocky outcroppings in the western Upper Peninsula to the gently rolling hills in the southeast. Retreating from Michigan about 9,500 to 15,000 years ago, the glaciers left in their path the Great Lakes and the terrain that mountain bikers enjoy today. The western Upper Peninsula boasts the highest altitudes with mountains such as Brockway Mountain on the Keweenaw Peninsula, where you can drive up a twisting road for views of Lake Superior, and the Huron Mountains near Marquette, home to the private Huron Mountain Club.

The Great Lakes, the greatest gift of the glaciers, surround Michigan like a moat. Offering 3,251 miles of Great Lakes shoreline, 36,350 miles of streams, and about 35,000 mapped lakes and ponds, it is not surprising that Michigan is known as the "Water Wonderland." Immense sand dunes rise from the lakes, and, although beautiful to view and challenging to hike on, sand is often an unwelcome companion on many Michigan mountain bike rides.

With so much water, Michigan is home to 166 different fish species, such as perch, bass, pike, crappie, and trout. Hunting rivals fishing for popularity, and cyclists need to be extremely careful during the November deer-hunting season. It is best to avoid the woods altogether during that time; at the very least, wear bright-orange clothing if you choose to cycle. Michigan is also a bird-watcher's delight, claiming 233 indigenous species and hosting many more during the spring and fall migrations.

With so many birds, it should be no surprise that trees dominate much of Michigan. At one time there were so many trees that clearings were found only in the southwestern prairies of the Lower Peninsula. Although logging and fires destroyed many of the early forests, more than half of Michigan is still covered with trees. The largest state forest system in the United States is found in Michigan and stretches 3.9 million acres. The abundance of leaves and branches poses a unique problem to Michigan cyclists—from sticks jamming derailleurs to leaves coating chains.

NORTH COUNTRY NATIONAL SCENIC TRAIL

Eventually to stretch about 4,200 miles, the North Country Trail (NCT), officially established in 1980, unfolds like a sandy ribbon from the plains of North Dakota to New York's Adirondack Mountains. Michigan's contribution to the NCT will be about 1,100 miles, more than any other state. Beginning in Ironwood, the trail meanders through the Upper Peninsula, touching Lake Superior in the Porcupine Mountains Wilderness State Park and Pictured Rocks National Lakeshore. Dipping into the Lower Peninsula, it crosses the Mackinac Bridge then follows Lake Michigan to Petoskey, where it heads inward through the Pere Marquette State Forest and onto the Huron-Manistee National Forest. As the NCT heads south of the Croton Dam and into Ohio, the route becomes mostly farmland and passes through a large percentage of private land.

As so often happens when mountain bikers use historically "hiker-only" trail systems, a dust cloud of controversy follows in the fat tire's wake. Whether mountain bikes are allowed on different portions of the NCT is up to the local governing body of that particular segment, such as the Department of Natural Resources (DNR) or the National Forest Service. The Huron-Manistee National Forest has opened segments of its NCT portions to mountain bikes. The DNR also allows mountain bikes on most of the NCT portions that fall within its lands—for example, in the Pere Marquette State Forest but not in the Wilderness State Park. At this time, however, no portion of the NCT within the boundaries of the Ottawa or Hiawatha National Forests is officially open to mountain bikes.

This does not necessarily mean that the Forest Service officials who work for those governing bodies are unfriendly to mountain bikers. It is simply that when the forest plans were written, mountain bikes were a new phenomenon and so were not included. A ranger with the Mackinaw State Forest said that he welcomes mountain bikes and believes that some of the trail systems that he manages would not be used at all if not for mountain bikers.

To keep mountain bikes legal on the NCT, it is crucial that mountain bikers follow all mountain biking etiquette (see Rules of the Trail). We have included what we consider to be some of the best portions of the NCT for mountain bikes, possibly the best mountain biking in Michigan. Each NCT segment featured in this book is listed under the geographical region in which it is located. Always check with the appropriate official before exploring other portions of the NCT. Most of the trail is not currently open to bikers—if in doubt, ask before you ride.

RAILS-TO-TRAILS: LINKING MICHIGAN'S COMMUNITIES

Michigan is blessed with an abundance of rail-trails and ranks third in the nation with 1,122 rail-trail miles, including ninety-three actual trails and more than thirty-eight projects on the board. The Michigan Rails-to-Trails Conservancy (RTC) Field Office (see Appendix C) opened its doors in 1988, and the Discover Michigan Trail, a statewide system of interconnected trails, is the office's goal.

The Michigan RTC provides local groups with assistance; educates the public about rail-trails; works closely with state and local government in planning trails; and sponsors the Michigander, a multiday fund-raising bike tour. Local groups such as the Top of Michigan Trails Council, Traverse Area Recreation and Transportation Trails, and friends groups throughout the state have joined the RTC in trail development, establishing Michigan as a leader in the rails-to-trails movement.

It would be impossible to list all Michigan's rails-to-trails and mountain biking trails in one book. Rail-trails are mentioned only if part of another ride. Contact the Michigan RTC for the most current rail-trails information.

MICHIGAN MOUNTAIN BIKING ASSOCIATION

Founded in 1990, the nonprofit Michigan Mountain Biking Association (MMBA) promotes all facets of mountain biking in Michigan, including trail etiquette, education, and advocacy. Working with a variety of groups, from land managers and park personnel to national mountain biking organizations, the MMBA has been responsible for building and maintaining many of the mountain biking trails in Michigan, particularly in the Lower Peninsula.

The MMBA's leadership has been innovative in implementing mountain biking programs such as the Mountain Kids, which helps disadvantaged children learn about the pleasures of mountain biking. The more than 1,300 members are spread out over ten chapters in the Lower Peninsula, with contacts in the Upper Peninsula. Annually they log well over 5,000 hours of volunteer work with activities, updates, and volunteer opportunities published four times per year in the *Bent Rim Bugle*. The MMBA also maintains an excellent Web site and list-serv that has updates on news and activities across the state. The MMBA is the best avenue for mountain bikers to get involved in the planning, support, and maintenance of Michigan's trail systems.

COMMERCIAL FOREST ACT

The Commercial Forest Act (CFA), also known as the Commercial Forest Reserve Act (CFR), gives property owners a cut in taxes in exchange for allowing public recreation on private land, typically logging and mining properties. The Upper Peninsula has more than 2.2 million acres of CFA land; the Lower Peninsula has about 480,000 acres. The law applies specifically to foot travel for hunting and fishing, but most landowners have graciously allowed mountain bikers to use their land.

Cyclists should remember, however, that they are on private land and tread lightly, staying on existing trails and roads and respecting NO TRESPASSING signs. Bikers should also bear in mind that CFA land is still commercial property; a secluded doubletrack one year could become part of a logging operation or be sold the next year. Cyclists can make sure that the land they wish to explore is actually CFA land by purchasing a booklet from the Michigan Department of Natural Resources (see Appendix B) that lists all CFA land. Permission for the rides listed in this book that veer onto CFA land, particularly in the Keweenaw Peninsula, were verified with the landowners during the summer of 2001.

Rules of the Trail

We heard them before we saw them—a group of about five mountain bikers talking loudly as they flew down the hillside, completely oblivious to all other users. Keith yelled a warning about the horseback riders we had seen earlier, but they did not acknowledge us. Later we spoke with the horseback riders and were told about the boorish bikers. We apologized for the cyclists, realizing that mountain bikers that treat others and the trails with such little respect might eventually get all mountain bikers banned from trails. In fact, thousands of miles of dirt trails already have been closed due to the irresponsible habits of a few riders.

Luckily, the scenario described above is rare. It is important, however, that all mountain bikers realize that when they don their helmets and sit on their fat-tire machines they become ambassadors for mountain biking. Here are some basic guidelines adapted from the International Mountain Bicycling Association Rules of the Trail. These guidelines can help prevent damage to land, water, plants, and wildlife; maintain trail access; and avoid conflicts with other backcountry visitors and trail users.

1. **Only ride on trails that are open.** Don't trespass on private land, and be sure to obtain any necessary permits. If you're not sure if a trail is closed or if you need a permit, don't hesitate to ask.

2. **Keep your bicycle under control.** Watch the condition of the trail at all times, and follow the appropriate speed regulations and recommendations.

3. **Yield to others on the trail.** Make your approach well known in advance, either with a friendly greeting or a bell. When approaching a corner, junction, or blind spot, expect to encounter other trail users. When passing others, show your respect by slowing to a walking space.

4. **Don't startle animals.** Animals may be easily scared by sudden approaches or loud noises. For your safety—and the safety of others in the area as well as the animals themselves—give all wildlife a wide berth. When encountering horses, defer to the horseback riders' directions.

5. **Zero impact.** Be aware of the impact you're making on the trail beneath you. You should not ride under conditions where you will leave evidence of your passing, such as on certain soils after rain. If a ride features optional side hikes into wilderness areas, be a zero-impact hiker, too. Whether you're on bike or on foot, stick to existing trails, leave gates as you found them, and carry out everything you brought in.

6. **Be prepared.** Know the equipment you are using, the area where you'll be riding, and your cycling abilities and limitations. Avoid unnecessary breakdowns by keeping your equipment in good shape. When you head out, bring spare parts and supplies for weather changes. Be sure to wear appropriate safety gear, including a helmet, and learn how to be self-sufficient.

BIKE MAINTENANCE:

In addition to following good trail etiquette, stay safe by keeping your bike in prime condition. Have regular bike checkups. Also carry the following items with you on your rides:

- A helmet. Always wear one; going without isn't worth the risk.
- Food and water
- Patch kit, extra tube, tire irons, and a hand pump
- Allen wrenches
- Chain breaker
- Chain lube

Consider carrying the following maintenance and safety items either with you or in your vehicle:

- Spokes
- Rags
- Extra chain
- Freewheel remover
- Brake and derailleur cables
- Screwdrivers
- Extra chain
- Crescent wrench
- Rain gear
- First-aid kit
- Compass
- Lighter or matches
- Space blanket

How to Use This Guide

You will find sixty-seven rides in this guidebook, with something for every level of rider. Most of the rides are loops, sometimes returning on dirt or paved roads. If you are a singletrack junkie or want to avoid roads altogether, it is usually possible to make a ride an out-and-back jaunt or arrange a car shuttle.

The arrangement of the book is self-explanatory, but it is a good idea to review the following format explanations before you begin riding, particularly the aerobic, difficulty, and hill ratings. Each ride is arranged in an "at-a-glance" format with the following information:

Number and name of the ride: Rides are cross-referenced by number throughout the book. The ride name reflects the name of the trail. Where more than one name exists, we've chosen the one that best reflects the nature of the trail.

Location: The general whereabouts of the ride—distance and direction from the closest city or town.

Distance: The total length of the ride and whether it is a loop or an out-and-back ride.

Time: An estimate of how long it takes to complete the ride. The time listed is the actual riding time and does not include rest stops. Strong, skilled riders may be able to do a given ride in less time, while other riders may take considerably longer. Also bear in mind that severe weather, changes in trail conditions, or mechanical problems may prolong a ride.

Tread: The type of road or trail: singletrack, wide ski trails, doubletrack, dirt road, and paved road.

Aerobic level: The level of physical effort required to complete The Ride—easy, moderate, or strenuous. This is how we define the ratings:

Easy: Flat or gently rolling terrain; no steeps or prolonged climbs.

Moderate: Some hills. Climbs may be short and fairly steep or long and gradual.

Strenuous: Frequent or prolonged climbs steep enough to require riding in the lowest gear; requires a high level of aerobic fitness, power, and endurance. Less-fit riders may need to walk.

These ratings are judgment calls, so a "moderate" ride might be an "easy" ride for one person or the opposite for someone else. Always remember that walking your bike is perfectly acceptable. Do not hurt yourself in the name of pride; however, do expect to get frothy with sweat and short of breath at times. As your fitness level increases, so will your fun. Always check with your doctor if you are unsure of your aerobic level.

Technical difficulty: The level of bike-handling skills needed to successfully complete a ride, enjoy yourself, and stay in one piece. The ratings are on a scale of 1 to 5 (plus or minus symbols cover the gray areas), with 1 being the easiest and 5 being the most difficult. A ride covering a wide variety of skills receives more than one rating; for example, 1+ to 3. Remember that walking is acceptable and preferable to getting into an accident.

Level 1: Basic bike riding skills needed. The tread is smooth and without obstacles, ruts, or steeps.

Level 2: Mostly smooth tread; wide, well-groomed singletrack or road/doubletrack with minor ruts or loose gravel or sand.

Level 3: Irregular tread with some rough sections; singletrack or doubletrack with obvious route choices and some steep sections. Occasional obstacles may include small roots, rocks, water bars, ruts, loose gravel or sand, and sharp turns or broad, open switchbacks.

Level 4: Rough tread with few smooth places; singletrack or rough doubletrack with limited route choices and steep sections, some with obstacles. Obstacles are numerous and varied, including rocks, roots, branches, ruts, sidehills, narrow tread, loose gravel or sand, and switchbacks.

Level 5: Continuously broken, rocky, root-infested, or trenched tread; singletrack and severe changes in gradient. Some slopes are so steep that wheels lift off ground. Obstacles are nearly continuous and may include boulders, logs, water, large holes, deep ruts, ledges, piles of loose gravel, steep sidehills, encroaching trees, and tight switchbacks.

Hill factor: Michigan does not have the extreme elevation gain of more mountainous states, but steep hills are common. The following ratings are included to let riders know the types of hills to expect on the majority of each ride:

Flat: Elevation gain is negligible.

Rolling: Rolling hills with gains of approximately 10 to 30 feet.

Hilly: Constant ups and downs, gaining 30 to 100 feet at a time.

Highlands: Extended relief with sustained climbs of 100 feet or more.

Highlights: Special features or qualities that make a ride worthwhile.

Land status: A list of managing agencies or landowners. Most of the rides in this book are on national forest land or state land, but some rides cross private land and Commercial Forest Act land. The status of a ride can change quickly, so please respect NO TRESPASSING signs if you encounter them.

Maps: A list of available maps, including U.S. Geological Survey (USGS) maps, that show each ride's area. These maps may be used for a more detailed view, though they may not show the ride's routes. In some cases no maps are available for specific rides.

Access: How to find the trailhead or start of the ride.

Notes on the trail: These paragraphs detail the qualities that make a ride unique. You'll find specifics on things you'll see along the way and a general description of natural surroundings. This section also notes if there is an entrance fee. Almost all Michigan state parks and recreation areas charge $4.00 for a vehicle daily permit (or $20.00 for an annual permit). All fees were accurate at the time of publication, but cyclists should call ahead for the most up-to-date information.

The ride: This section provides a mile-by-mile explanation of the ride, emphasizing key points, where to turn, and how not to get lost. The mileage for each ride was taken using a cyclocomputer, but not all bike computers are calibrated the same; use the mileage as a yardstick.

A map accompanies each ride. The maps are clean, easy-to-use navigational tools. Closed trails are not usually shown but may be listed in the ride description. Painstaking effort has been taken to ensure accuracy.

One last thing to keep in mind is that trails can change quickly. Although the information here was accurate when written, there is no guarantee that there won't be a new obstacle or trail closure tomorrow. Enough said. Now get out there and ride!

Legend

Interstate		Interstate
U.S. Highways		U.S. Highways
Miscellaneous Roads (Paved)		State Roads
Gravel Road		Forest Roads

Interstate   (5) (55) (555)

U.S. Highways   (5) (55) (555)

State Roads   (5) (55) (555)

Forest Roads   [41] [416] [4165]

Cities

Capitol	Large	Small
✪	◉	○

Roads column (left):

Interstate

U.S. Highways

Miscellaneous Roads (Paved)

Gravel Road

Unimproved Roads

Powerlines

Railroad Tracks

State Boundary

Wilderness Boundary

River/Creek

Lakes/Large Rivers

Oceans/Large Bodies of Water

Cliffs

Islands

Swamps

Route Legend

	Paved Road
	Maintained Dirt
= = = =	Unmaintained Dirt
– – –	Singletrack Trail
	Selected Route

Symbols column (right):

Airport ✈

Bridge ≍

Campground ▲

Golf Course ⚑

Hospital 🄷

Mountain / Peak ▲

Parking 🅿

Trailhead T

Picnic 🐂

Ranger Station ▶

Skiing ⚠

Structures ■

Waterfalls //

Gate —

Scale/Orientation

0   Mile   1

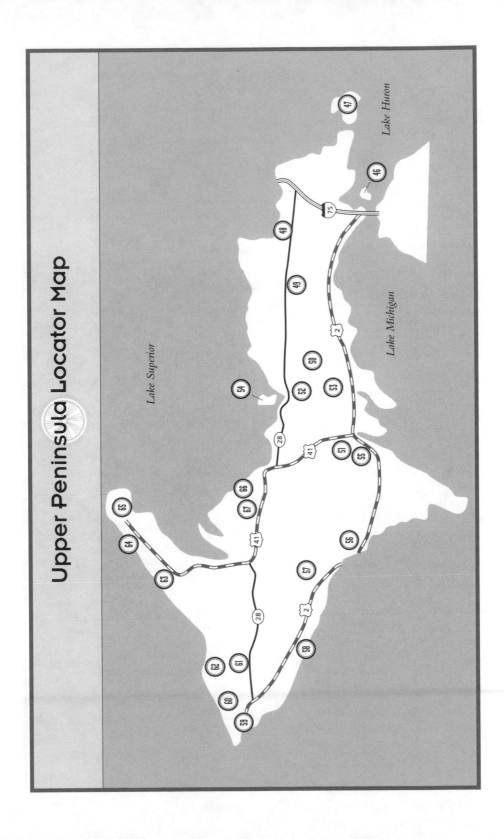

Upper Peninsula Locator Map

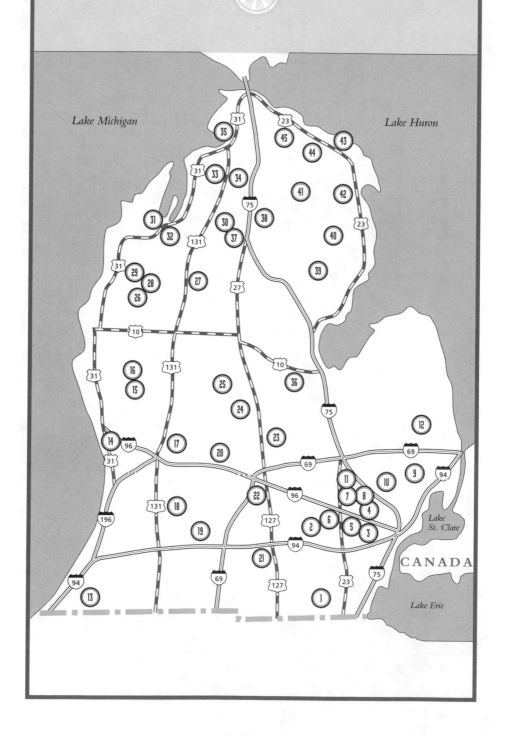

Lower Peninsula Locator Map

Lake Michigan

Lake Huron

Lake St. Clare

CANADA

Lake Erie

Southeastern Michigan:
Outstanding Recreation Areas Near Urban Sprawl

Detroit's industrial arm reaches far into southeastern Michigan, yet a factory's smokestack still seems distant when you're cruising along the forest-lined trails this area offers. About half Michigan's population lives in the greater Detroit area. Although the area's famous for automobiles, Motown, and professional athletics, few persons realize that the state and county parks in southeastern Michigan are a mountain biker's delight.

Stretching west to Jackson, north through the capital of Lansing, and east to the shores of Lake Huron, southeastern Michigan is a mixture of the urban and the rural. Once called the "earthly paradise of North America" by Detroit's founder, Antoine de la Mothe, sieur de Cadillac, the Detroit area still retains charm—from loyal Tiger baseball fans to lush, green forests.

Unfortunately, congestion is a problem on greater-Detroit trails. Heavy use has brought controversy, sometimes heated, among different trail-use groups. Luckily for mountain bikers, the Michigan Mountain Bike Association (MMBA) is particularly strong in southeastern Michigan. Through the MMBA's thoughtful advocacy, existing trails have remained open to mountain bikers, and more bike-specific trails are in the planning stages.

Despite the crowds, most of the southeastern trails will remind cyclists of the paradise to which Cadillac was referring. The rides roll along green hills, with glimpses of blue lakes tempting cyclists to jump in after a hot, sweaty ride. Retreating glaciers created a horseshoe-shaped area known as the Saginaw Lobe during the last Ice Age. Running from Flint down to the Indiana border then back up to Grand Rapids, this area is brimming with boaters, hikers, bikers, and campers taking advantage of the glacier-carved hills and lakes.

Although most of the trails stay open year-round, fall is an ideal time to explore southeastern Michigan; the temperature drops and the leaves start to show their orange and red tree bouquets. A typical year finds fall colors peaking by the middle of October. Stopping at a local cider mill for doughnuts and apple cider is the perfect conclusion to an autumn day on the trails, but don't disregard the winter months. Snow does not typically have much lasting power in southeastern Michigan, and exploring an uncrowded, frozen trail can be a delight.

Heritage Park Loop

Location:	2 miles north of Adrian.
Distance:	9.4-mile loop.
Time:	1–2 hours.
Tread:	2 miles of dirt road, 0.2 mile of doubletrack, 7.2 miles of singletrack.
Aerobic level:	Moderately easy.
Technical difficulty:	1–2 +; flat, wide trail to twisted, off-cambered singletrack.
Hill factor:	Flat to rolling.
Highlights:	Singletrack oasis among flat farm country.
Land status:	Heritage Park, City of Adrian.
Maps:	USGS Adrian; maps available from Adrian Locksmith and Cyclery in Adrian (see Appendix A).
Access:	From the intersection of Maple Street and Main Street/Michigan 52 in Adrian, drive north for 2.2 miles on Main Street/M–52. Take a hard right (south) after the Mobil Station onto North Adrian Drive and follow the signs to Heritage Park. Turn east into Heritage Park and continue to the parking area to the north, near the Center for the Aging.

Notes on the trail: Located in the extreme southeastern corner of Michigan, Heritage Park combines cornfields with conifers. The well-designed trail system—an eclectic mix of flat, wide trail, gravel road, and singletrack—has been nurtured by local riders. Hosting spring and fall mountain bike races, the singletrack portions of the route offer off-cambered riding on tree-lined knolls and twisting, tight turns through sometimes low-lying, muddy terrain. The route follows the most common flow of traffic, marked by white arrows on small black signs. Occasionally the trail is two-way, so be alert for cyclists cruising toward you and for hikers on the trails near Stubnitz Environmental Center. A few sections of singletrack are unmarked but fairly easy to follow. For a detailed introduction to Heritage Park, join local riders on Wednesday nights at 6:00 P.M.

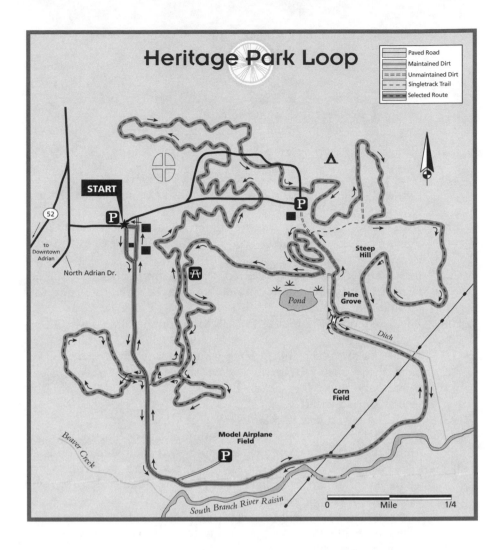

The Ride

0.0   Cycle back onto the access road and turn right at the T intersection. Head south on the broken gravel road, around the maintenance buildings and historic Adrian Town Hall.

0.35   Turn right onto a singletrack and follow the white arrow. Twist through the woods and an open field. Turn right at all intersections. Loop back to the road and the beginning of the singletrack.

0.7   Back at the road, turn right and continue cycling on the road through an open area. Stay with the road as it curves left.

1.0   Road splits; stay right and follow the river. Road on the left ends at model airplane field.

1.3 Road ends; continue cycling on the grass. Follow the edge of the cornfield and pass under the power lines twice.

2.1 Turn right into the woods and cross over a drainage ditch on a small wooden bridge. After a small hill, reach an intersection in a clearing near a pine tree grove, and turn left. Follow the edge of the field. Return route is on the right.

2.2 Stay right at another trail intersection, then almost immediately turn left onto a doubletrack heading uphill. The singletrack straight ahead is the return route.

2.4 Near the top of the hill and just before reaching the Stubnitz Environmental Center, turn left onto a singletrack and get ready for a twisting downhill.

2.8 Turn right at the bottom of the singletrack and follow the doubletrack. Soon the trail narrows into the Eagle Heritage Trail, prone to mud.

3.2 Reach a picnic shelter at the top of a hill, and continue straight. Dive back into the woods on a narrow singletrack. Twist and roll through the woods.

3.8 The trail loops back on itself. Look for a trail heading downhill on the left.

3.9 Turn right at a steep hill. A left turn dumps out to a road.

4.3 Back at the picnic shelter, cycle across the field to the left of the shelter and look for the singletrack heading straight into the woods and downhill.

4.9 Cross the paved access road to the Stubnitz Center.

5.3 Cross the paved exit road for the Stubnitz Center. Singletrack continues to twist in and out of the woods near the ball diamonds.

6.2 Cross back over the Stubnitz exit road. Soon the trail dumps out again onto the road. Stay right, and almost immediately turn right back onto the singletrack.

6.4 Cross the road for the last time at the edge of the parking lot. The trail dumps out to a group camping area; ride along the edge of the field. Turn right onto a wide trail and follow it through the woods to the east end of the open field.

6.9 Turn right onto a singletrack and back into the woods. Follow the arrow and beaten path.

7.4 Turn left and head down a fast descent to the open, grassy area and pine grove. Turn left, following the edge of the field, and ride around the pine trees.

7.6 Turn left; retrace your tracks down the hill and over the drainage ditch bridge. Turn left and cycle around the cornfield. Follow the broken gravel road back to the parking lot.

9.4 Arrive back at parking area.

Potawatomi Trail

Location:	15 miles north of Ann Arbor.
Distance:	17.5-mile loop.
Time:	2–4 hours.
Tread:	17.5 miles of singletrack.
Aerobic level:	Moderately strenuous.
Difficulty rating:	3; watch for rocks, roots, sandy hills, and drop-offs.
Hill factor:	Rolling to hilly.
Highlights:	Long cruiser is Michigan's most famous mountain bike trail.
Land status:	Pinckney Recreation Area.
Maps:	USGS Pinckney; maps available at park entrance.
Access:	From Ann Arbor drive north 6 miles on U.S. 23. Turn west onto North Territorial Road and go 10 miles to Dexter–Townhall Road. Turn north and continue for 1.2 miles to the Silver Hill park entrance. Turn left into the parking lot.

Notes on the trail: The Potawatomi Trail is the granddaddy of mountain biking trails in southeastern Michigan—and for a senior citizen, it stills packs a wallop. Sandy hills with exposed roots defeat all but the strongest of riders. Cruising past a chain of lakes, the trail crosses a narrow section of Halfmoon Lake on a quaint wooden bridge; motorized and self-propelled boats float along as cyclists dash down or grind up steep hills. The trail, marked with wooden numbered signs, is incredibly popular and suffers from overuse; however, sand traps, loose gravel, and rocks keep speed demons in check. Two shorter loops, Silver Lake and Crooked Lake, connect to Potawatomi and are easy-to-follow alternatives. The recreation area charges a $4.00-per-vehicle entrance fee.

The Ride

0.0 Ride back toward the entrance road at the south end of the lot. A large sign with a map marks the trailhead. The ride begins with a

Potawatomi Trail

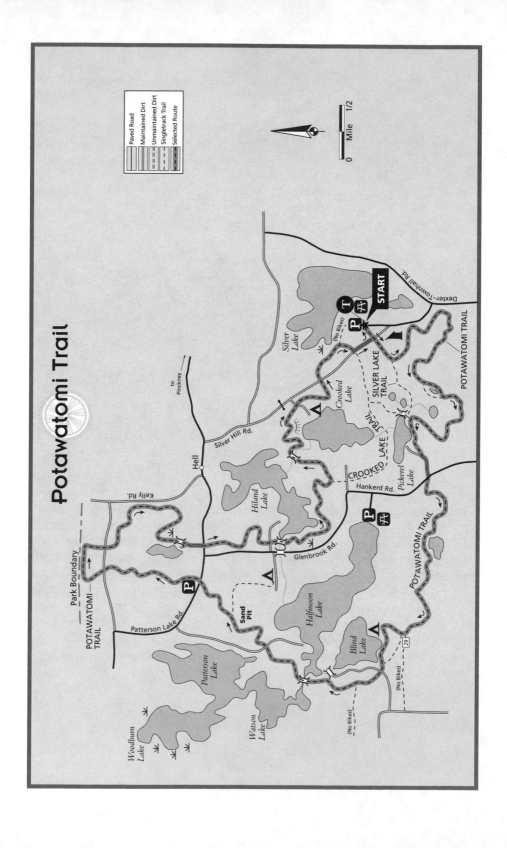

steep ascent to Silver Hill Road. Soon cross Silver Hill Road for another grind.

0.5   Reach an intersection; turn left and follow the well-worn trail. Continue straight for the shorter Silver Lake and Crooked Lake Loops.

1.0   Cycle around a gate and climb two short, steep hills.

4.1   Stay left as the trail splits. Cycle around the south end of Pickerel Lake. The trail merges with the Pickerel Lake access road; continue on Pickerel Road to Hankerd Road.

4.9   Turn right onto paved Hankerd Road. Soon turn left back onto the trail. Two miles of steep, slippery hills lie ahead.

6.8   Reach the bottom of a steep descent and turn right at Post 29.

7.1   Cycle past an outhouse on the left and Blind Lake backpacker campground on the right.

7.4   Cross a dirt road and climb a short hill to an overlook.

7.8   A hiking trail is on the left; continue straight.

8.2   Cross a narrow waterway between Halfmoon and Watson Lakes on a wooden bridge.

8.7   Cross a dirt road.

9.3   Stay to the edge of the trail to avoid a sand pit.

9.4   Stay left to continue on the trail. The trail on the right leads to Halfmoon Lake Campground.

9.8   Cross Patterson Lake Road.

10.6   Cross Doyle Road.

10.9   Turn right and parallel the University of Michigan property fence-line.

11.3   Loop back and cross Doyle Road.

12.6   Merge with Gosling Lake access road and continue to Patterson Lake Road.

13.0   Cross Patterson Lake Road.

13.9   Cross Highland Lake access road. The trail meanders and crosses two wooden bridges.

14.8   Turn left at an intersection with Crooked Lake Trail.

15.4   Cross a stream. Begin a long, steep climb up several switchbacks.

15.7   Reach the top and enjoy the scenic overlook of Crooked Lake and the countryside.

16.1   Cross Silver Hill Road.

16.6   Stay left at a trail intersection and cycle back to Silver Hill Road. The trail straight ahead continues to Silver Lake Beach and is for foot traffic only.

16.9   Turn left onto Silver Hill Road.

17.3   Road ends; turn left into the parking lot.

17.5   Ride ends.

Maybury Singletrack

Location:	Northville.
Distance:	5.6-mile loop.
Time:	30 minutes–1 hour.
Tread:	4.1 miles of singletrack, 1.5 miles of paved path.
Aerobic level:	Moderately easy.
Technical difficulty:	2.
Hill factor:	Rolling.
Highlights:	Short cruiser that leaves you wanting more.
Land status:	Maybury State Park.
Maps:	USGS Northville; maps available at park entrance.
Access:	From the intersection of Interstate 96 and Beck Road (exit 160), drive 3.9 miles south on Beck Road. Turn west onto Eight Mile Road and continue another 0.9 mile to the park entrance on the south side of the road. Continue about 0.7 mile to the farthest parking lot.

Notes on the trail: Maybury State Park has the honor of being the closest singletrack trail to the western Detroit suburbs. This honor is good and bad. The good news is that the small trail system is well maintained by the Michigan Mountain Biking Association. Constantly rolling, the buffed singletrack is a fast cruiser with a few technical, twisting sections. The bad news is that its proximity to a large population center has resulted in an overused, eroded trail with roots and rutted areas. Because of the heavy use, the trail is occasionally rerouted, and it is closed from December 15 through April 15. Luckily, the underused Novi North Park (Ride 4) is nearby, giving riders more trails to explore. Like all Michigan state parks, there is a $4.00-per-vehicle entrance fee.

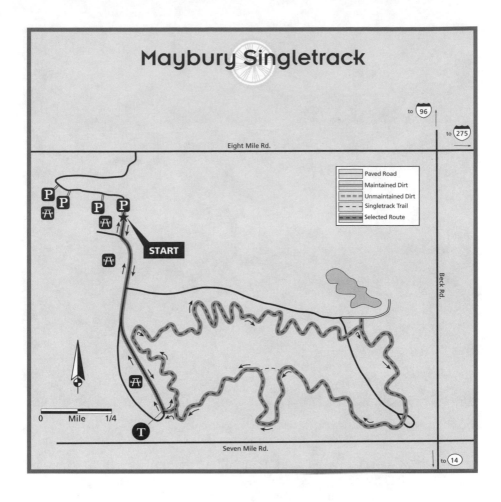

The Ride

0.0 Jump on the paved path and follow the signs to the mountain bike trail.

0.75 Arrive at the mountain bike trailhead on the left and cruise down a short hill. Turn left at the bottom of the hill; the next section is the most technical of the ride.

Kurt Radwanski cruises down the Maybury Singletrack.

2.95 Cross over a paved road. Soon follow the trail as it turns right and twists along a gentle downhill.

3.45 Cross over a paved cul-de-sac.

4.15 The trail splits; turn left to continue on the full loop. A right turn cuts the ride short.

4.85 Rcach the end of the loop. Gear up for another loop, or turn left and retrace your tracks back to the parking area on the paved path.

5.6 Arrive back at the parking area.

Novi North Park (Tree Farm)

Location:	0.5 mile from intersection of Novi and Old Novi Roads.
Distance:	6.7-mile loop.
Time:	45 minutes–1 hour.
Tread:	6.7 miles of singletrack and wide trail.
Aerobic level:	Moderately easy.
Technical difficulty:	2.
Hill factor:	Flat to rolling.
Highlights:	Urban-renewal trail rolls past old orchards and Christmas trees.
Land status:	City of Novi.
Map:	USGS Northville.
Access:	From the intersection of Interstate 96 and Novi Road in Novi, drive north on Novi Road for 1 mile. Turn north onto Old Novi Road and continue for 0.5 mile. Turn west onto South Lake Drive for 0.4 mile. Turn south into the Lakeshore Park entrance and continue until the road ends. Park here.

Notes on the trail: Not long ago, garbage dotted the 500-acre Novi North Park. Under the dedicated care of local Michigan Mountain Biking Association members, however, the park has become an example of urban renewal. Gone is most of the garbage, leaving a pleasant underused trail with trilliums and marigolds highlighting the spring months. The singletrack meanders through an old fruit orchard and a Christmas tree farm. Local riders are meeting ongoing interest from the City of Novi to develop the area into a golf course. The trail, however, needs more riders in order to justify its existence. Marked with black arrows on yellow diamonds and white mountain bike signs, the trail is easy to follow and offers bypasses for difficult sections. A vehicle entrance fee of $4.00 is charged to nonresidents from Memorial Day through Labor Day.

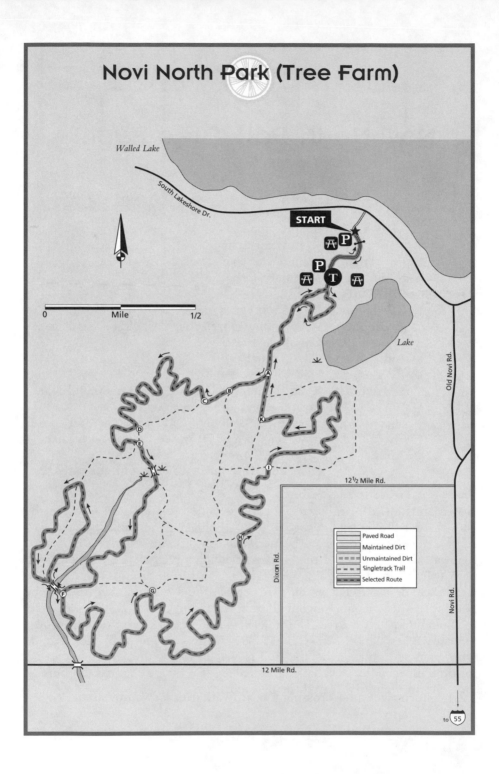

Sophia Radwanski takes a break at Novi North Park.

The Ride

0.0 Pick up the trailhead, marked with a large sign, at the south end of the parking lot. Stay left, following the yellow-and-black arrow onto a singletrack.

0.25 Turn left as the singletrack dumps out onto a wide trail.

0.5 Turn right at Post A. In a short distance reach Post B and turn right again.

0.7 Turn right onto narrower singletrack.

0.9 Turn right at Post C onto a more technical section with a twisting trail and logs to hop. To skip this section, continue straight.

1.9 Merge with the easier bypass at Post E. Stay left and follow the yellow-and-black arrow.

2.1 Turn right after crossing a boardwalk over a swampy area.

2.8 Turn right at Post F and cross the Rouge River on a wooden bridge. Stay right and follow Loop 754 counterclockwise through an open field.

3.7 Arrive back at Post F and turn right.

4.2 After rolling through an open, brushy area with the steepest climb of the ride, reach Post G and stay right.

5.0 Turn right at Post H.

5.5 Reach an intersection with a wide ski trail. Continue straight on the tight trail and ride through overgrown Christmas trees.

6.2 Turn right onto the wide trail at Post K and head back to the parking area.

6.7 Arrive back at the trailhead.

Island Lake Loops

Location:	5 miles southeast of Brighton.
Distance:	14.3-mile loop.
Time:	1–2 hours.
Tread:	14 miles of singletrack, 0.3 mile of paved road.
Aerobic level:	Easy.
Technical difficulty:	2; rutted and sandy singletrack.
Hill factor:	Rolling to occasionally hilly.
Highlights:	Singletrack cruiser snakes through hardwoods and follows Huron River.
Land status:	Island Lake Recreation Area.
Maps:	USGS Kent Lake; maps available at park entrance.
Access:	From the Interstate 96 and Kensington Road interchange (exit 151), drive 0.5 mile south on Kensington Road. After crossing the Huron River, turn east into the Island Lake Recreation Area. Turn south onto the road immediately following the entrance booth and continue toward the Island Lake Picnic Area. Drive about 1.25 miles. Turn north onto the paved road signed TRAILHEAD PARKING, and continue to the parking area.

Notes on the trail: The Blue and Yellow Loops at this popular trail system complement each other just like their namesake colors. Although each trail is enjoyable on its own, together they make a long singletrack cruiser

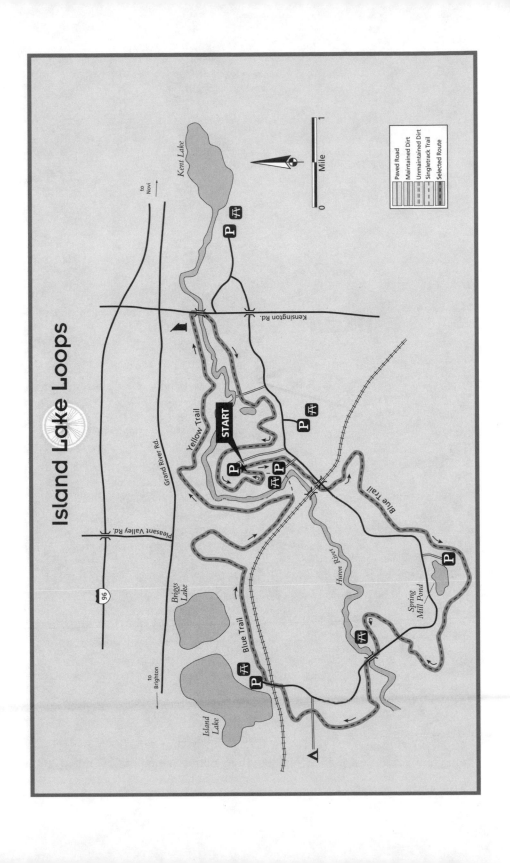

Twisting along the Island Lake trails.

with enough hills for a solid workout but not so many that water bottle arms get tendonitis. The prettiest section comes after a bridge crossing and meanders next to the river, with big trees sheltering the trail. The route is easy to follow; however, due to its popularity sections can become rutted. Fortunately, Michigan Mountain Biking Association members are active in repairing eroded trail, and occasionally the trail direction is reversed to further safeguard against erosion. There is a $4.00-per-vehicle entrance fee to the recreation area.

The Ride

0.0 Cycle toward the large signs marking the Blue and Yellow Trails on the south side of the parking lot (opposite side from the pit toilets). Follow the Blue Trail, marked with blue diamonds and black arrows.

0.7 Turn left at the paved road and briefly follow it under a railroad viaduct. Turn left back onto the trail; follow the black arrows and parallel the railroad tracks.

2.0 Cycle out of the woods and approach Spring Mill Pond.

3.9 Cross the main road after a steep downhill.

4.7 Reach Placeway Picnic Area. Turn back onto the main road and follow it for a short distance.

4.8 Pick up the trail on the left and prepare for a hilly section.

5.7 Cross a dirt road that leads to an organization campground.

6.3 Reach a stop sign. Turn left onto a paved road and continue toward the railroad tracks and Island Lake.

6.4 Cross the tracks and look for the trail on the right. Get ready for a fast cruise.

8.7 Reach an intersection with a post painted blue and yellow. Turn left onto the Yellow Trail; the Blue Trail continues straight and returns to the parking area. The next section twists through hardwoods, follows the Huron River, and crosses one of its tributaries on a long wooden bridge.

11.3 Reach Kensington Road; turn right and ride on the road's shoulder. After crossing the Huron River, look for the trail on the right.

12.0 After cruising through an open area, dive back into the woods and wind through the big trees.

12.2 Cross a dirt road that leads to the Huron River canoe launch.

14.2 The Yellow Trail merges with the Blue Trail.

14.3 Arrive back at the parking area.

Brighton Recreation Area Loops

Location:	5.5 miles southwest of Brighton.
Distance:	12.7-mile loop.
Time:	1–2 hours.
Tread:	12.7 miles of singletrack.
Aerobic level:	Moderate.
Technical difficulty:	Torn Shirt Loop is a 3+ with log jumps and steep hills; Murray Lake Loop rates a more mellow 2.
Hill factor:	Rolling to hilly.
Highlights:	Mountain biker–designed singletrack twists through forest and past inland lakes. Listen for the sandhill cranes that nest nearby.
Land status:	Brighton Recreation Area.
Maps:	USGS Brighton; maps available at trailhead.
Access:	From the Interstate 96 and Grand River Avenue interchange in Brighton, drive 0.25 mile south on Grand River Avenue. Turn west onto Challis Road. Go another 1.3 miles, then turn south at the stop sign next to Brighton Ski Area onto Bauer Road. Continue for another 2.9 miles. Turn west onto Bishop Lake Road and go 1.2 miles. Turn south at the large sign for the Bishop Lake Picnic Area. Turn right after the tollbooth and continue into the parking area.

Notes on the trail: Two singletrack trails, designed specifically for mountain bikes, opened during the summer of 1998 at this popular recreation area. The 7-mile Murray Lake Loop zigzags through a virtually obstacle-free forest. The hills are just enough of a challenge that bikers might have to walk their bikes if caught in the wrong gear. The descents occasionally plunge into a trough, propelling cyclists to the top of the next hill. The 5-mile Torn Shirt is a more demanding loop. Hills that leave you breathless, logs to hop, and rocks to avoid help make this the more challenging of the two loops. The ride described below combines the two loops, but both make excellent shorter rides on their own. The trails are marked, and there is a $4.00-per-vehicle entrance fee into the recreation area.

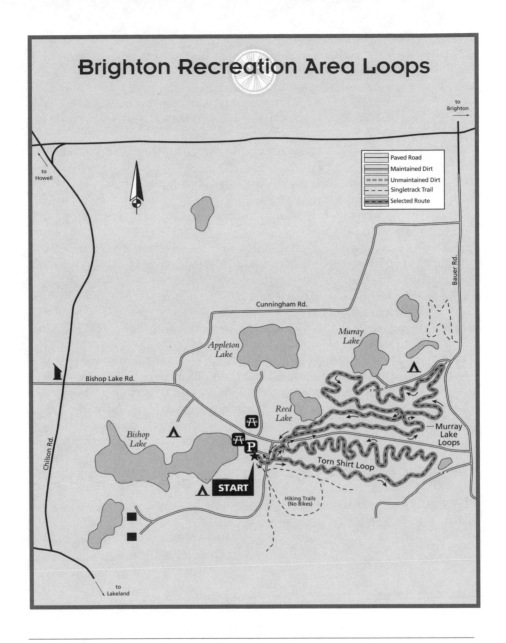

The Ride

0.0   Cycle up a small hill and pass the outhouse and water pump. Stay left after reaching a fork; the trail to the right is for hikers only. Cross a dirt road and continue up another short hill. The fork on the left is the return route.

0.15 Follow the arrow for the Torn Shirt Loop at a trail intersection. Murray Lake Loop turns to the left.

1.45 Test your skills at a ramped log climb.

3.0 Reach a clearing. For the next mile the trail bounces in and out of a clearing.

5.6 Reach intersection with Murray Lake Trail and turn right. Continue straight to return to the trailhead. Murray Lake Trail crosses the dirt road, parallels the road, and soon turns left into the woods.

5.75 Reach a fork in the trail; continue cycling to the right. The left fork is the return route.

7.25 Reach a fork. The trail to the left shortens the ride by 3.5 miles; stay right for the full loop.

8.2 Reach Murray Lake Campground, an excellent lunch stop complete with pit toilets.

8.75 Turn right at the T intersection and follow the well-worn path.

8.85 Turn left at the T intersection. Cycling straight dumps you out onto a dirt road.

10.2 Dive into a little gully. The next 0.8 mile is most technical of the Murray Lake Loop.

11.1 Meet back at the intersection with the shortcut loop, and bear right.

11.3 Reach a trail intersection. Continue straight for the easier route, or turn right, drop down, and then climb steeply. The more challenging option merges with the main trail in a short distance.

12.1 Reach a doubletrack that leads down to a lake. Turn right, then immediately left.

12.4 Reach Bishop Lake Road and retrace your tracks across the road. Turn right and follow the trailhead sign.

12.6 Reach the main trail intersection, and retrace your tracks across the road.

12.7 Arrive back at the trailhead.

Highland Recreation Area

Location:	9 miles east of Hartland.
Distance:	16.7-mile loop.
Time:	2–3 hours.
Tread:	16.7 miles of singletrack.
Aerobic level:	Moderate to strenuous.
Technical difficulty:	2+ (Loops A and B); 3+–4 (Loops C and D).
Hill factor:	Rolling to hilly.
Highlights:	Tight handlebar-grabbing singletrack that climbs steeply as it winds through dense woods.
Land status:	Highland Recreation Area.
Maps:	USGS Highland; maps available at trailhead.
Access:	From the intersection of Michigan 59 and U.S. 23 in Hartland, drive 9 miles east on M–59. Turn south onto Duck Lake Road and continue for 1 mile. Turn west onto Livingston Road and continue for 0.25 mile to the parking area on the right.

Notes on the trail: It is impossible to ride this trail system without bumping into a tree at least once. The four loops are on singletrack so narrow and twisty that handlebars can hook a tree at any moment. The Highland Trail System, developed in 1994, offers 16 miles of tough trails and several short, steep hills, making it the most challenging trail system in southeastern Michigan. Signs mark the beginning of each loop with mileage and elevation gain, so it is almost impossible to get lost. The route here takes in the entire trail system, including the more challenging Loops C and D. For a shorter and easier ride, cycle Loops A and B only, cutting the ride by about 7 miles. Unfortunately, this outstanding system is threatened by a proposed highway trunk line in west Oakland County (as of summer 2001).

The Ride

0.0 Cycle across Livingston Road past the large map and trailhead. Continue on the two-way singletrack and cycle over a small wooden bridge. Soon reach a fork and turn left onto Loop A. The

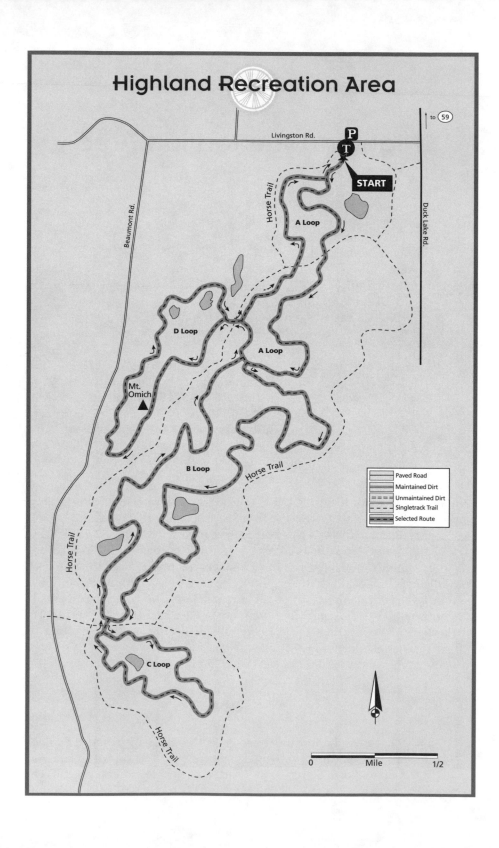

Erin cruises along the challenging trails at the Highland Recreation Area.

trail twists tightly, bouncing over rocks and roots for the next few miles.

2.7 Reach intersection with Loop B and continue straight. The trail picks up the pace with bigger climbs, rocks, and logs over the next 4 miles. This is a warm-up for Loops C and D. A right turn here leads back to the parking lot.

6.9 Arrive at the Loop C intersection and turn left. Cruise down a hill past the horse trail, and stay left at the marked intersection. Get ready for a challenge!

9.4 Back at the Loop B intersection, turn left onto Loop B. The next couple of miles brings Michigan's own slickrock and a series of whoop-de-dos.

11.4 Loop B merges into Loop A. Soon reach the intersection with Loop D and turn left onto a two-way trail.

11.6 Cross over a horse trail, head left, and follow the arrow. Offering the trail's highpoint, Mt. Omich, and more twists, this loop feels long on tired legs.

15.5 Cycle back over the horse trail. Retrace your tracks and turn left onto Loop A. The ride picks up the pace with more downhills and straightaways.

16.6 Loop A ends; merge onto a two-way trail.

16.7 End of ride.

Pontiac Lake Recreation Area

Location:	Waterford.
Distance:	11.1-mile loop.
Time:	1–1.5 hours.
Tread:	11.1 miles of singletrack.
Aerobic level:	Moderate.
Technical difficulty:	2 + –3; most consistently rocky trail in southeastern region.
Hill factor:	Rolling to hilly.
Highlights:	Thrilling rush through the woods with hilltop views.
Land status:	Pontiac Lake Recreation Area.
Maps:	USGS Pontiac Lake; maps available at park entrance.

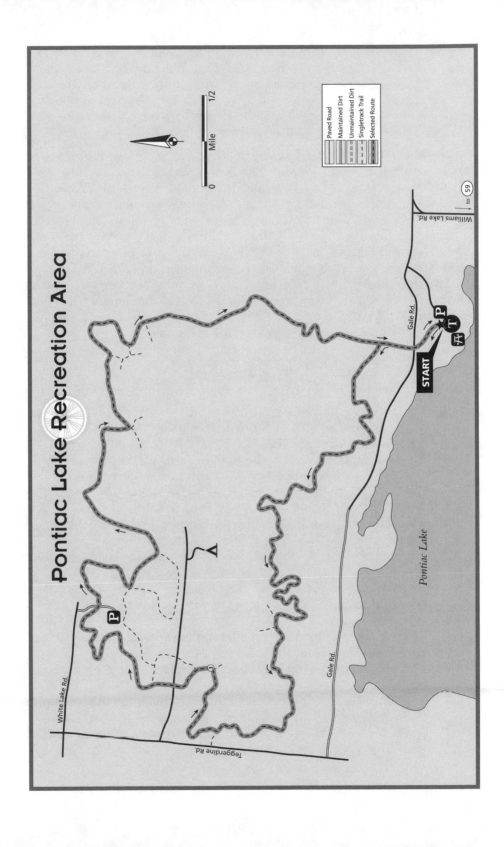

Pontiac Lake Recreation Area

Paved Road
Maintained Dirt
Unmaintained Dirt
Singletrack Trail
Selected Route

0   Mile   1/2

White Lake Rd.

Teggerdine Rd.

Gale Rd.

Gale Rd.

Williams Lake Rd.

to 59

START

P

T

Pontiac Lake

Access: From Michigan 59 and Williams Lake in Waterford, turn north onto Williams Lake Road and continue for 0.8 mile. Turn west onto Gale Road, and drive 0.3 mile to the park entrance on the south side of the road. Continue to the southwest corner of the parking lot.

Notes on the trail: Pontiac Lake Recreation Area's popular multiple-use trail system is receiving a face-lift. The Pontiac Lake chapter of the Michigan Mountain Biking Association and the Pontiac Lake Trail Riders are working with the Department of Natural Resources to realign and vegetate the old trails. It will probably be a few more years before the final plan is in place, but that isn't to say that mountain bikers can't enjoy the trails now. "Work-in-progress" maps are available at the park entrance, and the trail is still a thrilling rush as it works its way up and down the rolling Pontiac Lake terrain. Mountain bike, horse, and multiple-use routes are clearly marked. The 3,800-acre park also offers a modern campground, boating and fishing, and a rifle range. Like with all state recreation areas, there is a $4.00-per-vehicle entrance fee ($20.00 for an annual pass).

The Ride

0.0   Cycle toward the southwest corner of the parking lot. Pass the large trailhead sign and continue cruising on the flat singletrack. Soon cross over paved Gale Road.

0.35   The trail splits; stay left and follow the arrow. The upcoming section twists over several rocky switchbacks that climb through the woods.

2.4   Reach the top of a hill overlooking Pontiac Lake.

3.3   After crossing an intersection with a bridle trail, reach a split in the trail and stay left. A right turn will shorten the ride.

4.3   The trail on the left is for horses only. Stay right and climb a rocky hill.

5.0   Bridle trail merges from the right. Soon the trail splits again; stay left with marker 3. Cycling straight will shorten the ride.

5.2   Cross a paved road.

6.4   Cross dirt access road for a model airplane parking area.

6.9   Reach another fork in the trail; stay left.

8.25   Come to a four-way intersection and turn left with the mountain bike sign.

9.3   Reach another intersection and continue straight on the bike-only trail.

10.4   Reach the top of an open hill and get ready for a fast downhill.

11.1   Arrive back at the parking lot.

Stony Creek Loop

Location:	7 miles north of Utica.
Distance:	4.9-mile loop.
Time:	30 minutes–1 hour.
Tread:	2.2 miles of singletrack, 2.7 miles of double-track.
Aerobic level:	Easy to moderate.
Technical difficulty:	2; logs to hop and hills to negotiate.
Hill factor:	Rolling.
Highlights:	Banked, twisted singletrack that climbs to Macomb County's highest point.
Land status:	Stony Creek Metropark.
Maps:	USGS Utica; maps available at park headquarters.
Access:	From Michigan 59 and Michigan 53, drive 6 miles north on M–53 and turn west onto 26 Mile Road. Continue for 2 miles to the park entrance. Follow the park road, passing Stony Creek Lake on the right, for about 2 miles. Turn west into the West Branch Picnic Area and park in Parking Lot B.

Notes on the trail: Boasting Macomb County's highest point, this well-marked 14-mile trail system winds along tight singletracks and wide doubletracks through open, grassy meadows. The route climbs to an overlook then plunges down a series of fast, banked switchbacks. Climbing once again, riders bounce over exposed roots and clamber up a log ramp. A fine example of the Michigan Mountain Biking Association's maintenance, the trail system is sometimes rerouted due to erosion and heavy use. The park's vehicle entrance fee runs $2.00 on weekdays and $3.00 on weekends (an annual pass is available for $15.00).

The Ride

0.0   Cycle to the trailhead at the west end of the parking lot, and continue down the doubletrack.

0.35 Reach Post B and turn left toward Post L, climbing a few hills on the way.

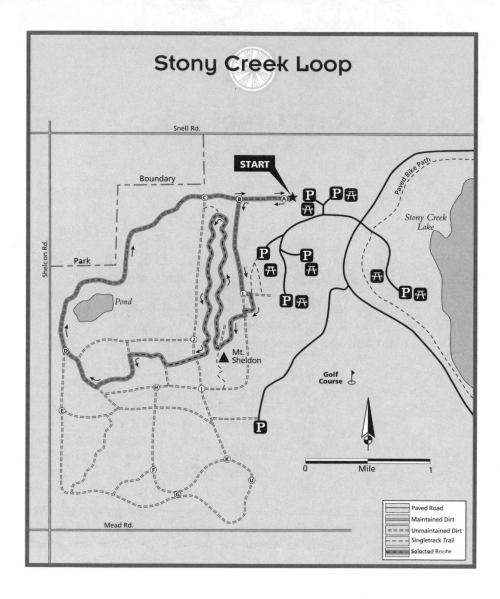

0.8 Arrive at Post L and turn left up a short hill. Turn right onto an unmarked singletrack. Turn left when the singletrack dumps back out at the doubletrack, then almost immediately turn right onto the marked singletrack.

1.1 Dump out onto a doubletrack. Turn left and climb to a clearing on Mt. Sheldon, Macomb County's highest point. Retrace your tracks down the hill and take a left onto the marked singletrack.

2.0 Reach a fork and bear left, climbing a hill. A ramped log climb lies ahead.

2.5 Cross a doubletrack.

2.75 Reach a T intersection and turn right onto wide singletrack.

3.1 Arrive at a clearing and follow the doubletrack to your left. The next section is mostly flat.

3.25 Reach a T intersection and turn right onto the doubletrack. Soon arrive at another intersection and cycle left toward Post D.

3.4 Reach Post D and turn right toward Post C.

4.5 Arrive at Post C and continue straight to Post B.

4.6 From Post B cycle uphill toward Post A.

4.9 Arrive back at parking lot.

Bald Mountain Loops

Location:	2 miles east of Lake Orion (North Loop), 3 miles south of Lake Orion (South Loop).
Distance:	7.7-mile loop (North Loop), 4-mile loop (South Loop).
Time:	1.5–2 hours (for both loops).
Tread:	7.5 miles of singletrack, 0.2 mile of doubletrack (North Loop); 3.8 miles of singletrack, 0.2 mile of doubletrack (South Loop).
Aerobic level:	Easy to moderate.
Technical difficulty:	2; sand and loose rocks create tricky descents.
Hill factor:	Rolling.
Highlights:	Sit back and enjoy these singletrack cruisers.
Land status:	Bald Mountain State Recreation Area.
Maps:	USGS Lake Orion; maps available at park headquarters.
Access:	
North Loop:	From the intersection of Interstate 75 and Michigan 24 (Lapeer Road), drive 5 miles north on M–24. Turn east onto Clarkston Road and continue for 2.2 miles. Turn north onto Adams Road and go another 0.5 mile. Turn east onto Stony Creek Road, then immediately north onto Harmon Road. Continue 0.5 mile north to the parking area, at the intersection of Harmon and Predmore Roads.

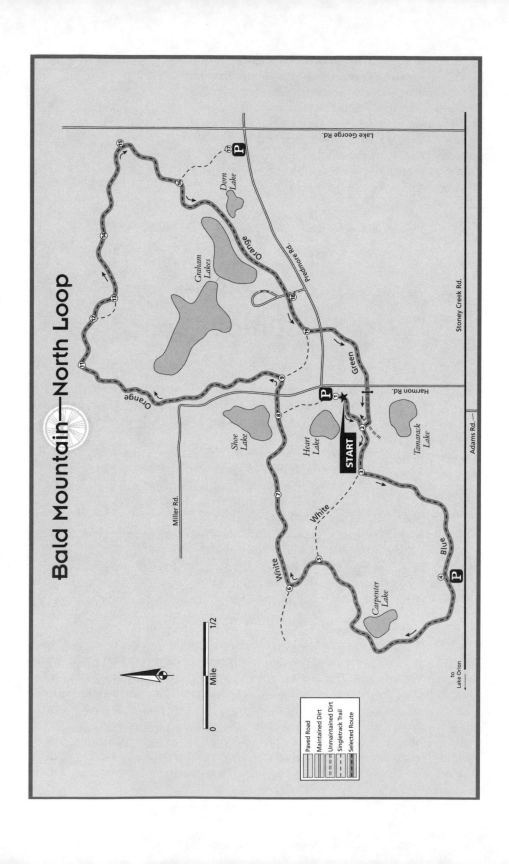

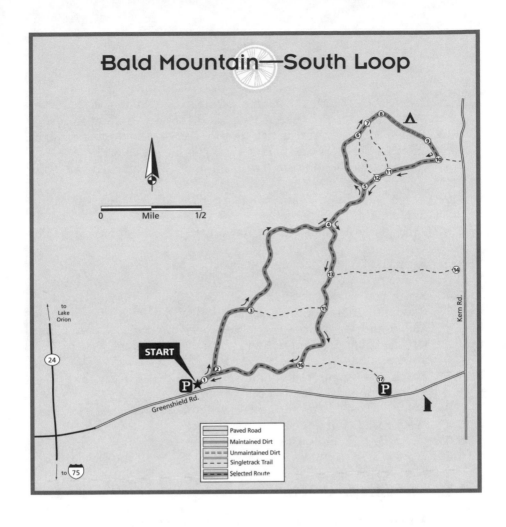

Bald Mountain—South Loop

to Lake Orion

24

to 75

START

P

Greenshield Rd.

Kern Rd.

0   Mile   1/2

Paved Road
Maintained Dirt
Unmaintained Dirt
Singletrack Trail
Selected Route

South Loop: From the intersection of I–75 and M–24, drive
3.5 miles north on M–24. Turn east onto
Greenshield Road and continue for about 0.75
mile. Parking area is to the north.

Notes on the trail: Cruising past inland lakes and creeks, these two tree-lined loops offer riders a rollicking good time. Rocky descents, sand traps, and a few steep hills keep you alert, but for the most part these two cruisers promise a fast forest ride. The 4,600-acre park is a pristine escape from the greater Detroit bustle, although the gun noise from a nearby shooting range occasionally interrupts the pastoral image. The loops are marked with numbered posts and trail maps. Springtime at Bald Mountain can be muddy, so cyclists are advised to hop over to nearby Stony Creek (Ride 9) during that time. Entrance to the park requires the standard $4.00 daily vehicle permit.

The Ride

North Loop

0.0 Pedal to the south end of the parking lot toward Post 1 on the White Loop. Soon arrive at Post 2 and continue straight to Post 3.

0.55 Reach Post 3 and turn left toward Post 4. Continuing straight shortens the loop. The next portion is hilliest part of the ride.

1.3 Arrive at Post 4 and bear left. Soon pass Carpenter Lake on your way to Post 5.

1.6 Reach a T intersection and stay right. Ignore the upcoming unmarked trail on the left.

2.3 Arrive at Post 5 and turn left toward Post 6, back onto the White Trail.

2.6 Reach Post 6 and turn right, continuing to Post 7.

3.0 Cruise by Post 7.

3.4 Reach Post 8, next to Shoe Lake. White Loop turns right, back to the parking lot. Continue straight, crossing over Miller Road, to Post 9 and the Yellow Loop. Soon arrive at Post 9, part of the Orange Loop, and continue straight to Post 10. Reach Post 10 after a steep hill and continue to Post 11.

4.5 Reach Post 11 and turn right toward Post 12. The trail forks at Post 12; both options meet up again at Post 13.

4.8 Arrive at Post 13 and turn right toward Post 14.

5.2 From Post 14 continue straight to Post 15.

5.6 Reach Post 15 and turn right toward Post 16.

6.0 From Post 16 continue straight to Post 18. A left turn leads to the east parking area.

6.8 After crossing a dirt road, reach Post 18. Continue cycling toward Post 19.

7.0 Arrive at Post 19 and turn left onto the Green Loop toward Post 2. Cross Predmore Road.

7.3 Cross Harmon Road. Pedal around the gate and continue cycling on a doubletrack.

7.5 Caution! As doubletrack turns left look for Post 2 on the right. Make a hard right and head back toward Post 1.

7.7 Arrive back at parking lot.

South Loop

0.0 Head north on the singletrack. Pass Post 1 and continue on to Post 2. Soon arrive at Post 2 and turn left toward Post 3.

0.5 Reach Post 3 and stay left toward Post 4. Cycling straight drastically shortens the ride.

1.1 After a fun downhill, reach Post 4 and turn left toward Post 5. A right turn toward Post 13 shortens the loop.

Bruce Kantor lets it roll on Bald Mountain's fast trails.

1.3 Arrive at Post 5 and turn left toward Post 6.

1.6 Reach Post 6 and turn left, heading downhill toward Post 7. Cruise by Post 7 and on to Post 8. Reach Post 8 after another fun downhill and turn right toward Post 9 on a doubletrack. Pass a campground on the left.

1.9 Look for Post 9 and a singletrack on the right. Continue on the singletrack toward Post 10. Soon reach Post 10; turn right and cycle toward Post 11.

2.3 Reach Post 11 and continue straight to Post 12. Shortly reach Post 12 and continue to Post 5. At Post 5 continue straight to Post 4.

2.6 Reach Post 4 and turn left toward Post 13.

2.9 Arrive at Post 13 and cycle straight to Post 15.

3.1 From Post 15 turn left toward Post 16.

3.4 Reach Post 16 and continue straight to Post 2.

3.8 Arrive at Post 2 and turn left to Post 1.

4.0 Arrive back at the parking area.

Holdridge Lakes Loops

Location:	2 miles east of Holly.
Distance:	2.2-mile loop (North Loop); 5.8-mile loop (West Loop); 16.3-mile loop (East/Gruber's Grinder Loop).
Time:	15–30 minutes (North Loop); 45 minutes–1 hour (West Loop); 2–4 hours (East/Gruber's Grinder Loop).
Tread:	24.3 miles of singletrack.
Aerobic level:	Easy (North Loop); Moderate (West Loop); Moderately Strenuous (East/Gruber's Grinder Loop).
Technical difficulty:	1 (North Loop); 2+ (West Loop); 3+ (Gruber's Grinder).
Hill factor:	Flat to rolling.
Highlights:	Three trails with something for every ability—from 4-foot log climbs to fast cruising.
Land status:	Holly Recreation Area.
Maps:	USGS Davisburg; maps available at trailhead.
Access:	From the intersection of Interstate 75 and Grange Hall Road in Holly, drive 0.5 mile west on Grange Hall Road. Turn north onto Hess Road and continue for about 1.5 miles to the trailhead on the left.

Notes on the trail: A lot of love has gone into this well-maintained trail system. Offering three loops, the trails are quintessential southern Michigan. The singletrack rolls through dense forest, with the most difficult trail butting up next to I–75, a reminder that civilization is nearby. The North Loop winds through tall grasses and is perfect for beginners. The West Loop's popularity with intermediate riders is obvious from its buffed singletrack. The East Loop (Gruber's Grinder) offers plenty of challenges for advanced riders, including 4-foot log climbs, tight turns, and short switchbacks. Luckily, if you get in over your head, there are plenty of places to bail out. Like for all Michigan state parks, there is a $4.00-per-vehicle entrance fee.

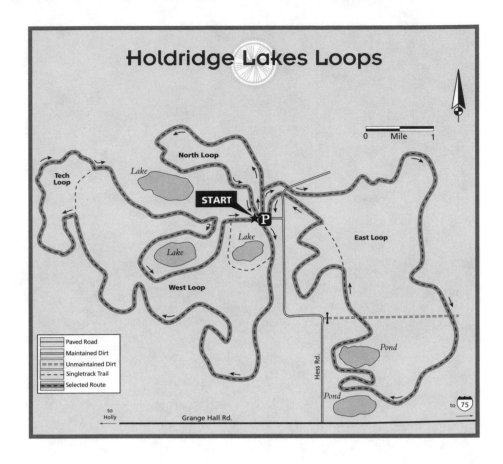

The Ride

East Loop (Gruber's Grinder)

0.0 Cycle to the trailhead on the north side of the parking lot. North Loop and Gruber's Grinder share the same trailhead.

0.5 Reach the intersection with Gruber's Grinder (East Loop) and turn right. North Loop continues to the left. Soon cross over Hess Road and the fun begins. Get ready for log hops, tight turns, and short switchbacks.

2.0 Arrive at I-75, a reminder that you are still in congested southeastern Michigan.

4.5 and 5.5 Enjoy the trail's largest ramped log climbs.

7.7 Reach Old Shields Roadbed at Marker 7. Stay left to continue on the loop; a right turn cuts the ride short.

9.8 Stay right at a trail rerouting.

10.3 Arrive at a T intersection and turn left, then immediately right.

47

Keith climbs one of several log ramps on Gruber's Grinder.

10.4 Thorndog cutoff turns left; stay right to continue the loop.

10.8 Too Tired cutoff turns right; stay left to continue on the loop. Watch out for a tricky log hop with a steep descent just past Marker 14. Prepare for the hilliest portion of the ride.

16.0 Cross Hess Road.

16.3 Back at the trailhead. Cycle to the south end of the parking lot to the West Loop trailhead.

West Loop

16.5 Reach Marker 1 and bear left, staying on the long loop.

19.4 Turn left at a T intersection. A right turn shortens the loop. Shift into a granny gear for the Wall, steepest hill on all the loops, just around the next bend.

19.7 Arrive at Marker 4 and turn left onto the technical portion of the loop. Cycling straight shortens the loop.

20.4 Reach a T intersection and turn left.

20.9 Turn right at Marker 6 and head toward Paul's Slide on the Lakeshore Long Loop, a pretty section with exciting downhills.

22.1 Arrive back at the parking lot. Cycle to the North/East Loop trailhead on the north end of the parking lot.

North Loop

22.6 Pass the turnoff for the East Loop (Gruber's Grinder) and continue straight. Twist and turn through the high brush back into the woods, and pass a lake with an inviting bench.

24.3 The trail dumps out at the parking lot.

Ruby Campground Singletrack

Location:	11 miles west of Port Huron.
Distance:	5-mile loop.
Time:	30–90 minutes.
Tread:	4.6 miles of singletrack, 0.4 mile of dirt road.
Aerobic level:	Moderate.
Technical difficulty:	2–4. Steep, slippery switchback climbs and technical descents.
Hill factor:	Rolling with two steep, extended climbs and descents.
Highlights:	Rugged singletrack with gut-wrenching climbs and nail-biting descents.
Land status:	Private. Landowner graciously allows mountain bikers to use designated trails, but please respect property and stay on established trails.
Maps:	USGS Ruby; maps available at The Bicycle & Fitness Barn in Port Huron (see Appendix A).
Access:	From the intersection of Interstates 94 and 69 in Port Huron, drive 5.3 miles west on I–69 to Taylor Road exit. Continue north on Taylor Road for 0.1 mile, then turn west onto LaPeer Road and go 2.4 miles. Turn north onto Cribbins Road and continue for 3 miles. Turn west onto Imlay City Road and continue for 0.4 mile to the Ruby Campground entrance on the north. Continue down the hill and park in the visitor parking area, near the campground office.

Notes on the trail: Developed by local riders about six years ago, this ride offers steep switchback ascents and descents that plunge straight down small but rugged hills. Luckily, the most difficult segments of the ride include bypass options. The challenges, however, don't end with steep hills. Log hops, roots, and slippery, claylike soil add to the technical mix. Beyond the technical challenges, riders will find a picturesque route, crossing Mill Creek twice and meandering along a tree-lined singletrack with section names like Aaron's Island, Tommy's Trilogy, and Amyr Odyssey. Cyclists need to thank campground owners Ron and Marie Bur-

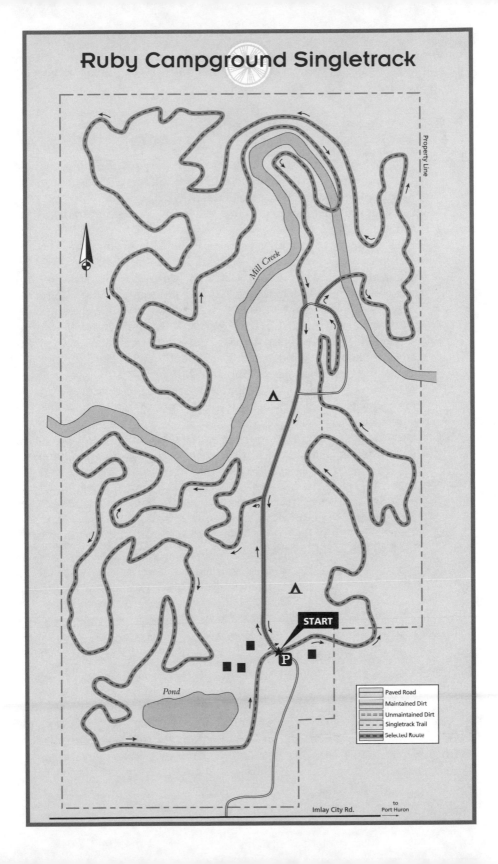

ton for generously opening their property to mountain bikes, including an annual race in July. Keep tabs on new singletrack development by checking in with Dave at The Bicycle & Fitness Barn.

The Ride

0.0 Cycle along the campground access road, past the playground. Just before reaching Campsite 1, turn left onto the singletrack heading uphill and into the woods. Break out of the woods at the playground area and continue following the singletrack as it weaves in and out of trees and next to the river.

1.8 Back at the visitor parking area, cross the campground access road and look for the trail to the left of the green pole barn.

2.3 The trail splits. For the more difficult route, stay right and climb steeply. Turn left to bypass the hill and shorten the ride. The route described below climbs the hill.

2.6 After a steep descent the trail merges with the bypass. The trail soon splits again, with the bypass continuing straight. A hard right climbs steeply to a ridge, with an equally steep, rutted descent. The route described here climbs the hill.

2.9 After riding through the campground, reach the first creek crossing. Bridges are in the works. If they're not in place, expect to get your feet wet.

3.5 Gear down for another steep switchback climb to the top of a bluff. Meander along the bluff and get ready for an equally steep descent.

4.6 Reach the second water crossing. If the bridge is not yet installed, walk or ride across the creek. Follow the singletrack along the creek where it soon dumps out to the campground access road. Turn right onto the road. Cycle past the trailhead and continue back to the parking area.

5.0 End of ride.

Southwestern Michigan:
Variety Rules from Farm Fields to Man-made Obstacles

From flat farm fields to rolling hills, southwestern Michigan surprises mountain bikers with its variety. Dominated by trails maintained by the Michigan Mountain Biking Association (MMBA), southwestern Michigan, for the purposes of this book, includes everything south of Michigan 10 and roughly west of U.S. 27.

Butting up against northern Indiana, extreme southern Michigan is punctuated by farms. Sitting in the middle of this farmland is the T. K. Lawless Singletrack, an oasis of forest-covered hills. Traveling farther north, cyclists explore an urban adventure at Ella Sharp Park, home to thirteen short, distinct loops. State Recreation Areas like Fort Custer, Ionia, Yankee Springs, and Bass River host their own twisting singletracks, courtesy of the hard work of local MMBA volunteers and the DNR. Each of these trail systems has its own flavor—from the steep, sandy climbs at Yankee Springs to the open, boulder-strewn last half of the Ionia trails.

Southwestern Michigan's trails, however, are not only about fast cruising along buffed singletrack. At Deerfield County Park a trail rolls through a covered bridge! As the trails move northward, the terrain becomes more rugged and rolling in the Huron-Manistee National Forest. A North Country Trail segment is a breathtaking ramble, and the Hungerford Lake Trail offers fast downhills.

Perhaps, the most unique trail is found farther south at Burchfield Park. Strewn with obstacles, the trail system boasts more man-made apparatus than any other trail in Michigan. With additional singletrack in development, it is the perfect place to practice balancing skills. In short, Burchfield reflects what southwestern Michigan is all about: variety.

T. K. Lawless Singletrack

Location:	4.5 miles southeast of Vandalia.
Distance:	10.4-mile loop.
Time:	1.5–3 hours.
Tread:	10.4 miles of singletrack.
Aerobic level:	Moderately easy.
Technical difficulty:	2 +.
Hill factor:	Rolling.
Highlights:	Popular county park holds a wallop of a fun trail with whoop-de-dos and tight, twisted singletrack.
Land status:	Dr. T. K. Lawless County Park.
Map:	USGS Vandalia.
Access:	From downtown Vandalia, drive 2.5 miles east on Michigan 60. Turn south onto Lewis Lake Road and continue for 1 mile. Turn east onto Monkey Run Street and continue about 1 mile to the park entrance on the left. Pass the tollbooth and continue back to the parking area.

Notes on the trail: Located in a mellow county park surrounded by flat farmland, the Lawless singletrack surprises visitors with its rolling terrain. Using a limited space, the buffed singletrack twists on itself, running over the same hills many times and making the climbs feel much bigger than they are. Natural obstacles like sand, roots, and whoop-de-dos are enhanced with man-made ones, including a teeter-totter and strategically placed logs. Maintained by the Cass County Parks Department and volunteers, this popular, buffed trail is easy to follow; yellow arrows point out the correct path. Mountain bike races take place in June and August, and the trail closes from late fall through spring. A $2.00 entrance fee is charged ($1.00 for county residents), and park management takes its helmet rule seriously.

The Ride

0.0   Trailhead is located at the south end of the parking lot, marked with large map. Pedal along the singletrack to the right of the map. Cross Monkey Run Street and follow the arrows to the right.

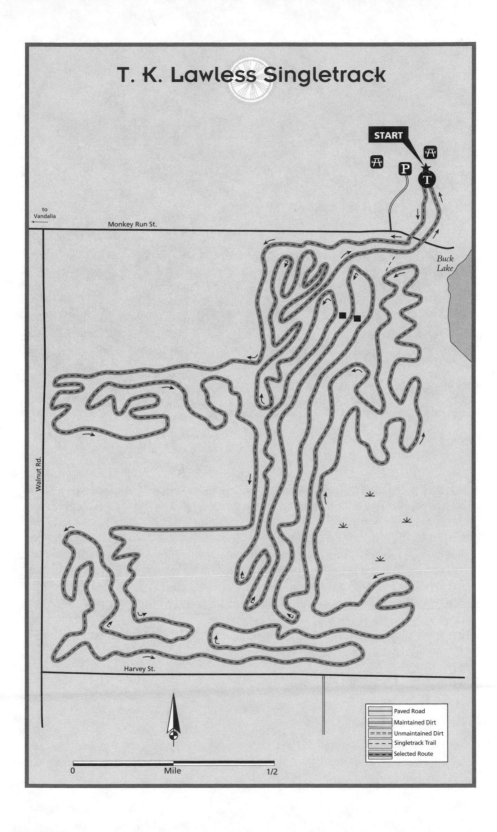

Teeter-totter sets the tone for the T. K. Lawless Singletrack.

0.5   Test your skills on a teeter-totter obstacle.

2.2   After twisting and turning through the woods, come out to a cornfield and head straight between the fields. The next segment is faster, with less twisted trail.

3.6   Reach a section of whoop-de-dos, followed by speedy downhills.

6.0   Reach a T intersection; turn left to continue on the full loop. A right turn leads to the parking area.

6.6   Hit big whoop-de-dos, followed by banked S-curves.

7.6   Cycle between old pit toilets and head downhill on a wide trail.

8.1   Turn right onto a narrow singletrack.

10.0   Turn left onto a wider trail. Soon the trail narrows again; cruise past the shortcut intersections.

10.3   Cross Monkey Run Street.

10.4   Arrive back at parking area.

Bass River Recreation Area

Location:	18.6 miles south of Grand Haven.
Distance:	5.4-mile loop.
Time:	30 minutes–1 hour.
Tread:	5.4 miles of singletrack.
Aerobic level:	Easy.
Technical difficulty:	2+.
Hill factor:	Flat.
Highlights:	Tight and twisted singletrack with whoop-de-dos and narrow tree passages.
Land status:	Bass River Recreation Area.
Map:	USGS Nunica.
Access:	From the intersection of U.S. Highway 31 and Michigan 104 in Grand Haven, drive 8 miles south on U.S. 31. Turn east onto Michigan 45 and continue for 7 miles. Turn north onto 104th Avenue and continue for 3.3 miles. Turn east onto a dirt road, marked with RECREATION AREA signs. Continue for 0.3 mile to the stop sign; park on the west side of the stop sign.

Notes on the trail: Twisting continuously, this tight, mostly flat trail system was designed for mountain bikers by mountain bikers. Maintained by the Michigan Mountain Biking Association, the narrow singletrack is home to whoop-de-dos, sand mounds, narrow tree passages, and roots. The small trail system is really two trails. The North Loop is a little straighter than the South Loop and twists through dense pine trees before crossing over the dirt access road. The South Loop twists relentlessly, making the short trail seem much longer. The route described here begins with the North Loop then merges with the South Loop. The trails are marked with blue markers and mountain bike signs, making it impossible to get lost.

The Ride

0.0 Cycle past the stop sign and turn left onto the North Loop. Pedal along the open singletrack and pass a pond on the right. Continue into the dense pine trees.

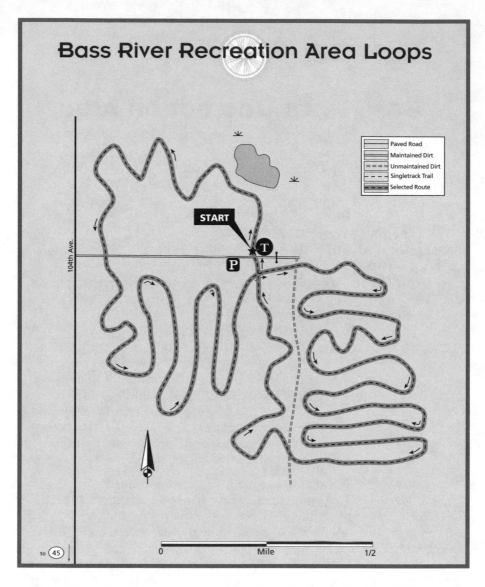

Bass River Recreation Area Loops

Paved Road
Maintained Dirt
Unmaintained Dirt
Singletrack Trail
Selected Route

START

104th Ave.

P   T

to 45

0   Mile   1/2

0.8 Cross the dirt entrance road and continue on the North Loop as it twists through the trees.

2.2 Reach an intersection with the South Loop near the trailhead. Continue straight across the trail and onto the South Loop. The return route is on the right.

2.8 Turn left onto a doubletrack, then almost immediately turn right back onto the singletrack and up a short, sandy mound. The trail continues to twist through the woods.

4.5 Reach the doubletrack again and turn right, then left.

5.1 Cross another doubletrack and continue straight.

5.4 Arrive back at the trailhead.

North Country Trail: Michigan 20 to South Nichols Lake

Location:	2.75 miles west of White Cloud.
Distance:	35.6-mile loop.
Time:	3–6 hours.
Tread:	19.2 miles of singletrack, 4 miles of paved road, 12.4 miles of dirt road.
Aerobic level:	Moderately strenuous (due to length).
Technical difficulty:	2.
Hill factor:	Flat to rolling.
Highlights:	Mellow section of the North Country Trail with all of the NCT's beauty.
Land status:	Huron-Manistee National Forest, Baldwin Ranger District.
Maps:	USGS White Cloud, Woodland Park; maps available at forest offices and NCT Association (see Appendix C).
Access:	From the intersection of Michigan 20 and Michigan 37 in the north end of White Cloud, drive 2.75 miles west on M–20. Trail parking is on south side of M–20.

Notes on the trail: Combine buffed singletrack and fast, twisting downhills with the natural beauty of the North Country Trail and you have the perfect mountain biking mixture. This is the flattest section of the NCT in this book, making it also the easiest. The route passes through a variety of vegetation, including dense forest and bucolic meadows. It brushes up next to low-lying areas, and its highest hills are found near Six Mile Road. The route returns on dirt and paved roads that pass by the NCT Schoolhouse, available as a hostel for trail users. It is also possible to make the ride an out-and-back run, cycling as far as you want, or leave a second vehicle at the South Nichols Lake trailhead. The M–20 trailhead requires a $3.00 parking pass, which is available at Rosenberg True Value Hardware (1164 East Wilcox Avenue) in White Cloud. Like all portions of the NCT, this trail is marked with blue paint and NCT signs. Note: The NCT section south of M–20 is closed to mountain bikes.

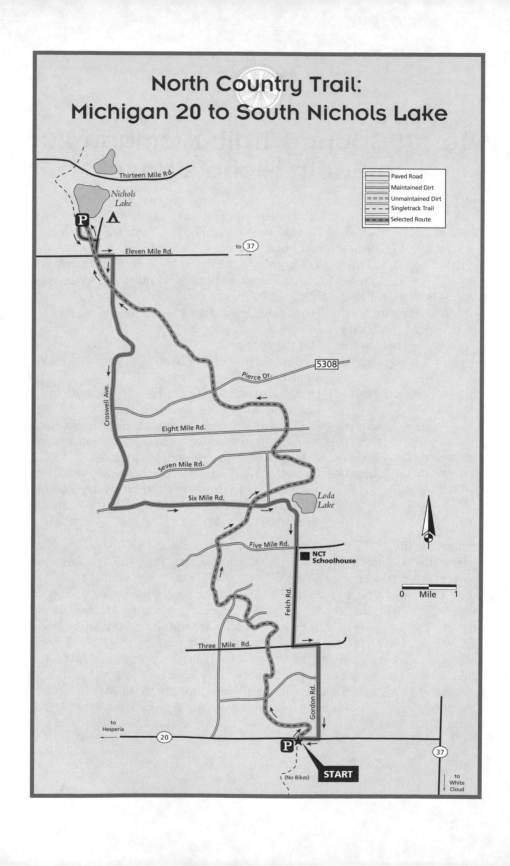

North Country Trail:
Michigan 20 to South Nichols Lake

Paved Road
Maintained Dirt
Unmaintained Dirt
Singletrack Trail
Selected Route

Thirteen Mile Rd.

Nichols Lake

Eleven Mile Rd.   to 37

Croswell Ave.

5308

Pierce Dr.

Eight Mile Rd.

Seven Mile Rd.

Six Mile Rd.

Loda Lake

Five Mile Rd.

NCT Schoolhouse

Felch Rd.

Three Mile Rd.

Gordon Rd.

to Hesperia   20

37

to White Cloud

(No Bikes)

START

0   Mile   1

The Ride

0.0   Cycle across M–20 and pick up the trail on the north side of the road.

1.0   Head down the stairs and cross a creek on a narrow footbridge.

1.3   Cross a dirt road.

2.0   The trail widens after crossing a sandy doubletrack.

2.2   The trail turns right into the woods on a tight singletrack.

3.1   Cross paved Three Mile Road.

4.4   Reach a clearing. The trail twists and turns through the woods.

6.9   Cross sandy Five Mile Road. The trail continues a twisted roller-coaster ride.

7.8   Watch out for the sand pit at the bottom of a hill. Stay right and follow the trail back into the woods. Get ready for the steepest climbs of the ride.

8.5   Reach Six Mile Road and turn right onto the sandy dirt road. Almost immediately turn left back onto the singletrack.

10.9   Cross sandy Seven Mile Road.

13.5   Turn right as the singletrack dumps out onto a doubletrack, then immediately turn right back onto the singletrack.

13.9   Reach Eight Mile Road and continue straight.

15.3   Reach a primitive campground and turn right down a rutted hill. Cross a stream on a narrow bridge and climb a short, sandy hill.

16.1   Test your skills by climbing a 4-foot ramped log climb.

17.8   Cross dirt Croswell Avenue and continue straight.

18.5   Cross paved Eleven Mile Road and onto the access road for Nichols Lake trailhead. The trail picks up again almost immediately on the left.

19.0   Cross paved boat launch access road.

19.2   Reach Nichols Lake boat ramp and trailhead parking area—good spot to enjoy lake views and relax before the long ride back. Singletrack junkies can retrace their tracks back to the trailhead. Those looking for a shorter route, turn left. Ride away from the lake and up the paved road.

19.5   Turn right.

19.9   Turn left onto paved Eleven Mile Road.

20.3   Turn right onto dirt Croswell Avenue.

23.8   Cross over Eight Mile Road and continue straight.

26.0   Turn left onto dirt Six Mile Road. Get ready for a roller coaster to the end.

28.9   The NCT comes in on the right. If you need more singletrack, turn right and head back to the trailhead. The road route continues straight.

29.8   Loda Lake Wildlife Sanctuary is on the left as the road turns right and becomes Felch Avenue.

Log ramp provides an end-of-singletrack challenge as the NCT nears South Nichols Lake.

30.7	Felch crosses over Five Mile Road and becomes paved. Almost immediately, look for the NCT Schoolhouse on the left.
32.8	Turn left, as Felch Avenue ends, and onto Three Mile Road.
33.3	Turn right onto dirt Gordon Road.
35.3	Turn right onto M–20.
35.6	Turn left into the parking area and the end of the ride.

Hungerford Lake Mountain Bike Trail

Location:	7 miles west of Big Rapids.
Distance:	7-mile loop.
Time:	1–2 hours.
Tread:	7 miles of narrow and wide singletrack.
Aerobic level:	Moderate.
Technical difficulty:	2.
Hill factor:	Rolling to hilly.
Highlights:	Fast downhills on tight mountain bike–only singletrack.
Land status:	Huron-Manistee National Forest, Baldwin Ranger District.
Maps:	USGS Woodville; maps available from forest office (see Appendix B).
Access:	From the intersection of U.S. 131 and Michigan 20 at the west edge of Big Rapids, drive west 5.2 miles. Turn north onto Cypress Avenue and continue for 0.5 mile. Turn east onto Hungerford Lake Road and drive 0.5 mile to the end of the road. Turn north onto Forest Road 5134 and continue for 0.2 mile to the parking area (where the pavement ends).

Notes on the trail: This mountain bike–only trail sweeps and swoops through the Hungerford Lake Recreation Area. Although marked with mountain bike signs, the trail can be confusing at times, since almost all the intersection posts and maps have been vandalized. As long as you follow the mountain bike signs, however, you can't get lost. Horse's hooves

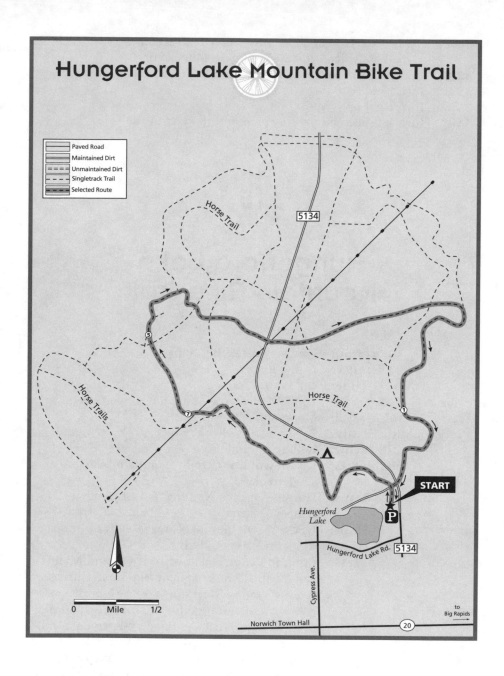

Hungerford Lake Mountain Bike Trail

Legend:
- Paved Road
- Maintained Dirt
- Unmaintained Dirt
- Singletrack Trail
- Selected Route

Horse Trail

5134

Horse Trail

Horse Trails

START

Hungerford Lake

Hungerford Lake Rd. 5134

Cypress Ave.

Norwich Town Hall

to Big Rapids

20

0   Mile   1/2

also occasionally pock the path; sand, churned from passing horses, is the other major challenge. Despite these minor negatives, the trail offers many exciting downhills. The route here takes in the shorter 7-mile loop; a 12-mile loop is possible by staying left at the 3.1-mile mark.

Keith checks his speed on the Hungerford Lake Mountain Bike Trail.

The Ride

0.0 Pedal north on the trail and follow the mountain bike/skier signs. Soon pass an unmarked trail on the left; continue straight. Shortly cross a dirt road and continue straight.

0.5 After a long, steady climb and a fast downhill, look for the trail continuing on the left.

0.9 Reach a fork in the trail. The trail on the right dumps out to a campground and another trailhead. Turn left and continue on the singletrack.

1.5 The trail splits; stay left. Soon cross the horse trail.

2.0 Cross underneath power lines at a very sandy portion of the trail. Reach Post 7 in a short while; turn right and follow the mountain bike sign.

2.5 Arrive at an intersection with horse and ski trails, and follow the mountain bike signs. Soon reach Post 5 and turn right onto a wide ski trail.

3.1 Turn right back onto a narrow singletrack. Stay left for the 12-mile loop.

3.3 Reach an intersection with a horse trail and unnumbered post. Cross the horse trail and stay left.

3.8 Cross a dirt road and pedal underneath power lines to an unmarked post; continue straight.

5.1 Turn right at a T intersection.

6.1 Reach a four-way intersection with Post 1 and a horse trail. Turn left onto a wide trail.

6.8 Cross Forest Road 5134 to a dirt road. Immediately turn left onto a tight singletrack.

7.0 Arrive back at parking lot.

Cannonsburg Ski Area Singletrack

Location:	10 miles northeast of Grand Rapids.
Distance:	3.7-mile loop.
Time:	30 minutes–1 hour.
Tread:	3.7 miles of narrow and wide singletrack.
Aerobic level:	Moderate to strenuous.
Technical difficulty:	2+.
Hill factor:	Hilly.
Highlights:	Steep climbs on twisted singletrack with a finale of sweeping views.
Land status:	Private. Landowner graciously permits mountain bikers to use trails; please respect property and stay on established trails.
Map:	USGS Cannonsburg.
Access:	From the intersection of Interstate 96 and U.S. 131 in Grand Rapids, drive 1.5 miles north on U.S. 131. Take the first exit onto West River Drive, which later becomes Cannonsburg Road, and continue east for about 8.5 miles. Turn south into the entrance of the Cannonsburg Ski Area. Park near the lodge.

Notes on the trail: Offering steep, sustained climbs in and out of trees, this trail maximizes a small area by twisting and turning on itself.

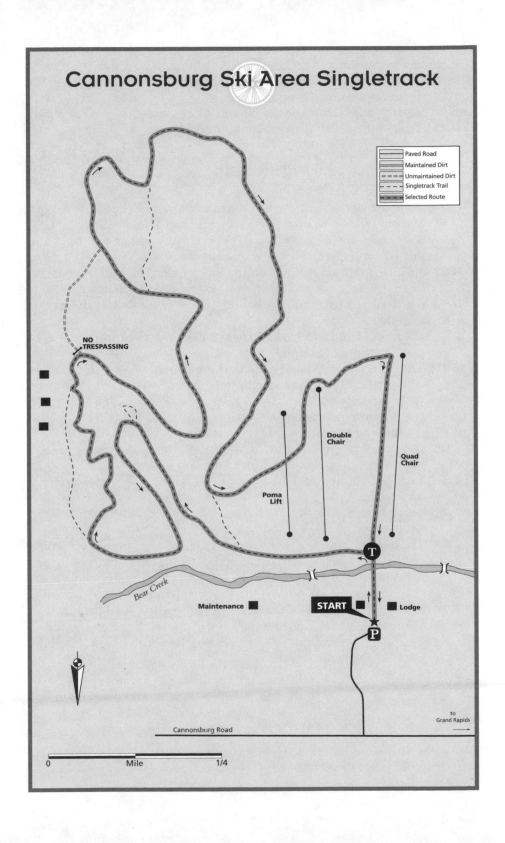

Cannonsburg Ski Area Singletrack

Paved Road
Maintained Dirt
Unmaintained Dirt
Singletrack Trail
Selected Route

NO
TRESPASSING

Double
Chair

Quad
Chair

Poma
Lift

T

Bear Creek

Maintenance ■

START ■ ■ Lodge

P

to
Grand Rapids

Cannonsburg Road

0   Mile   1/4

Unmarked and at times confusing, the route rolls through the hills next to the small Cannonsburg Ski Area. Cannonsburg management has welcomed mountain bikers by allowing the development of singletrack trails and hosting an annual mountain bike race in October. Cannonsburg offers panoramic views, which come at the end of the route. A fast, plunging downhill ends the ride with an exclamation point.

The Ride

0.0 From the parking area, cycle down the steps, between the lodges, and over the creek on a bridge. Turn left and follow the worn path along the base of the ski area. Pass the maintenance buildings and climb into the woods on a wide, sandy trail.

0.5 Reach a fork and stay left on the worn path. The trail flattens out and begins a steady descent on a twisting, sandy singletrack.

0.9 The trail turns right at the bottom of a very sandy hill and begins climbing again.

1.1 Come to another fork and turn right onto a narrower, sandy singletrack that heads uphill.

1.4 The trail turns right and widens at the bottom of a twisting, sandy singletrack. Homes are on the left. Soon reach a T intersection with another doubletrack and turn right. The doubletrack on the left is marked with a NO TRESPASSING sign. Shortly the trail dives to the left and into the woods.

2.05 Reach a T intersection with another trail and turn right. Almost immediately reach another fork and stay to the right.

2.3 Turn left at another T intersection. Soon turn right at another T intersection.

2.7 Come to a clearing on a wide, sandy trail and turn right. Head downhill on sandy, banked turns.

3.1 The trail splits after a steady downhill on a wide path. Continuing on the trail takes you past the maintenance area and back to the parking lot. For big views, turn left and pedal uphill and underneath the poma lift. Follow the first chairlift to the top.

3.3 Turn right at the top of the first chairlift and cycle around the lift. Continue pedaling up the sandy hill. Turn left to reach the top of the quad chairlift. Enjoy the views and then cruise back down the slope on the route of your choice.

3.7 Arrive back at the parking area.

Yankee Springs Recreation Area

Location:	4.5 miles south of Middleville.
Distance:	13.1-mile loop.
Time:	1.5–2.5 hours.
Tread:	12.9 miles of singletrack, 0.2 mile of dirt road.
Aerobic level:	Moderate.
Technical difficulty:	3; root-infested, rutted, and rocky.
Hill factor:	Rolling to hilly.
Highlights:	Fast roller-coaster ride among tall red pines.
Land status:	Yankee Springs Recreation Area.
Maps:	USGS Middleville; maps available at trailhead.
Access:	From the intersection of Michigan 442 and Michigan 611/Yankee Springs Road in Middleville, drive 4.5 miles south on M–611/Yankee Springs Road. Turn west at the entrance to Deep Lake Campground and continue to the mountain bike staging area.

Notes on the trail: Bopping in and out of trees and rolling along a picturesque ridgeline, this fun and fast mountain bike–only trail cruises among tall red pines and past the Devil's Soup Bowl, a sunken area surrounded by thick trees. The most strenuous climbs come in the middle section, as the trail rolls above a ravine on a narrow ridge. The popular, buffed trail is marked with numbered posts and arrows, making it virtually impossible to get lost. Riders, however, will find plenty of other challenges, including log jumps and rutted ascents and descents with sandy runouts. Rubber mats in the sandiest sections help riders climb particularly steep hills. Cyclists who want to cut the ride short have several options. As with all Michigan state recreation areas, there is a $4.00-per-vehicle entrance fee.

The Ride

0.0 From the parking area, cycle back up the access road to the start of the trail and turn left. Begin a fast cruise in and out of trees. Ignore the faint singletrack on the left and follow the buffed trail. Soon follow the trail as it sweeps left.

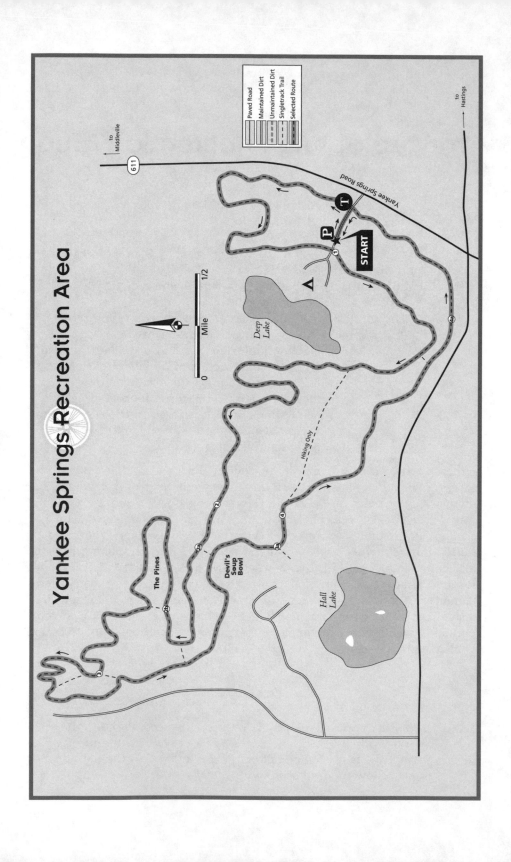

2.0 After passing the campground on the right, cross the access road and arrive at Post 1. The trailhead parking area is on the left. Cruise down a fast, fun descent and follow the buffed singletrack past two posts. Soon pass the first of several shortcuts and continue straight.

4.5 Reach Post 2 and continue straight to Post 2a.

4.7 Arrive at Post 2a. A left turn, heading to the Devil's Soup Bowl, cuts the ride short. Continue straight for the full loop. The trail rides through a pretty ravine area, swooping up and down a ridge.

6.0 Reach Post 2b. A left turn cuts the trail short. Stay right to continue the full loop and climb a steep hill leading to The Pines.

8.2 Reach Post 3. A left turn cuts the ride short. Stay right to continue the full loop. The trail twists through woods and under power lines. At an intersection with several trails, follow the mountain bike signs and stay on the buffed trail.

10.6 After passing by the Devil's Soup Bowl, arrive at vandalized Post 3a, which may or may not be marked. Continue straight and follow the worn path.

10.8 After a fast descent and rocky ascent, arrive at Post 4. Stay right with the buffed singletrack and head toward Post 4a on a fast and fun downhill.

12.0 Reach Post 4a after paralleling Gun Lake Road. Continue straight as the trail twists and rolls to the finish.

13.1 Turn left at a small stop sign, and cycle back to the parking area.

Fort Custer Recreation Area

Location:	2.5 miles from Augusta.
Distance:	16.8-mile loop.
Time:	2–4 hours.
Tread:	1.5 miles of paved road, 0.2 mile of dirt road, 15.1 miles of singletrack.
Aerobic level:	Moderate for distance; shorter loops are possible.
Technical difficulty:	1–2+.
Hill factor:	Flat to rolling.
Highlights:	Rainbow of loops with something for everyone.
Land status:	Fort Custer Recreation Area.
Maps:	USGS Augusta; maps available at park headquarters for 25 cents.
Access:	From Michigan 96/Dickman Road and Augusta Drive in Augusta, drive a quarter mile east on M–96 to park entrance. Turn south into the park and continue on the main park road for 2.3 miles. Turn east (right) onto the trailhead access road and continue to the parking area.

Notes on the trail: Offering a rainbow of loops, this well-organized and popular 16-mile multiple-use trail system offers something for everyone. The difficult Red Loop challenges riders with logs, whoop-de-dos, steeper climbs, and twisting Granny's Garden. The mellower Green Loop rolls next to Eagle Lake with a steep switchback climb and two shallow creek crossings. The Blue and Yellow Loops complete the rainbow with mostly obstacle-free trails, perfect for the novice cyclist. Cyclists should be aware that the trail signage is under review and could change in the near future. The daily entrance fee runs $4.00 per vehicle; a $20.00 annual pass, good at all state parks, is also available.

The Ride

0.0 Pedal to the southeast corner of the parking lot to the large trail map. Continue to Post 1 and turn right. Pedal onto the Red Trail and twist toward Post 2.

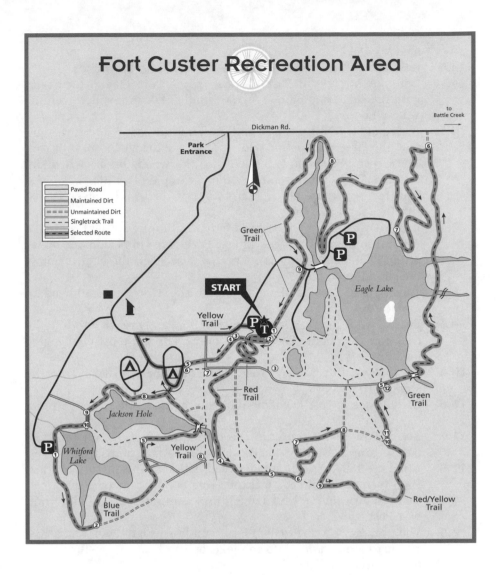

Fort Custer Recreation Area

0.25 Reach Post 2 and continue on the Red Trail. Get ready for banked S-curves.

0.6 Cruise by Post 3 and continue on the Red Trail as it meanders through trees.

1.6 Gear down for the Cardiac Climb.

1.9 Reach Post 5 after climbing a hill, and continue climbing.

2.05 Arrive at Post 6 and turn left onto technical Granny's Garden. Continuing straight will bypass this section and take you to Red Trail Post 9.

2.8 Make a sharp right turn at Post 7 as the trail widens and climbs a sandy hill. Share the trail again with the Yellow Loop.

3.1 Turn right with the wide trail at Post 8. Prepare to cruise for the next 2 miles.

3.5 Reach Red Trail Post 9 and turn left, back into the woods.

4.7 Continue straight at Post 10. Soon reach Post 11 and turn right with the Red Loop onto a narrow singletrack as it splits from the Yellow Loop.

5.1 Arrive at Red Trail Post 12 and Green Trail Post 5 and turn right onto the Green Loop on a wide trail. Eagle Lake is in front of you. The Green Trail soon turns left into the woods on a narrow singletrack. Cross a bridge, and climb a couple of switchbacks. Get your feet wet twice at creek crossings as the trail follows the east side of Eagle Lake.

7.1 Reach Post 6 and make a hard left. Continuing straight will take you out to the Battle Creek Linear Park. Take in peek-a-boo views of the lake, ending in a long, pretty descent to the shore. Follow the shoreline to Post 7.

8.1 Turn right at Post 7 and a boat launch site; turn right and head up a sandy hill.

9.5 Reach Post 8 and turn left. Almost immediately reach a fork in the trail and stay right. The next section holds the most challenging log hops.

10.5 Reach Post 9 at a paved road and cruise back to Post 1 on the straight trail.

11.0 Arrive back at Post 1. Follow the well-marked Yellow Loop to Post 5.

11.7 Reach Post 5 and ride into the campground. Turn left onto the paved campground road and cycle next to the campsites.

11.9 After site 159, turn left onto a paved path that shortly turns to dirt. Soon turn right onto the Jackson Hole Loop. Cross over a double-track to a primitive boat launch and continue on the wide trail, past Post 8.

12.5 The trail meets a dirt road at Post 9 and turns left. Soon reach Post 10, just before riding into the lake on the boat ramp. Turn right, back onto the wide trail.

12.9 Reach a parking area for the Whitford Lake Hiking Trail. Stay left and cross the parking lot to the trailhead at Post 1.

13.5 The trail rolls again and heads back into the woods.

14.0 Stay left at Post 2 and continue to Post 3.

14.6 Reach Post 3 and continue straight across the road. Soon cruise by Post 4.

14.8 Arrive at Post 5 and a T intersection. Stay right and cycle around Jackson Hole Lake. A left turn takes you back to Whitford Lake trailhead.

15.2 Watch out! The bridge is out at the bottom of hill. Walk your bike over the logs. Trails on the right are connectors from the Yellow Loop; always stay left.

15.5 Back at the beginning of the Blue Loop, turn right, toward the campground. At the paved campground road, turn left and follow the EXIT signs.

16.0 Reach an intersection with the campground road and main park road. Turn right and head back toward the parking area.

16.7 Reach the trailhead parking access road and turn right.

16.8 End of ride.

Ionia Recreation Area

Location:	3.1 miles west of South Ionia.
Distance:	7.9-mile loop.
Time:	1–1.5 hours.
Tread:	7.9 miles of singletrack.
Aerobic level:	Moderately easy.
Technical difficulty:	2–2 + .
Hill factor:	Flat to rolling.
Highlights:	Boulder-strewn area unlike any other Michigan ride.
Land status:	Ionia Recreation Area.
Maps:	USGS Ionia, Saranac.
Access:	From the intersection of Michigan 66 and Riverside Drive in South Ionia, turn west onto Riverside Drive and continue for 3.1 miles to the trailhead parking area on the north side of the road.

Notes on the trail: Boulders dot the open fields that surround this narrow trail system. Consisting of two loops, the trails maximize a long, skinny space. Maintained by Dan's Bike Shop in Ionia, the two loops run through a mostly open, stony area, with few of the dense trees that are so common on Michigan trails. Beginning on the easier Brown Loop, the route follows a buffed, twisting trail, then picks up the Yellow Loop and dips into the trees for the first time. Pedaling up and down a ridge, riders encounter the most challenges of the ride, including tight tree passages, short and steep climbs, log jumps, and sand. Following the railroad tracks, the trail finally climbs the ridge for good and begins the return route. Completely in the open, the second half of the Yellow Loop passes large

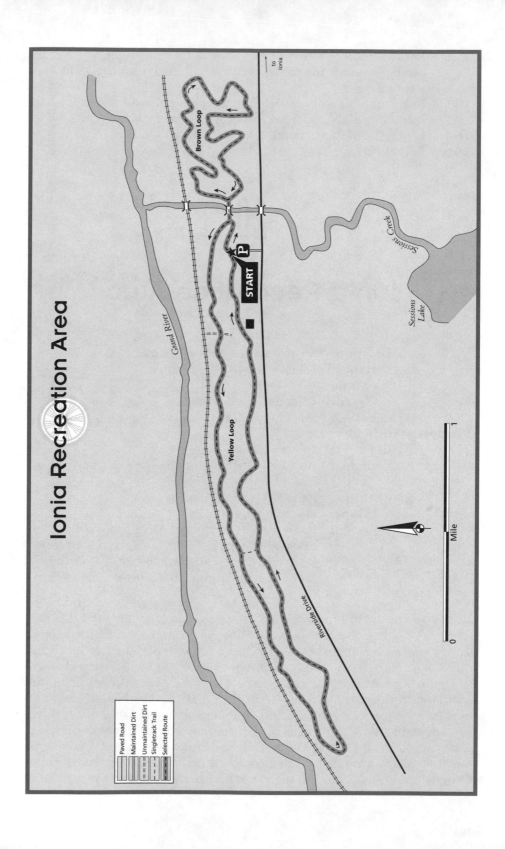

Ionia Recreation Area

Paved Road
Maintained Dirt
Unmaintained Dirt
Singletrack Trail
Selected Route

Grand River

Brown Loop

to Ionia

Sessions Creek

Sessions Lake

START

P

Yellow Loop

Riverside Drive

Mile

0   1

Erin cruises along fast, open trail at the Ionia Recreation Area.

boulders on a straight, mostly open trail with gravel and loose stones. It is impossible to get lost on this easy-to-follow trail system. Like all Michigan state parks, there is a $4.00-per-vehicle entrance fee, which must be paid at park headquarters (see Appendix B), since the parking area does not have a self-pay station.

The Ride

0.0 Pick up the trail at the northeast corner of the parking lot, next to the trail map.

0.2 Reach the intersection with the Yellow and Brown Loops. Stay right for the Brown Loop and cross over the bridge. Ride in a clockwise direction, following the arrows.

2.5 The loop ends; turn left and cross the bridge. Stay right for the Yellow Loop.

3.0 Cross an old doubletrack and head into the woods as the trail begins to roll.

4.0 Continue straight over a wide trail. A left turn will shorten the ride by about 2.5 miles.

5.2	Turn left in a clearing and begin the return route. Watch for loose gravel from here to the end.
6.5	The shortcut rejoins the trail on the left.
7.5	Cruise by an old schoolhouse next to the road.
7.9	Arrive back at the parking lot.

Ella Sharp Singletrack

Location:	Jackson.
Distance:	13.2-mile loop.
Time:	1.5–3 hours.
Tread:	1.7 miles of paved road, 0.2 mile of dirt road, 11.3 miles of singletrack.
Aerobic level:	Moderate.
Technical difficulty:	1 to 2+.
Hill factor:	Flat to rolling.
Highlights:	A baker's dozen of twisted singletrack.
Land status:	Ella Sharp City Park.
Maps:	USGS Jackson; rough map available from Michigan Mountain Biking Association (see Appendix A).
Access:	From the intersection of Stonewall and Horton Roads in Jackson, turn north onto Stonewall Road. Drive 0.25 mile to the Ella Sharp Park entrance. Turn east and continue to the stop sign. Turn north onto Oakwood Street toward the pool, then almost immediately turn east onto Birchwood Drive. Continue to the parking area about 0.25 mile down the road. Park across from a No Dumping sign and Loops 1 and 2 trailhead.

Notes on the trail: Think of this ride as a selection of pastries at a bakery. You can savor one or devour a baker's dozen. Connected by paved roads, the ride consists of thirteen different trails for all skill levels in a pretty urban park. It is possible to do a short ride by combining a few loops, or you can complete all the loops by riding the route described here. Each trail is clearly signed with its own trailhead, and orange dots painted

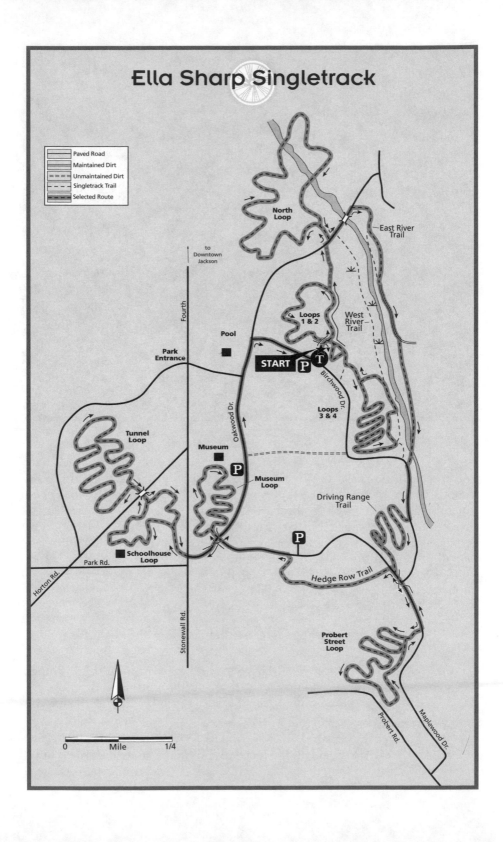

Tunnel Loop's namesake.

on trees mark almost every route. The most confusing section comprises Loops 1–4, which is where the route begins. Once this segment is completed, it is clear sailing through the rest of the ride, but expect to encounter short, steep hills, twisted singletrack, and logs to hop. The trails, developed from old horse routes, twist repeatedly, maximizing a small area. This trail system is so popular that it is rare not to meet other bikers and hikers. Other activities available in the park include swimming, golf, soccer, a museum, and a planetarium.

The Ride

0.0   Cycle across Birchwood Drive to the Loops 1–2 trailhead. Plunge down a rough, wide trail. Turn left at the bottom and follow the orange "1" painted on a tree. Shortly reach a sand pit, which the trail circles and twists around. Cycle around it in a counter clockwise direction and pick up the singletrack on the opposite end.

0.8   Cross over the first downhill of the ride. Loop 2 begins here and twists like a figure eight.

1.1 Watch out! Just before a steep uphill, follow the trail as it branches to the left. This is the connector to Loop 3 and easy to miss. The trail stays below road level, then climbs up a hill in an open area and begins Loop 3. The next two loops are the most twisted. Loop 3 merges with Loop 4, marked with a large painted "4" on a tree.

2.0 After twisting and turning, reach a T intersection and turn left onto the unmarked West River Trail.

2.1 This section of the West River Trail is closed. Stay left and head back toward the road.

2.2 Reach the connector trail between Loops 2 and 3. Turn right and head toward Loops 1 and 2. Stay right at all intersections, and pedal back to the sand pit.

2.5 At the sand pit stay right and cycle the doubletrack out to a paved road.

2.7 Turn right onto the paved road, then immediately turn left onto the marked North Loop. When the trail splits, stay left and cycle up a steep hill.

3.1 Before reaching private property, turn right and follow the orange dots. The next section crosses the river twice on bridges.

4.7 Back at the paved road, turn left and cross the river. Look for the East River trailhead on the right and cycle up a steep hill. Turn right at the top of the hill. You can stay high or cycle down next to the river; all options lead to the same place.

5.0 The trail merges with a dirt road next to a building. Continue straight.

5.2 Follow the trail as it continues into the woods and the road curves to the left.

5.4 Pass through a fence. Ride out to Birchwood Drive and turn left.

5.6 Turn right onto marked Driving Range Trail, a tight singletrack.

6.1 The trail splits at the top of a hill. Stay left and head downhill.

6.3 Turn left when the trail dumps out onto paved Maplewood Drive. Continue straight at the intersection with Birchwood.

6.5 Turn right onto Probert Street Loop, and turn right at the first intersection. The trail on the left is the return route. Follow the orange dots as the trail plunges down steep hills with tight turns and equally steep ascents.

7.5 Arrive back at Maplewood Drive and turn left. Cruise past the Birchwood intersection and continue on Maplewood Drive.

7.7 Just past where the Driving Range Trail dumps out, reach marked Hedge Row Trail and turn left.

8.0 Hedge Row dumps out at a field. Cycle across the field to paved Maplewood Drive and turn left.

8.2 Cross Oakwood Drive to the marked Museum Loop trailhead. The trail splits; stay to the left (the return is on the right). Watch for low-hanging branches.

9.0 Turn right onto Oakwood Drive. Continue to the intersection with busy Stonewall Road. Watching for cars, cross the road to the marked trailhead for Schoolhouse and Tunnel Loops. Turn right, following the power lines.

10.7 Reach an intersection. Turn left, heading downhill toward the Tunnel Loop, and cruise through the old tunnel. Continuing straight takes you out of the loop.

10.8 Turn left after passing through a tunnel. Cycling straight dumps you out to a field.

12.2 End of loop. Cycle back through the tunnel and up the hill; turn left, following the OUT sign.

12.5 Arrive back at the intersection of Stonewall Road and Oakwood Drive. Cross Stonewall and take Oakwood Drive to Birchwood Drive.

13.0 Turn right onto Birchwood.

13.2 Arrive back at parking area.

Burchfield Park Singletrack

Location:	5 miles south of Lansing.
Distance:	5.9-mile loop.
Time:	30 minutes–1 hour.
Tread:	5.7 miles of singletrack, 0.2 mile of double-track.
Aerobic level:	Moderately easy.
Technical difficulty:	3–4.
Hill factor:	Mostly flat with a few hills.
Highlights:	Challenging obstacle-strewn singletrack; perfect for bike control practice.
Land status:	Ingham County Park.
Map:	USGS Aurelius.
Access:	From the intersection of Interstate 96 and M. L. King Jr. Boulevard in Lansing, drive 0.25 mile south on Eaton Rapids Road to the stoplight. Turn east onto Bishop Road and go 0.5 mile. Turn south onto Grovenburg Road. After 3.75 miles pass the main Burchfield Park

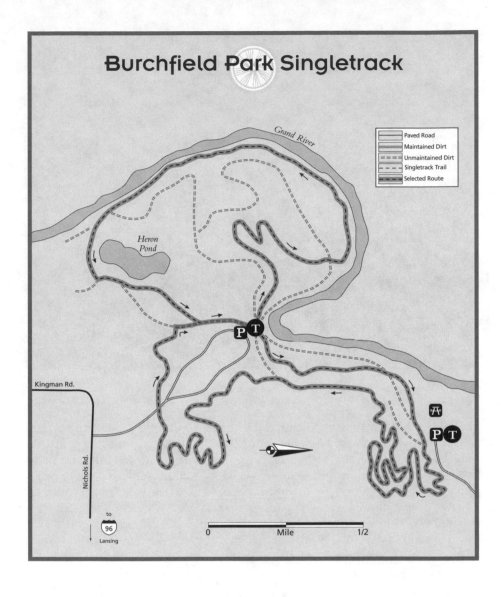

Burchfield Park Singletrack

Grand River

Heron Pond

Kingman Rd.

Nichols Rd.

to
96
Lansing

	Paved Road
	Maintained Dirt
	Unmaintained Dirt
	Singletrack Trail
	Selected Route

0   Mile   1/2

entrance on the west side of the road. Turn
west onto Nichols Road at 4.65 miles and follow the signs to the River Bend Natural Area.
In 0.4 mile turn north into the River Bend Natural Area and continue to the parking area.

Notes on the trail: This trail is like a B horror movie: plenty of monstrous
obstacles with imaginative names like Kentaro's Monster and Dragon's
Back. The trail offers every imaginable apparatus from laddered climbs

Erin attempts one of Burchfield Park's many challenging obstacles.

and rock piles to twists and turns. Fortunately, the most difficult apparatuses always have a bypass. Developed by local Michigan Mountain Biking Association members, the trail is marked with mountain bike signs and yellow tape, and each section of obstacles is named, such as Treehugger's Log. At times, however, the trail becomes so fast that it is easy to miss an obstacle and blindly cruise by an apparatus on a bypass. The obstacles mentioned below are only a taste of what you will find, so stay alert. This trail system is dynamic, with new singletrack and obstacles in the works. There is a $2.00 entrance fee to the park.

The Ride

0.0 From the trailhead/map kiosk, turn right and follow the wide ski trail. Turn right almost immediately onto a singletrack, marked with ADVANCED MOUNTAIN BIKE signs.

0.15 Merge back onto the wide ski trail. In a very short distance, pick up the advanced mountain bike trail on the left and parallel the river. Follow the signs as you cross over the ski trail, brush up next to a parking lot, and climb a hill.

0.5 Turn right back onto the narrower singletrack. Meet the first of many obstacles—a log hop, shortly followed by a rocky climb.

1.0 The trail splits; stay right. Straight takes you back to the parking area. Shortly reach ZGDT Rockpile; cycle over it or go around it.

2.2 Arrive at Kentaro's Monster, a log hopper's playground. After this section, the trail straightens out and becomes much faster. Stay alert or you'll miss some of the obstacles.

3.0 Reach Dragon's Back, one of the laddered log bridges, and test your skills.

3.4 Reach dirt access road for River Bend trailhead. Turn right and then immediately left back onto the singletrack. The trail twists sharply through the woods.

3.8 After a rock pile, the singletrack dumps out onto a doubletrack. Turn right and cycle back to the River Bend trailhead.

4.0 Arrive back at the trailhead. Turn left and in a short distance reach a four-way intersection. Continue straight and follow the ADVANCED MOUNTAIN BIKE sign. Almost immediately reach a Y intersection and stay right.

4.7 Reach another four-way intersection. Continue straight and follow the yellow tape. Soon cruise next to the river on the prettiest portion of the ride. Follow the signs and yellow tape and you won't get lost.

5.4 Arrive at a multiple-trail intersection and stay with the middle trail. Follow the sign to River Bend. In a very short distance turn left at a T intersection and follow the yellow tape.

5.6 Turn left at another Y intersection and cruise down a hill. Turn right at the bottom of the hill and climb a short, steep hill. Turn right at the top of the hill.

5.7 Stay left at a Y intersection, follow the yellow tape, and coast down a hill. Soon reach a familiar intersection and turn left toward the River Bend trailhead.

5.9 Arrive back at the parking area.

Sleepy Hollow State Park

Location:	12 miles southeast of St. Johns.
Distance:	10.9-mile loop.
Time:	1–2 hours.
Tread:	10.9 miles of singletrack and wide ski trails.
Aerobic level:	Moderately easy.
Technical difficulty:	2-.
Hill factor:	Mostly flat to occasionally rolling.
Highlights:	Gentle cruiser, ending with Lake Ovid overlooks.
Land status:	Sleepy Hollow State Park.
Maps:	USGS Price; maps available at park headquarters.
Access:	From the intersection of Michigan 21 and U.S. 27 in St. Johns, drive south on U.S. 27 for 6 miles to the Price Road exit. Continue east on Price Road for 5.5 miles to the park entrance. Turn north and drive 0.4 mile past the tollbooth. Turn east, following the HIKING TRAIL sign, onto a dirt road and continue back to the parking area.

Notes on the trail: Park management at this 2,600-acre park has opened its doors to mountain bikers, allowing cyclists on the entire 16-mile hiking trail system. This route follows the perimeter Red Trail as it cruises through open fields and in and out of hardwoods. It is an excellent trail for beginners looking for a longer, virtually obstacle-free, mostly singletrack ride. More experienced cyclists will find it a good early season conditioner. Although the trail is marked with posts and maps, there are a few confusing intersections. However, a wrong turn is usually obvious within a short distance. The prettiest section and most challenging hills come toward the end of the ride when the trail follows man-made Lake Ovid. A $4.00-per-vehicle entrance fee is charged.

The Ride

0.0   Cycle to the trailhead at the east end of the parking lot. Turn left at Post 1 and follow the Red Trail.

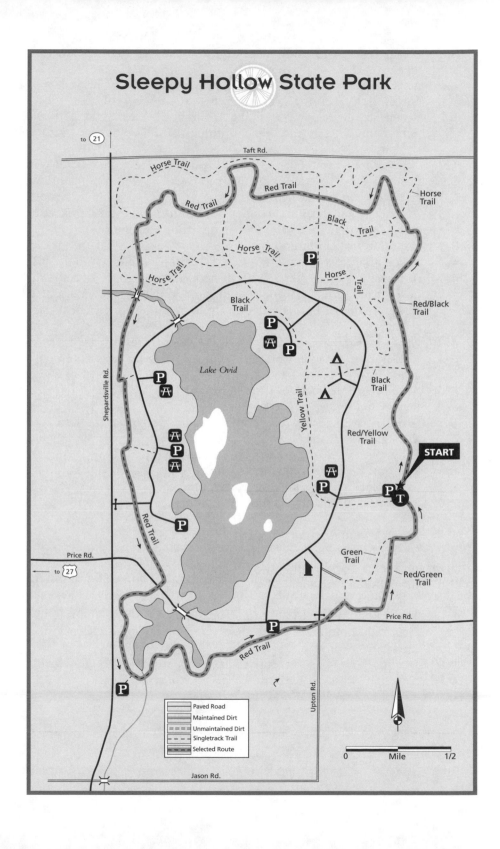

Sleepy Hollow State Park

0.9	Reach Post 3 and continue straight on the Red Trail. A left turn takes you to a campground.
1.6	After crossing a bridge and climbing a hill, turn right and head downhill. Continuing straight leads to the horse trails.
1.7	Reach an intersection with the Black Trail. Turn right onto the tighter singletrack and head uphill. The Black Trail continues straight.
1.9	Cross a horse trail. Soon cross a wooden bridge across a creek.
1.95	Reach a T intersection and turn right. Cross over another bridge and continue on the Red Trail.
2.8	After cruising through an open field, cross the horse trail once again. The trail enters the woods and rolls a bit more.
3.9	Continue straight at Post 9.
4.1	Reach an intersection with a foot trail. Stay left and go up the hill.
4.5	At a swampy area, merge with the horse trail. In a short while the horse trail turns left and the mountain biking trail continues straight. Almost immediately the trail splits at a white post; stay right.
4.8	Cross over the Maple River on a wooden bridge.
5.3	Red Trail turns right. Continuing straight dumps you out at picnic grounds.
5.6	At another intersection, turn right with the Red Trail. A left turn takes you to more picnic grounds.
6.1	Cross a paved access road and continue straight on the Red Trail through the brush.
6.7	Cross paved Price Road and continue straight.
6.8	The trail turns right next to a pond. Cycle along one of the prettiest sections of the trail and cross a bridge.
7.0	Turn left at the T intersection. A right turn takes you out to a parking area.
7.5	Reach an intersection. Stay left and cross a bridge.
8.0	Cycle along a ridge with a tree-dotted pond on the left. The trail rolls with biggest hills yet.
9.6	Reach a marked intersection; continue straight through the field. A left turn takes you out to a road.
9.8	The trail dumps out to the intersection of Price and Upton Roads. Turn right onto Price Road, then immediately turn left back onto the trail.
9.9	Reach a T intersection. Stay right and continue on the Red Trail.
10.7	Stay right with the Red Trail at another T intersection.
10.9	Arrive back at Post 1 and the parking area.

Jailhouse Trail

Location:	Ithaca.
Distance:	3.9-mile loop.
Time:	30–45 minutes.
Tread:	3.9 miles of singletrack.
Aerobic level:	Easy.
Technical difficulty:	2.
Hill factor:	Flat with a few small hills.
Highlights:	Buffed singletrack with small-town charm.
Land status:	City of Ithaca.
Map:	USGS Ithaca.
Access:	From the intersection of East Center Street/Business 27 and South Pine River Street in downtown Ithaca, turn south onto South Pine River Street. Continue for 0.75 mile. Turn west into the fairgrounds and follow the JAIL-HOUSE TRAIL sign. Continue straight to the intersection with the yellow directory sign and turn south. The Jailhouse Trail starts to the west, just beyond the horse barns.

Notes on the trail: Located practically in downtown Ithaca, a small farming community, the Jailhouse Trail shares its space with the fairgrounds, giving it a folksy feeling. The short, buffed trail is almost completely flat except for a couple of small hills. A few log jumps and ramps punctuate the trail as it twists and turns through a grove of young trees, occasionally dumping out to open fields. Developed by the Michigan Mountain Biking Association, the trail is marked with large red arrows, and it's perfect for novice riders new to singletrack. This popular sand-free trail also hosts an annual bike race.

The Ride

0.0 Pick up the trail at the south end of the fairgrounds. Look for the large wooden trailhead in an open area. Singletrack takes off into the woods and follows a red arrow.

1.1 Reach the steepest hill of the ride.

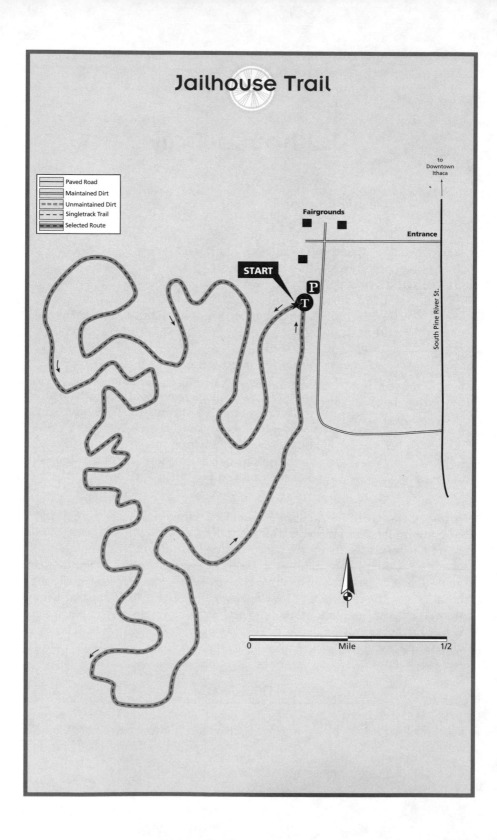

2.0 The trail starts to twist and turn.

3.2 The trail straightens out and cruises through a field.

3.6 Turn left onto a doubletrack. Almost immediately turn left, back onto a singletrack.

3.9 Arrive back at trailhead. Get ready for another lap!

Deerfield County Park

Location:	6.6 miles west of Mt. Pleasant.
Distance:	5.7-mile loop.
Time:	30 minutes–1 hour.
Tread:	1.4 miles of doubletrack, 4.3 miles of wide and narrow singletrack.
Aerobic level:	Moderately easy.
Technical difficulty:	1+.
Hill factor:	Flat with one long hill and a few minor ones.
Highlights:	Tranquil river setting with suspension bridges, a covered bridge, and a rolling ridge.
Land status:	Isabella County Parks.
Map:	USGS Mount Pleasant.
Access:	From the intersection of Business 27 and Michigan 20 in Mt. Pleasant, drive 6.3 miles west on M–20. Turn south into the park entrance, pass the tollbooth, and pay the entrance fee. Continue for 0.3 mile to the first parking area on the north.

Notes on the trail: This tranquil 590-acre park sidles up next to the Chippewa River and rolls through small hills. Two suspension bridges and one covered bridge cross the river, perfect for entertaining young children. The first half of the route closely follows the mellow River Trail, ideal for families. The second half rolls more pronouncedly along the Wildwood Pathway, a National Recreation Trail with narrow singletrack and a log jump. Interconnecting trails, begging for exploration, crisscross the park. The park, an island of trees among farmland, is also extremely popular with hikers, so display your most courteous biking behavior. There is a $4.00-per-vehicle entrance fee.

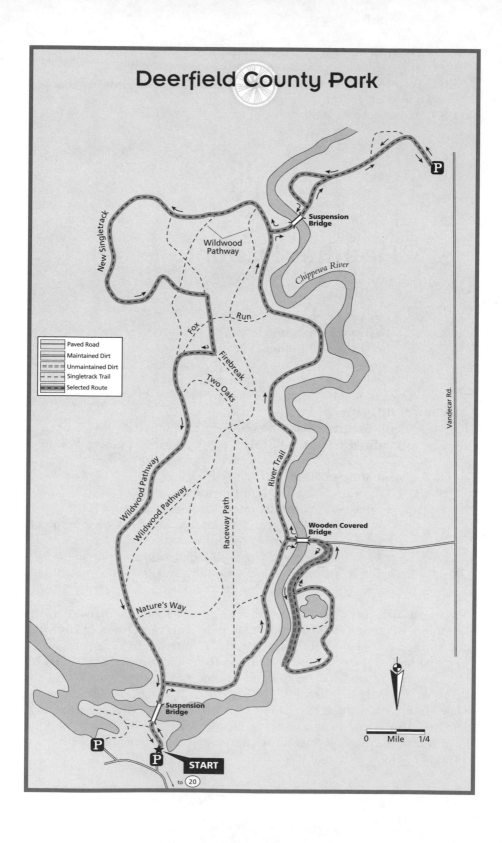

Deerfield Park's covered bridge.

The Ride

0.0 Pick up the trail at the south end of the parking lot. Soon reach the first suspension bridge and walk your bike over it.

0.2 Turn right onto River Trail.

0.4 Stay right at the intersection with Raceway Path.

0.8 Turn right at an intersection with the Covered Bridge Trail and cruise down a hill. Cycle through the wooden covered bridge. Immediately after the bridge, turn right onto an unnamed doubletrack.

1.2 Veer left onto a singletrack. Climb a hill through a small grove of evergreens.

1.6 Back at the doubletrack, turn right and cycle toward the covered bridge. Turn left and retrace your tracks over the bridge.

1.8 Turn right back onto the River Trail and meander next to the river.

2.1 Pass through the campground area and stay right at all intersections with other trails.

2.7 Reach another intersection. Wildwood Pathway goes left. Turn right down a fun, rooty singletrack and walk your bike over the second suspension bridge.

3.3 Reach the south parking area and picnic grounds. Turn around and retrace your tracks over the suspension bridge and up the rooty singletrack.

3.9 Back at the intersection with Wildwood Pathway, turn right and zip by a trail on the left.

4.2 The trail splits. Wildwood goes left. Turn right, climbing a steep, sandy hill. Turn right at the top of the hill.

4.6 After a rolling descent, reach an intersection with Wildwood Pathway. Continue straight, up a hill and over a log jump. Turn right at the top of the hill. Take the second right down a hill back toward Wildwood Pathway.

4.8 Arrive back at Wildwood Pathway and turn left. Cruise by Two Oaks Crossover.

5.3 Stay right at the beginning of the Wildwood Pathway and head back toward the first suspension bridge. Cruise by a sign for Nature's Way Loop.

5.5 Back at the intersection with the River Trail, stay right toward the bridge. Walk over the suspension bridge. Turn left at the end of the bridge and cycle toward the parking area.

5.7 Arrive back at the parking area.

Northwestern Michigan:
Lake Michigan Sunsets, Inland Lakes, and Plush Resorts

Lake Michigan, soaring sand dunes, dense forest, and rolling hills have attracted tourists to northwestern Michigan since the late 1800s. Today mountain bikers benefit from the area's history of tourism and the active lifestyle of the locals. Hill-hugging segments of the North Country Trail (NCT) reveal breathtaking views, mountain bike trails dot elegant four-season resorts, and forest pathways wind through deep forest.

It should be no surprise that northwestern Michigan—everything west of Interstate 75 and north of U.S. 10—is home to an abundance of trail choices, including the most sections of the NCT open to mountain bikers. With so many NCT segments to choose from, only a handful could be included in this book. Clustered around the Petoskey/Harbor Springs area and near Traverse City and Cadillac, these segments roll through hardwoods on mostly buffed singletrack. A 3-mile descent on the NCT near Kipp Road is one of the most thrilling downhills in Michigan.

Northwestern Michigan also hosts well-marked cross-country skiing pathways that become mountain biking havens in the summer. Located throughout northern Michigan, pathway highlights include the Cadillac Pathway and Big M Ski Area.

Unlike southern Michigan, there are relatively few mountain bike–specific trails in northwestern Michigan. The VASA Singletrack Trail, the mountain biking companion to the famous VASA Ski Trail, has gained most of the attention over the past few years for its well-maintained singletrack. A cooperative effort between the Department of Natural Resources and the Michigan Mountain Biking Association, the trail is a perfect example of how local biking advocates are developing trails.

Buffed singletrack can also be found at some of the luxurious golf and ski resorts, such as Boyne Mountain and Crystal Resort, that call northwestern Michigan home. Boyne Mountain stands out among the three with viciously steep hills and banked descents. Ultimately, the best way to discover northwestern Michigan mountain biking is to join one of several local bike stores, such as Fitness Source & Cycle in Petoskey (see Appendix A), on weekly group rides.

Big M Loop

Location:	7 miles southwest of Wellston.
Distance:	11.75-mile loop; other loops are possible.
Time:	1.5–3 hours.
Tread:	11.75 miles of narrow and wide singletrack.
Aerobic level:	Moderately strenuous.
Technical difficulty:	2.
Hill factor:	Hilly to highlands. Trail rolls constantly with a few sustained climbs.
Highlights:	A hill climber's delight with many fun descents and 360-degree views.
Land status:	Huron-Manistee National Forest, Manistee Ranger District.
Maps:	USGS Udell; maps available at forest office (see Appendix B).
Access:	Drive 4 miles west of Wellston on Michigan 55. Turn south onto East Udell Hills Road and continue for 3 miles to the Big M parking area on the right.

Notes on the trail: This old downhill skiing area is a challenging cross-country skiing area in the winter and an equally invigorating mountain biking route in the summer. Cyclists should be prepared for many aerobic climbs, particularly to the top of Capper's Peak, with its 360-degree views of the Manistee Forest. The route is fairly well marked with maps at most of the intersections and clear diamond markers with colored dots. With more singletrack in development, the area is open to mountain bikes from April 15 through September 30. Bikers should show caution on the long, steep descents, which often cross rutted doubletracks and are sometimes covered in leaves by late September.

The Ride

0.0 From the trailhead pedal along Lumberjack Trail. Stay right at the first intersection.

0.7 The trail begins its roller-coaster ride.

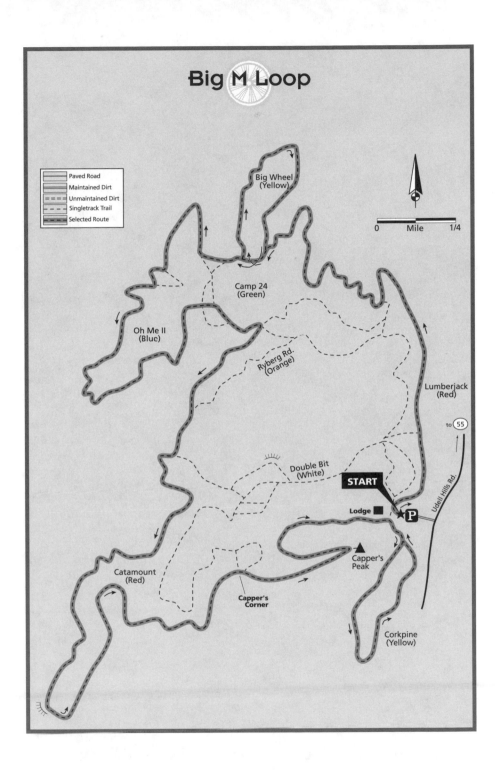

Fall leaves hide obstacles on Big M trails.

1.15 Reach Post 3 at the edge of a clearcut. Turn right onto Camp 24. Continue through the clearcut and back into the woods as the trail begins the first of many long climbs.

2.45 Arrive at Post 4 and turn right onto Big Wheel. Ride in a clockwise direction.

3.5 Turn right back onto Camp 24. Almost immediately arrive back at Post 4 and continue straight.

3.7 Reach Post 5 and turn right onto the trail marked with two black diamonds. Watch for whoop-de-dos and hidden holes. The easier route is on the left.

4.85 Arrive at a trail intersection. Continue straight and follow the diamond.

6.0 Back at the Camp 24 Loop. Turn right and head downhill.

6.25 At Post 6 turn right onto Double Bit. You will soon reach an intersection with Ryberg Road; stay right with Double Bit.

6.8 Stay right with the wide Double Bit at another intersection with Ryberg Road.

6.9 Turn right onto Catamount Trail. Get ready for more climbing and big views.

8.1 Reach first viewpoint.

9.4 Reach Capper's Corner and turn right onto tight singletrack that follows the ridgeline. Do not head downhill.

9.8 Drop your bike and walk up the sandy hill on the left to the top of Capper's Peak for views of the Manistee National Forest. Enjoy the vistas and retrace your tracks back to your bike. Prepare for a quick 250-foot elevation loss as you continue down the hill.

10.4 Pedal past the lodge and turn right onto Corkpine for a short, cool down loop.

10.55 Turn right and follow the CORKPINE sign.

11.75 Arrive back at parking area.

Cadillac Pathway

Location:	3 miles east of Cadillac.
Distance:	10-mile loop.
Time:	1 hour.
Tread:	9.9 miles of narrow and wide singletrack, 0.1 mile of doubletrack.
Aerobic level:	Easy to moderate. A few hills leave you gasping for breath.
Technical difficulty:	2.
Highlights:	Best DNR-designated pathway in the Pere Marquette Forest.
Hill factor:	Rolling.
Land status:	Pere Marquette State Forest, Kalkaska Unit.
Maps:	USGS Cadillac North, Jennings; maps available at trailhead and DNR office (see Appendix B).
Access:	From the intersection of U.S. 131 and Michigan 55 in downtown Cadillac, drive 2.5 miles north on U.S. 131. Turn east onto Boon Road and follow the sign to the Cadillac Pathway. Drive 3.5 miles to the well-signed trailhead on the east side of the road.

Notes on the trail: The Cadillac Pathway is the most enjoyable pathway in the Pere Marquette Forest. The scenery isn't particularly spectacular; instead it offers consistently smooth trails, narrow singletrack, and fast, exhilarating descents. The singletrack becomes even narrower about halfway through the ride as it leaves the main trail and winds through hardwood trees. Like other pathways, it is clearly signed with blue diamonds and maps on numbered posts at every intersection. Families with young mountain bikers can explore the many shorter loops.

The Ride

0.0 Begin at Post 1 near the large information board. Continue straight on the flat trail to Post 2. In a short distance emerge from the woods and arrive at Post 2. Cycle to Post 3.

0.5 From Post 3 stay right toward Post 4. Get ready for the first hill of the ride.

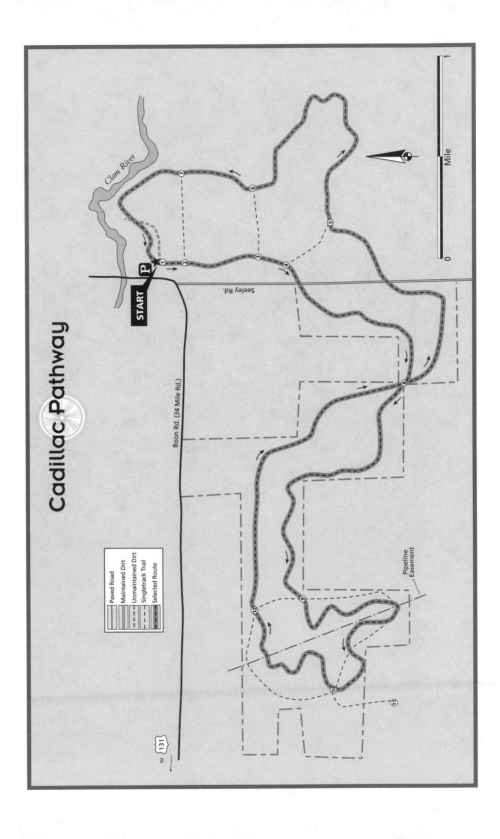

Cadillac Pathway

Keith cruises along Cadillac Pathway's gentle beginning.

0.65 Reach Post 4 and turn right toward Post 8.

0.75 Cross Seely Road.

1.6 Arrive at Post 8 and follow the sign to Post 9. The trail rolls continuously from this point on.

3.1 Reach Post 9 and continue cycling downhill toward Post 10. Shortly turn right at an unmarked, narrower singletrack trail.

3.5 The singletrack rejoins the ski trail at a pipeline service road. Continue on the wide main trail. Soon turn right as the singletrack once again splits off from the main trail.

3.8 Cross a wider ski trail.

3.95 The singletrack rejoins the main trail at Post 10. Turn right back onto the singletrack trail, hidden behind a distinctive three-pronged tree.

4.4 Rejoin the wider ski trail at the pipeline service road. Coast down first of many fun descents past Post 12.

4.65 Cruise past Post 12. Continue toward Post 8 and climb steadily at times.

6.3 At Post 8 continue cycling to Post 5. Ease off the brakes for another fast downhill.

7.05 Cross Seely Road.

7.4 Reach Post 5 and turn right. Cycle up a hill to Post 6.

8.75 Turn right at Post 6 and cycle past pine trees on your way to Post 7.

9.1 From Post 7 continue cycling straight toward Post 1.

9.6 Follow the trail to the left as it dumps out onto a doubletrack along the Clam River.

9.7 Pick up the singletrack paralleling the doubletrack to the right.

10.0 Arrive back at the parking lot.

North Country Trail:
Marilla Trailhead to Dilling Road

Location:	6.8 miles southwest of Mesick.
Distance:	29.1-mile loop.
Time:	3–5 hours.
Tread:	15.4 miles of singletrack, 11.9 miles of dirt road, 1.8 miles of paved road.
Aerobic level:	Moderate to strenuous (for length); possible to shorten ride with car shuttle.
Technical difficulty:	3+; hill-hugging narrow singletrack is exhilarating but potentially treacherous.
Hill factor:	Highlands.
Highlights:	Sustained climbs and big views give a mountain feeling among hills.
Land status:	Huron-Manistee National Forest, Manistee Ranger District.
Maps:	USGS Yuma, Marilla; maps available at the trailhead and forest office in Manistee and Cadillac. NCT guidebooks available from North Country Trail Association (see Appendix C).
Access:	From the intersection of Michigan 37 and Michigan 115, just west of Mesick, turn west onto M–115 and drive 1.3 miles. Turn south onto Hodenpyl Dam Road and go 5.5 miles. Turn left into the trailhead parking area.

Notes on the trail: Who says there aren't any mountains in Michigan? This ride has enough sustained climbs along a smooth, hill-hugging 15-mile singletrack trail to make riders forget that they are in a state with a high point of less than 2,000 feet. Cyclists are rewarded with views of the Manistee River, Hodenypyl Dam, and Udell Hills. The last half of the ride is on paved and dirt roads; but it can just as easily be an out-and-back ride, or you can leave a car at the Dilling Road Trailhead for a car shuttle. The trail is well marked with blue and gray diamonds and mile markers; however, the mileage we recorded differed slightly from what was posted. Watch for traffic on the dirt and paved roads.

North Country Trail:
Marilla Trailhead to Dilling Road

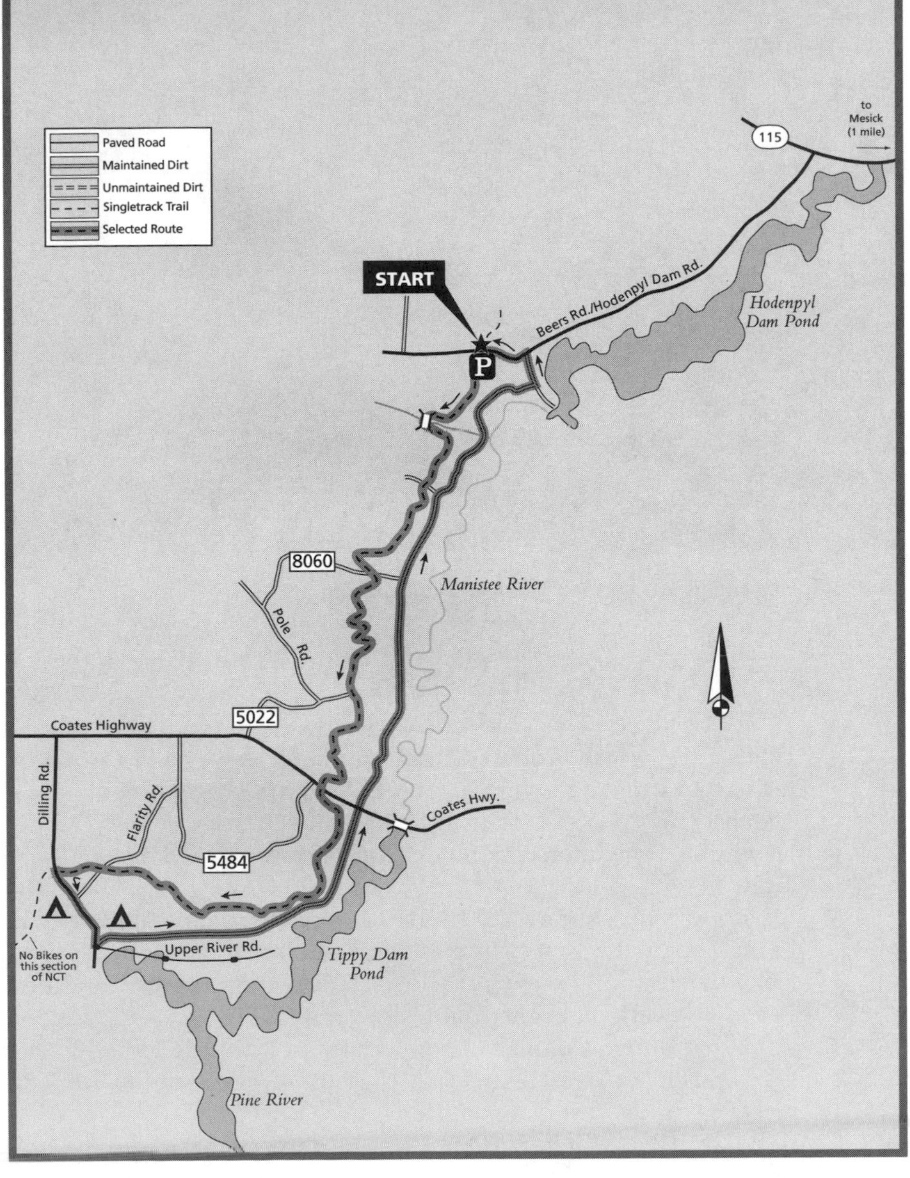

Paved Road
Maintained Dirt
Unmaintained Dirt
Singletrack Trail
Selected Route

to Mesick
(1 mile)

115

START

Beers Rd./Hodenpyl Dam Rd.

P

Hodenpyl
Dam Pond

8060

Manistee River

Pole Rd.

Coates Highway

5022

Dilling Rd.

Flarity Rd.

5484

Coates Hwy.

Upper River Rd.

Tippy Dam
Pond

No Bikes on
this section
of NCT

Pine River

Bruce Kantor climbs a ridge on the North Country Trail.

The Ride

0.0 Follow the North Country Trail markers past the information board and cycle on a gentle downhill. Views begin almost immediately.

1.1 Stay right at the intersection with the "hikers only" Manistee River Trail.

1.3 Cross a wooden bridge and begin a 1-mile climb on a tight switchback. This is the first of four sustained climbs and fast descents along narrow, hill-hugging singletrack over the next several miles.

8.8 Reach an overlook of the Manistee National Forest.

8.9 The High Bridge Connector Trail comes in from the left.

9.2 Cross paved Coates Highway at the end of a downhill. Immediately regain the lost elevation.

11.1 Reach overlook of Tippy Dam. Watch for trees jutting into the trail on the next downhill.

11.6 At the bottom of a hill cross a doubletrack.

12.6 Reach a high point and begin a long, fast downhill on a wide portion of the trail. The upcoming sharp right turn back onto the narrow trail at the bottom of the hill is easy to miss.

13.1	Make a sharp right turn.
14.6	Turn left onto a doubletrack, then almost immediately right back onto the singletrack.
15.4	Climb a small hill to the end of the singletrack at Dilling Road. The NCT continues on the other side of the road but isn't open to mountain bikes. Turn left and pedal downhill on Dilling Road.
16.4	Turn left toward the Tippy Dam Campground, marked by a sign. Straight leads to the shores of the Tippy Dam and Pond, a pretty 0.5-mile side trip and picnic site.
16.5	Stay left on the sandy Upper River Road/Forest Road 8100 and follow the power lines.
20.8	Cross the paved Coates Highway. Continue cycling the Upper River Road for another 7 miles as it rolls gently in and out of the forest and along the river.
27.8	Turn left at the unmarked dirt road as the Upper River Road ends.
28.3	Turn left onto paved Beers Road and pedal up a steep hill.
29.1	Watch for traffic and turn left into the parking area, just before the crest of the hill.

Crystal Mountain Trails

Location:	Crystal Mountain Resort.
Distance:	7.4-mile loop.
Time:	1–2 hours.
Tread:	0.2 mile of dirt road, 0.9 mile of paved road, 2.2 miles of singletrack, 4.1 miles of double-track/wide ski trail.
Aerobic level:	Easy for first 4.9 miles; moderately strenuous for last 2.5 miles.
Technical difficulty:	1 to 2 for first 4.9 miles; last 2.5 miles rate a 3.
Hill factor:	First half is flat; second half is hilly to high-lands.
Highlights:	Charming four-season resort hosts trail system with something for all abilities.
Land status:	Private. Landowner graciously allows mountain bikes to use designated trails; please respect property and stay on established trails.

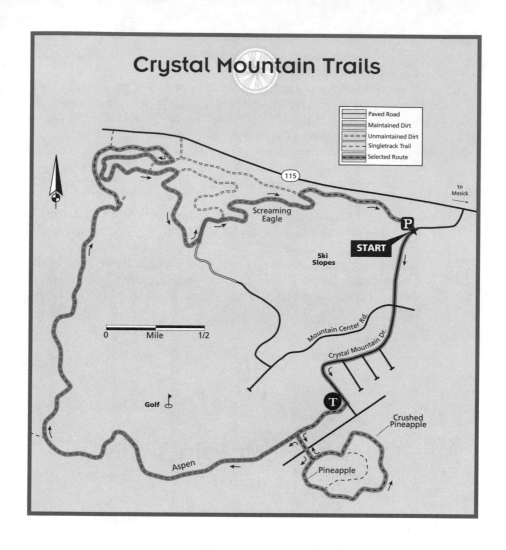

Crystal Mountain Trails

Maps: USGS Thompsonville; maps available at the Activities Desk in the Inn at the Mountain.

Access: From the intersection of U.S. 31 and Michigan 115, just south of Benzonia, drive 6 miles east on M–115. Turn southwest onto Crystal Mountain Drive and continue back to the large gravel parking lot near the Inn at the Mountain and at the base of the ski lifts. Park here.

Notes on the trail: This ride offers two distinct personalities. The first 4.9 miles provide a mostly flat, laid-back ramble, perfect for families and beginning mountain bikers. The last 2.5 miles, however, abruptly put an end to the mellow ride. Climbing steeply up and down Crystal's cross-country ski trails, the last section ends with a fast singletrack rush through

Erin cruises down a fast, bumpy hill at Crystal Mountain Resort.

the woods. Sand dots the trails, and families should consider making the first 4.9 miles an out-and-back ride. Cyclists should not leave the resort, however, without exploring Crystal's other amenities—from elegant condominiums to world-class golf.

The Ride

0.0 From the parking area, cycle south on Crystal Mountain Drive.

0.3 At a four-way intersection continue straight on Crystal Mountain Drive.

0.9 Turn right onto the singletrack trail, marked by a trailhead and signs for Aspen and Pineapple Trails.

1.2 Turn left at a trail intersection. Watch for traffic, and cross over a paved road. (To skip this side trail, continue straight on Aspen Trail.) Soon turn right onto Crushed Pineapple. The easier Pineapple continues straight.

1.8 Crushed Pineapple merges with Pineapple.

2.1 Back at Aspen Trail, turn left. For the next 2 miles ignore all other doubletracks coming in from the left.

4.7 Stay left on the narrower singletrack as the trail splits.

4.9 Reach an intersection with a map. A left turn leads to M–115. Stay right and climb the hill. This is a good spot for beginners or families to turn around and retrace their tracks.

5.3 Arrive at a T intersection with a map, and turn right up the wide trail. Almost immediately turn right again and follow the SCREAMING EAGLE signs up a steep hill.

5.8 After some grueling climbs and fast descents, reach a T intersection and turn right. Soon make a big, sweeping 180-degree left turn.

6.3 Turn left at a T intersection with a dirt road, and climb a steep hill.

6.5 Reach a mapped intersection at the top of the hill, and turn right toward Screaming Eagle.

6.85 Turn right and follow along the power lines for a fast downhill.

7.0 After making a sweeping left turn, head back into the woods and turn right at a trail intersection. A left turn takes you back to the 4.9-mile point.

7.4 Arrive back at parking area.

North Country Trail: Antrim/Kalkaska County

Location:	2 miles south of Alba.
Distance:	32.2-mile loop.
Time:	4–6 hours.
Tread:	16.9 miles of singletrack, 1.5 miles of double-track, 5.6 miles of dirt road, 8.2 miles of paved road.
Aerobic level:	Moderate. Shorter out-and-back ride is also possible.
Technical difficulty:	2+ for sand and brush.
Hill factor:	Flat to hilly.
Highlights:	Scenic singletrack that shows why the North Country Trail offers some of the best mountain biking in the state.
Land status:	Pere Marquette State Forest, Kalkaska Unit, Mackinaw State Forest.
Maps:	USGS Alba, Starvation Lake; North Country Trail Hiker Guide (see Appendix C).
Access:	From the intersection of U.S. 31 and Antrim County Road 42 in downtown Alba, drive 1 block east on C 42. Turn south onto Cinder Hill Road and continue for 2.1 miles. Look for the North Country Trail blue blazes on the trees, and turn east onto a sandy road. Park here.

Notes on the trail: This ride is proof that the North Country Trail (NCT) offers mountain bikers some of the prettiest scenery and most interesting terrain in Michigan. Pedaling south from Starvation Lake, the NCT rolls past Eagle Lake and into deep forest. The north section of the ride from Alba to Starvation Lake lacks some of the scenery of the southern section and is much brushier. The first 1.5 miles roll steeply, but the rest of the ride is either flat or gently rolling. If you only have time for a short ride, cycle the Starvation Lake to Kalkaska County Road 612 section. The return route is on paved and dirt roads, although it can just as easily be ridden out and back or as a shuttle. The trail is signed with NCT blue diamonds.

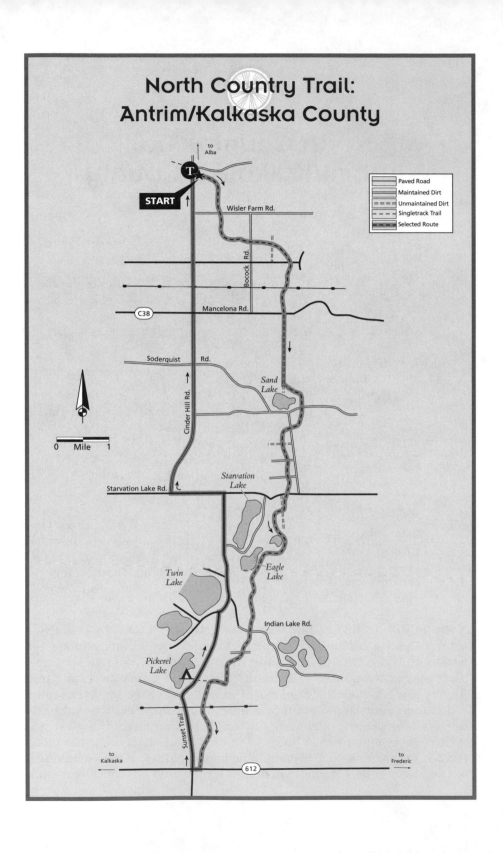

The Ride

0.0 Pedal south and follow the blue diamonds. Get prepared for a steep, cambered climb. The NCT section west of here quickly becomes a doubletrack with old trailers as the only scenery.

1.1 Cross Wisler Farm Road.

2.2 Cross Bocock Road.

3.15 Cross another road with a farm field on the right.

3.7 Cross a paved road. A left turn leads to the Lakes of the North development.

4.2 Reach power lines and continue straight.

4.8 Arrive at paved Mancelona Road/County Road 38. Continue on the doubletrack on the other side of the road.

6.3 Trail turns left and becomes a very brushy singletrack once again.

6.6 Cross a road and bear to the left.

7.0 Cross another road.

7.4 Cross a doubletrack.

8.2 Cross a dirt road.

8.4 Cross yet another road.

9.0 Cross Starvation Lake Road and turn right into the pine trees.

9.1 The trail turns left and parallels a doubletrack.

9.4 Turn right with the trail as it crosses the doubletrack you have been paralleling.

9.85 Look for the blue markers as the trail takes a sharp left turn.

10.4 Cycle past a pond. The next mile rolls by small inland lakes.

10.8 Pedal along the shore of Eagle Lake.

12.3 The trail turns to the right as you cross through a pipeline easement. Sit back and enjoy a fun, twisting descent.

12.75 After another downhill, the route opens up with an access road on the left.

13.1 Cross a pipeline easement once again.

13.3 Pedal across paved Indian Lake Road.

13.5 Pass an oil well on the left. The trail becomes narrower. Keep your eyes open for the blue markers, and make sure your handlebars don't hook a tree.

14.4 Cross a road.

14.9 Cross a dirt road and continue straight.

15.9 Cross an ORV trail.

16.2 After a climb, reach a turnoff to the right for Pickerel Lake Campground. This leads to Sunset Trail Road, part of the return route, and cuts the ride short by a few miles. The route continues to the left toward County Road 612/Manistee Lake Road.

17.0 Cross under power lines.

18.4 Turn right onto C 612/Manistee Lake Road. Then turn right immediately onto Sunset Trail.

Tree-hugging singletrack is common on this portion of the NCT.

21.9 Turn right at an intersection with Twin Lake Road and continue on Sunset Trail.

22.1 At a fork in the road, continue cycling on Sunset Trail by turning left and following Big Twin Lake. Indian Lake Road branches to the right.

22.5 Pedal straight uphill, following Sunset Trail and away from Big Twin Lake. Twin Lake Road continues to the left and wraps around Big Twin Lake.

24.5 Turn left onto Starvation Lake Road as Sunset Trail ends.

25.5 Turn right onto "seasonal" Cinder Hill Road marked by a large arrow with CINDER HILL printed in small letters. Continue on Cinder Hill for 6.7 miles to the parking area.

29.2 Cinder Hill Road becomes paved for about 1 mile after crossing Mancelona Road/C 38.

32.2 Arrive back at your vehicle.

Grand Traverse Pathways

(Lake Ann Pathway, Sand Lakes Quiet Area, Muncie Lakes Pathway, and Lost Lake Pathway)

Grand Traverse County is blessed with picturesque cross-country skiing trails that become equally scenic mountain-biking trails once the snow has melted. The four trails described here are so close together and easy to follow that we decided to include them under one heading. Located on Pere Marquette State Forest land, the trails are marked with blue triangles and numbered posts, and maps are available at the trailheads. We have recommended a loop for each pathway that you can ride by simply following the numbered posts in the order listed below.

Aerobic level: Moderate except for Sand Lakes Quiet Area, which is easy.

Technical difficulty: 1 + ; sand slows you down, especially on the Muncie Lakes Pathway.

Hill factor: Rolling to hilly.

Land status: Pere Marquette State Forest, Traverse City Unit.

Maps: USGS Lake Ann, Grawn, Jacks Landing; maps available at trailheads.

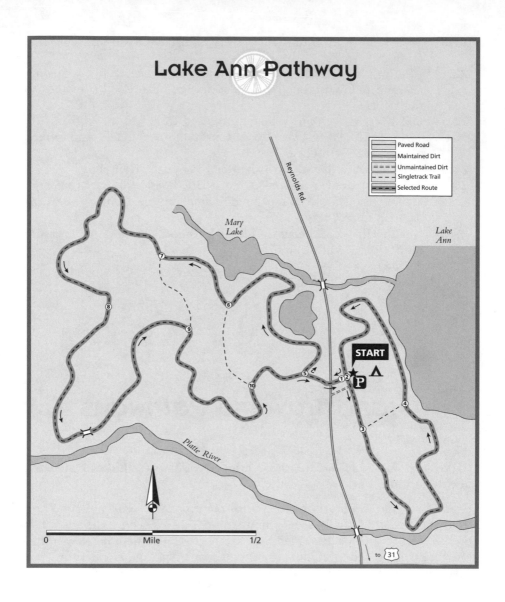

Lake Ann Pathway

Paved Road
Maintained Dirt
Unmaintained Dirt
Singletrack Trail
Selected Route

Reynolds Rd.

Mary Lake

Lake Ann

START

Platte River

0   Mile   1/2

to 31

Lake Ann Pathway

Location:	9 miles northwest of Interlochen.
Distance:	5.1-mile loop.
Time:	30 minutes–1 hour.
Tread:	5.1 miles of wide singletrack.
Access:	From the intersection of U.S. 31 and Michigan 137 north of Interlochen, drive 4.5 miles west on South U.S. 31. Turn north onto Reynolds Road and continue for 4.5 miles. Trailhead parking is on the right.

Skier's benches, designed for northern Michigan's abundant snowfall, dot the pathways.

Notes on the trail: This ride is really two loops combined into one. The first 1.5 miles is a mellow romp next to Lake Ann while the rest of the trail is a roller coaster ride past Shavenaugh Lake and Mary's Lake that will make you wish it was longer than 5 miles. Consider riding this one the same day as the nearby Lost Lake Pathway for a longer workout.

The Ride

Follow the posts in this order: 1 to 2 to 3 to 4 then back to 2. Cross Reynolds Road to Post 5, then continue to 6 to 7 to 8 to 9 to 10 then back to 5. Cross Reynolds Road one more time and cycle back to your vehicle.

Lost Lake Pathway

Location:	About 3 miles northwest of Interlochen.
Distance:	6.7-mile loop.
Time:	1 hour.
Tread:	6.7 miles of wide singletrack.
Access:	From the intersection of U.S. 31 and Michigan 137 north of Interlochen, drive 1.5 miles west

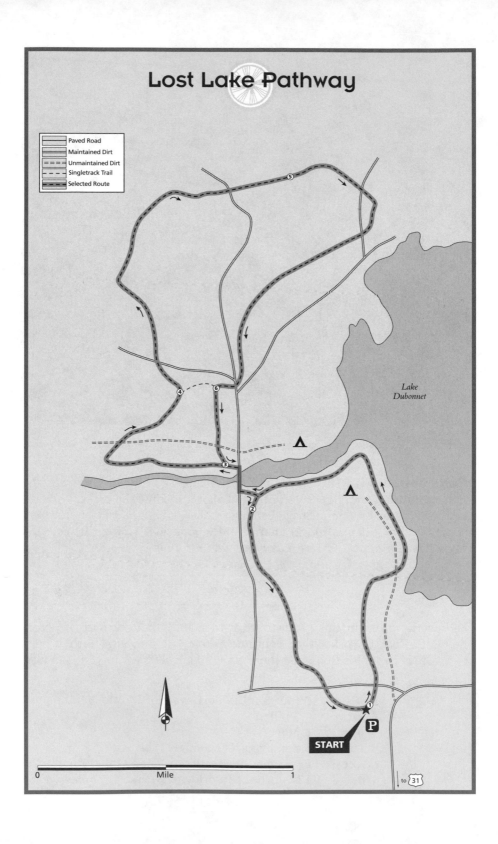

Lost Lake Pathway

Paved Road
Maintained Dirt
Unmaintained Dirt
Singletrack Trail
Selected Route

Lake Dubonnet

START

P

to 31

0   Mile   1

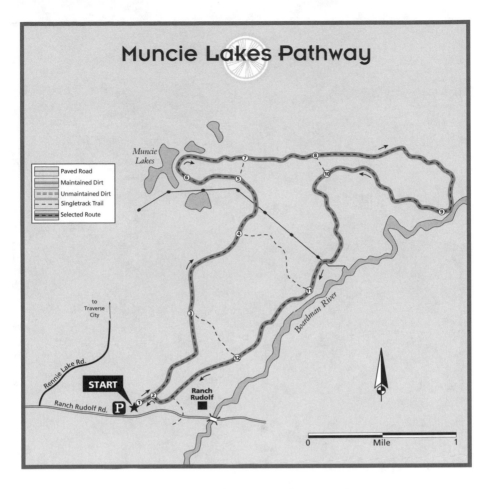

on South U.S. 31. Turn north onto
Wildwood/Gonder Road and continue for 1
mile. Trailhead parking is on the left.

Notes on the trail: Pleasant ramble through the forest, particularly when
combined with the Lake Ann Pathway.

The Ride

Pedal from Post 1 through the campground to Post 2. Turn right onto the
dirt road and cross the river. Look for Post 3 on the left; continue cycling
to Post 4 then 5 to 6 then back to 3. Retrace your tracks over the river and
turn right to Post 2. Then it is on to Post 1 and back to the parking area.

Muncie Lakes Pathway
Location: 10 miles southeast of Traverse City.
Distance: 8.7-mile loop.

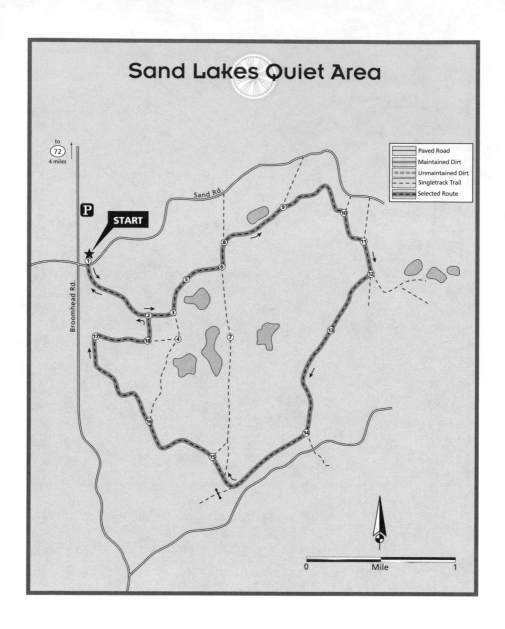

Sand Lakes Quiet Area

Time: 1–2 hours.

Tread: 8.7 miles of wide singletrack.

Access: From the intersection of U.S. 31, Michigan 72, and Four Mile Road, just east of the state park in Traverse City, drive 2.1 miles south on Four Mile Road to a stop sign. Turn east onto Hammond Road and continue for 1 mile. Turn south onto Highlake Road at the yield sign. After 0.5 mile, turn east onto Supply Road.

Drive 3 miles on Supply Road then turn south onto Rennie Lake Road. When Rennie Lake Road ends, turn east onto Ranch Rudolf Road for 0.7 mile to the parking area on the left.

Notes on the trail: This ride probably provides the best workout of the four pathways because the sand sometimes feels like quicksand; hills add to the aerobic challenge. The Shore-to-Shore Trail, stretching from Lake Huron to Lake Michigan, crosses the pathway. A bench along the Boardman River provides a peaceful place for a picnic.

The Ride

Cycle from Post 1 to 2 to 3 to 4 to 5 to 6, pedaling past the Muncie Lakes. Continue on to Posts 7, 8, 10 and 11, where the path meets the Boardman River. After enjoying the views, continue to Post 12 and 2 then back to 1.

Sand Lakes Quiet Area

Location:	About 10 miles southeast of Acme.
Distance:	8.3-mile loop.
Time:	1 hour.
Tread:	8.3 miles of wide and narrow singletrack.
Access:	From the intersection of U.S. 31 and Michigan 72 in Acme, drive 5.7 miles east on M–72 through Williamsburg. Turn south onto Cook Road and continue for 1.4 miles. Turn east onto Broomhead Road. In another 0.5 mile reach an intersection. Turn south, continuing on Broomhead Road. Reach the trailhead parking in 2.1 miles.

Notes on the trail: This route, the easiest but prettiest of the four trails, occasionally narrows to twist through dense trees and briefly joins the Shore-to-Shore Trail. The route follows the perimeter of the trail system, but it is possible to cut the ride short by taking one of the inner trails. If you venture off the outer loop, however, be prepared for more hills.

The Ride

Starting at Post 1, continue to 2 then 3 and 5. The first Sand Lake is on the right. Continue cycling to Post 6 then to 8 to 9 to 10 to 11 to 12 to 13 to 14. At this point the trail joins the Shore-to-Shore Trail. Cycle to Post 15, where the Shore-to-Shore Trail splits off. Continue to Post 16 to 17 to 18 to 2, then back to 1 and the parking area.

VASA Singletrack

Location:	7 miles southeast of downtown Traverse City.
Distance:	13-mile loop.
Time:	1–2 hours.
Tread:	13 miles of singletrack.
Aerobic level:	Easy to moderate.
Technical difficulty:	2; logs to hop and sandy patches.
Hill factor:	Flat to rolling.
Highlights:	13 miles of smooth, twisting singletrack.
Land status:	Pere Marquette State Forest, Traverse City Unit.
Maps:	USGS Mayfield, Jack's Landing; maps available in mailbox at trailhead.
Access:	From the west side of Traverse City at the U.S. 31, Michigan 37, and Michigan 72 intersection, drive 6 miles north on U.S. 31/M–72. Turn south onto Four Mile Road and continue for 2.1 miles to a stop sign. Turn east onto Hammond Road for 1 mile. Turn south onto Highlake Road at the yield sign. After 0.5 mile, turn east onto Supply Road. The trailhead parking will be on the left in 1.7 miles.

Notes on the trail: The VASA Singletrack is an excellent example of the smooth, well-maintained trails that have been built by the Michigan Mountain Biking Association in cooperation with the Department of Natural Resources. Thirteen miles of twisting singletrack wind along a groomed trail with banked corners, allowing you to turn almost without braking. There are plenty of gentle whoop-de-dos on the straight portions of the trail for an added thrill. Blue triangles with orange dots and numbered posts mark the trail, making it easy to follow. The trail passes over the VASA cross-country ski trail, where the world-famous VASA ski race takes place every winter; about 1,000 skiers compete on 12-, 27-, and 50-km courses. If you feel like a race but cross-country skiing isn't your thing, consider joining about 2,000 mountain bikers for the annual Iceman Cometh Challenge in November (see Appendix C).

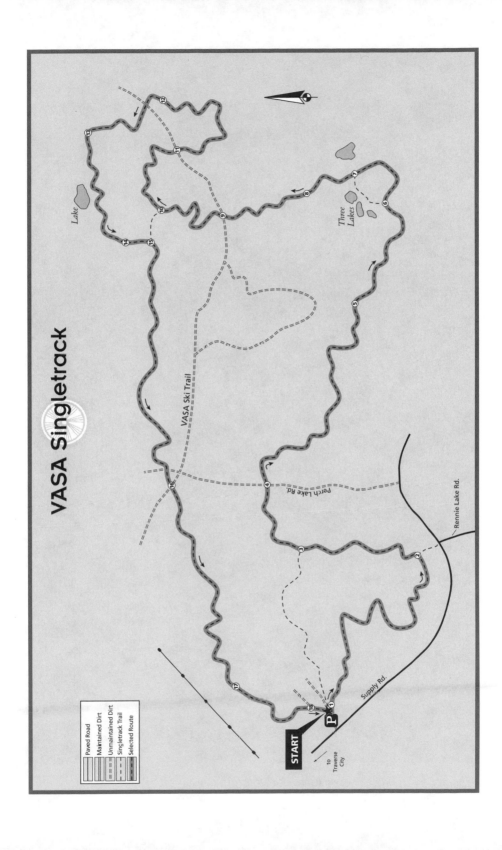

The fast VASA offers few obstacles—just fast, fun cruising.

The Ride

0.0   Pedal to the large map located next to the picnic benches in the middle of the parking lot. The ride begins here at Post 1.

1.2   Arrive at Post 2 after a fast and flat section.

2.0   At Post 3 stay to the right and pedal toward "the rock."

2.75 Post 4; cross Perch Lake Road.

3.8   Post 5.

4.5   Arrive at Post 6 and two options: the "hi-way," slightly longer with a steep hill, or the "lo-way," a pleasant ramble past three lakes. Both options take you to Post 7.

5.2   Turn right at Post 7 and continue to Post 8.

5.65 After a short climb, reach Post 8. The trail continues through a clearcut.

6.2   Arrive at Post 9, the first of several VASA ski trail crossings.

6.8   Reach Post 10 and continue straight. A left turn cuts the ride short by about 2.5 miles.

7.5   After crossing the ski trail, reach Post 11.

8.5   Reach Post 12, "the rock."

8.7   Arrive at Post 13. Get ready for more hill climbs between here and Post 16.

9.5   Reach Post 14.

9.6   Arrive at Post 15. The shortcut from Post 10 comes in on the left.

11.1 Cross a road to Post 16. The hilliest portion is over; sit back and enjoy the mellow whoop-de-dos.

12.5 Reach Post 17 under the power lines and cycle into the trees.

13.0 Arrive at Post 18 and back at the parking lot.

Boyne Mountain Loop

Location:	1 mile south of Boyne Falls.
Distance:	9.7-mile loop.
Time:	1.5–2.5 hours.
Tread:	0.5 mile of paved road, 9.2 miles of singletrack and ski trail.
Aerobic level:	Moderately strenuous. Only thighs of steel pedal up these steep hills.
Technical difficulty:	3+ to 4; late-summer sand poses problems.
Hill factor:	Highlands; constant hills with a few 200-foot climbs.
Highlights:	Fast, banked switchbacks and mountaintop views.
Land status:	Boyne Mountain Ski Area. Landowner graciously permits mountain bikers to use trails; please respect property and stay on established trails.
Maps:	USGS Boyne Falls; maps available at Boyne Country Sports in the resort village.
Access:	From the intersection of U.S. 131 and Michigan 75 in Boyne Falls, continue driving south on U.S. 131 for 0.8 mile. Turn west onto Boyne Mountain Drive and continue for another 0.8 mile. Turn north onto Mountain Pass Drive for a 0.1 mile and park at the Activity Center parking lot.

Notes on the trail: The sculpted slopes of the Boyne Mountain Ski Area are visible from miles away, but what is not apparent is the skinny singletrack hiding in the nearby forest. Hand cut by local fat-tire enthusiasts, these trails create a maze of steep cross-country ski trails and singletracks. The route here follows portions of the Grand Prix Race Loop and Superbowl Loop; however, as development marches forward at Boyne, sections of the Grand Prix Loop are disappearing. An alternative route is described just in case a large portion of Grand Prix disappears altogether. Orange, green, and blue dots and red arrows, used for annual mountain bike races, mark the trails.

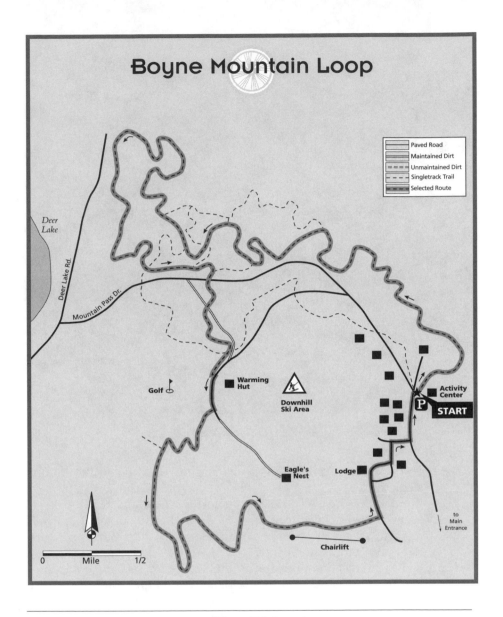

The Ride

0.0   Pedal to the north end of the parking lot and continue across a grassy area to the trailhead. Cyle along the well marked Pancake Trail, following the red arrows into the woods. The trail crosses a field and several sand traps.

0.65 Turn right onto the Xmas Trail with the maintenance buildings on the left.

Peering down at the resort from the top of Boyne Mountain.

0.9 Pass the Blue Trail. Continue around the sand pit to the Rumba singletrack.

1.1 Rumba joins Twister Trail for a short distance and then takes off again to the right onto Rumba II. In a short distance, Rumba II rejoins Twister at an intersection with Littlehammer Trail. Turn right onto Littlehammer.

1.5 Reach intersection with Innsbruck Trail. Stay left and cycle up a hill onto an unsigned singletrack, paralleling Mountain Pass Drive. The singletrack hits the ski trail again and heads left. Shortly reach one of many steep climbs on the route.

1.7 After the steep climb, stay to the left and follow the ski trail, which turns into a twisting singletrack.

2.15 Turn right onto Innsbruck, toward the South Rim singletrack. Continue cycling downhill on Innsbruck and cross over unmarked singletrack trails.

2.55 *Alternative route* for shorter ride or if next section of Grand Prix is gone: Turn left onto a singletrack, possibly marked with red arrows. After a short distance, turn left onto a ski trail (Innsbruck). Pick up the directions again at Mile 5.55.

2.7 Turn right onto an unmarked ski trail. Soon turn left onto an unmarked singletrack, just before the ski trail climbs a steep hill. In a short distance, the singletrack rejoins Innsbruck.

3.05 Turn left onto the Rootville singletrack. The next 2.35 miles follow a tight, twisting singletrack that passes through several clearcut areas. The trail disappears through these sections but appears again on the other side of the clearcuts.

5.4 Singletrack dumps out onto a ski trail intersection with Littlehammer, Grinder, and Innsbruck. Continue straight on Innsbruck.

5.55 Reach an intersection and continue straight, crossing over the Mountain Pass Drive.

5.7 Turn right onto Vistas Ski Trail. Soon cross a dirt road and continue climbing Vistas.

6.0 Continue straight on Grinder, while Vistas turns to the right. Almost immediately reach an intersection and turn right. Continue on Grinder and follow the signs to Superbowl and No Mercy. Get ready for a sustained climb to the top. Pass an intersection with Dave's Grind and Vistas. Continue climbing.

6.4 Pedal on the paved golf trail, riding past the first tee until the trail turns into dirt.

6.6 Turn right onto Superbowl/No Mercy Loop and head into the woods. The tight trail follows a serpentine, sometimes steep path through the woods. Cross an unmarked ski trail.

7.1 Cross the Cold Springs/Vista Ski Trail. Golf course is still on the right.

7.4 Pass through the Norwegian Woods and reach an intersection with Superbowl and No Mercy Loops. Turn left and continue on the Superbowl Loop.

8.1 Cross a ski trail and continue following the singletrack as it twists through the trees.

8.8 The trail dumps out next to a chairlift. Cruise downhill.

9.2 Reach the main road to the lodge. Turn left and cycle past the lodge. Pedal around the condos toward the Activity Center.

9.7 Arrive back at the parking lot.

34

North Country Trail:
Springvale to Thumb Lake Road

Location:	11.5 miles northeast of Petoskey.
Distance:	14.6-mile loop.
Time:	2–3 hours.
Tread:	5.3 miles of singletrack, 2.7 miles of double-track, 3.7 miles of dirt road, 2.9 miles of paved road.
Aerobic level:	Moderate to strenuous.
Technical difficulty:	3; hazards include sand, logs, and rocky sections.
Hill factor:	Hilly to highlands. Return is on mostly flat roads.
Highlights:	Steep terrain mixes with lush landscape for classic North Country Trail cycling.
Land status:	Mackinaw State Forest, Indian River Unit.
Maps:	USGS Thumb Lake; maps available at local bike stores (see Appendix A).
Access:	From the intersection of U.S. 131 and Charlevoix County Road 48 in Boyne Falls, drive 5 miles east on CR 48. Turn north onto Slashing Road and continue for 2.5 miles. Turn west onto Chandler Hill Road for 0.4 mile, then turn north onto Howard Road. Continue for 3.1 miles and turn east onto Springvale Road. Go 0.6 mile to Smithingill Road. Park here.

Notes on the trail: The North Country Trail (NCT) once again delivers with this aerobically challenging ride where sweeping descents mingle with grueling climbs. Early in the ride, cyclists shift into their granny gears for a 0.5-mile, 200-foot grind up a sandy hill. The top of a ridgeline offers a chance to rest, but the climbs aren't over yet. There are equally exciting descents, so fast that the trees become a green blur. Like most of the NCT, this segment is marked with blue diamonds or blue paint. There are a few route-finding challenges, but if blue isn't visible after a few minutes of riding, you know you took a wrong turn. The loop returns on relatively flat paved and dirt roads; if you feel like a challenge, make it an out-and-back ride.

North Country Trail:
Springvale to Thumb Lake Road

to
Petoskey

Smithingill Rd.

Cobb Rd.

START

P

	Paved Road
	Maintained Dirt
	Unmaintained Dirt
	Singletrack Trail
	Selected Route

Springvale Rd.

Howard Rd.

Walton Rd.

N

0   Mile   1

Chandler Hill Rd.

Thumb Lake

Slashing Rd.

to
Vanderbilt

Thumb Lake Rd.

C48

to
Boyne Falls

The Ride

0.0 Cycle across the road to the NCT sign. Continue into the dense woods on a doubletrack and immediately turn left. Soon turn right onto a singletrack.

0.35 Turn right onto a doubletrack.

1.1 Reach a fork and stay right, following the blue markers.

1.75 Reach another intersection and stay right onto the tight single-track.

2.1 Trail joins a doubletrack.

2.3 After a long, gentle downhill, reach a trail intersection. Turn left onto a doubletrack.

2.4 Reach another intersection and continue straight up a sandy hill.

2.6 After a sandy downhill, cross a creek. Immediately turn left and follow the creek up a hill.

2.9 Cross Walton Road and continue on the singletrack.

3.2 Arrive at a doubletrack and turn left.

3.3 At another intersection, turn left and cycle over a berm. Look forward to a grueling climb and a fast downhill.

4.6 Control your speed near the bottom of the hill and look for the trail, meandering through the woods on the right. Cycling straight takes you to Chandler Hill Road.

4.75 Watch for cars as the trail crosses Chandler Hill Road.

4.9 Reach an intersection and turn right, heading downhill, onto a doubletrack. Shortly turn left onto a singletrack.

5.3 After a wooded, rolling section, turn left onto a dirt road and cycle around a gate.

5.7 After a rocky downhill, you have an option. Turn left onto a cliff-hugging singletrack (route described here), or continue straight on a steep sandy road. Both routes join at the 6-mile point.

6.0 Reach an intersection and turn right back onto the dirt road. Continue straight onto a singletrack as the road turns left.

6.4 Watch out! After a fast downhill, trail turns left back into the woods. The trail shortly dumps out onto a doubletrack. Cycle around a gate and over a bridge. The trail picks up on the left.

6.9 Tricky creek crossing!

7.5 Cross a dirt road.

8.0 Trail ends at the intersection of Thumb Lake and Slashing Roads. Turn right onto Slashing Road. The next 6 miles are mostly level.

10.5 Turn left onto Chandler Hill Road.

10.9 Turn right onto sandy Howard Road.

14.0 Turn right onto Springvale Road. Your vehicle comes into view after a few twists in the road.

14.6 Arrive back at parking area.

35

North Country Trail: Kipp Road to Van Road

Location:	5.5 miles north of Petoskey.
Distance:	36.1-mile loop.
Time:	3.5–6 hours.
Tread:	17.8 miles of singletrack, 0.8 mile of double-track, 3.7 miles of dirt road, 13.8 miles of paved road.
Aerobic level:	Strenuous.
Technical difficulty:	3.
Hill factor:	Hilly to highlands. Ride starts with challenging half-mile climb.
Highlights:	Epic ride with many thigh-burning climbs and thrilling descents through lush forest and spring wildflowers.
Land status:	Mackinaw State Forest, Indian River Unit.
Maps:	USGS Harbor Springs and Larks Lake; maps available from North Country Trail Association (see Appendix C).
Access:	From the intersection of Michigan 119 and U.S. 31 in Petoskey, continue north on U.S. 31 for 3.5 miles. In Conway, turn north onto North Conway Road toward the Emmett County Road Commission garage. After 1 mile turn west onto Hathaway/Powers Road and continue for 0.5 mile. Turn north onto Kipp Road and continue for another 0.5 mile. Look for the trailhead on the left, and park along Kipp Road.

Notes on the trail: This epic ride is perfect in the spring, when trilliums line the trail and morel hunters shout greetings as you cruise by. Where spring and summer are lush with ferns and trees bending to touch the path, fall finds the forest in a frenzy of orange, red, and gold. The return route includes dirt and paved roads and passes by a Michigan Centennial Farm on Larks Lake Road and the Pellston Correctional Facility, probably Michigan's prettiest prison setting. Although this route is a loop, it is easy

North Country Trail:
Kipp Road to Van Road

Larks Lake

Rugged Rd.

Van Rd.

Van Rd.

Van Rd.

Gregory Rd.

Robinson Rd.

North Larks Lake Rd.

Robinson Rd.

South Larks Lake Rd.

Pleasantview Rd.

Stutsmanville Rd.

Brutus Rd.

C81

North Conway Rd.

Boyne Highlands

Nubs Nob

START

P

Pleasantview Rd.

Harbor Springs

119

Hathaway Rd.

Kipp Rd.

West Conway Rd.

31

to Alanson

Little Traverse Bay

119

Petoskey

Legend
- Paved Road
- Maintained Dirt
- Unmaintained Dirt
- Singletrack Trail
- Selected Route

0 Mile 1

to make it an out-and-back ride. Simply cut the ride short at any point, but don't miss cruising down those first 3 grueling miles. This downhill section just might be the most exhilarating in Michigan, but control your speed and be aware of other bikers and hikers on this popular stretch of the well-marked North Country Trail (NCT).

The Ride

0.0 Cycle past the NCT sign and continue into the deep woods. The first 0.5 mile rolls through the forest and crosses two sandy doubletracks. After the second doubletrack, begin a sustained climb for another 0.5 mile. Climbing continues off and on for the next 2 miles.

3.3 Reach a six-way intersection with Nubs Nob's cross-country ski trails and snowmobile trails. The NCT continues on the left. Cross a sandy road and cycle through a clearcut. The trail dives back into the woods and descends to paved Brutus Road.

5.0 Cross Brutus Road. Climb steeply along a ridgeline, then get ready for a fun, fast descent.

5.5 Reach a boggy area. Consider walking if it is muddy.

7.0 Arrive at Stutsmanville Road and turn left onto the dirt road.

7.4 Cross over Pleasantview Road and continue on the now paved Stutsmanville Road.

8.0 The NCT continues on the right. Even though it looks inviting, this section is low-lying and often wet. Riding on it will result in extensive trail damage, so continue on the paved roads.

8.2 Turn right onto South Larks Lake Road. Cycle past charming country homes as the road rolls through the countryside.

10.2 Turn left at the NCT sign onto a sandy doubletrack, then immediately right onto a singletrack and back into the woods. The trail continues to climb, but there are an equal number of sweeping downhills.

14.4 Watch for traffic and cross the paved Robinson Road. This segment sees less use, making route-finding more challenging.

15.1 Turn right onto a doubletrack.

15.5 Look for the blue paint on the trees. Veer to the right and continue on the faint singletrack. This is easy to miss!

16.2 The trail turns into a sandy doubletrack and continues up a hill.

16.6 The trail turns right and back into the trees.

16.8 The trail dumps out onto Gregory Road. Continue straight on sandy Gregory as it turns into Van Road.

17.5 Turn right with Van Road. Cycling straight will lead to Rugged Road.

20.1 Turn right onto paved North Larks Lake Road/Van Road.

Kurt Radwanski rushes past lush ferns that dominate the forest in summer.

20.8	Turn right onto the continuation of North Larks Lake Road, near Center Township Hall. Look for the Michigan Centennial Farm soon on the right.
24.0	Turn right onto Robinson Road and head downhill.
24.5	Cycle past Camp Pellston Correctional Facility on the right. Bear left onto South Larks Lake Road.
28.0	Turn left onto Stutsmanville Road.
28.8	Turn right onto Pleasantview Road/County Road 81.
29.6	Turn left onto Brutus Road and cycle up a long hill.
31.1	After reaching a crest and cruising downhill, turn right at the NCT sign. This is easy to miss! Retrace your tracks back to the trailhead.
32.8	Arrive back at the Nubs Nob intersection.
33.4	The trail forks. Stay to the right and follow the blue markers. Get ready for a long, fun downhill.
36.1	Arrive back at your vehicle.

Northeastern Michigan:
Lake Huron, Sunrises,
and Solitude

If northwestern Michigan is synonymous with trendy tourist centers, northeastern Michigan is its sleepy cousin. Down-to-earth towns like Posen, the potato capital of Michigan, dot the landscape. The beaches lining Lake Huron are rockier than those along Lake Michigan, and the trails in the Huron National Forest and Pigeon River State Forest see less traffic than forest pathways in northwestern Michigan.

The mountain bike rides in this part of the state—north of U.S. 10 and east of U.S. 27/75—in general reflect this down-to-earth atmosphere. Grassroots efforts in the Grayling area have resulted in handmade singletrack trails in the Hanson Hills Recreation Area. Nearby, local fat-tire advocates are also developing singletrack at Aspen Park near downtown Gaylord.

Gaylord also happens to be the one town in northeastern Michigan where resorts are the rule rather than the exception. Somewhat of a transition area between northwestern and northeastern Michigan, Gaylord is home to several glitzy golf and ski resorts. The Otsego Club and Resort has been home to an exciting mountin bike trail, but its future is in question; we did not include it in this book. However, local Michigan Mountain Biking Association members are busy building a 6-mile singletrack at Gaylord's Aspen Park, scheduled to open May 2002.

Just north of Gaylord lies Pigeon River State Forest. Site of a bitter oil dispute in the 1970s, the forest boasts the epic 80-mile High Country Pathway and the largest elk herd east of the Mississippi.

Many other designated pathways highlight the Huron National Forest and Mackinaw State Forest in this part of Michigan. Norway Ridge, Chippewa Hills, and Ocqueoc Falls are easy-to-follow trails that offer the best of Michigan—from rolling hills and hardwoods to cascading falls and inland lakes. The Black Mountain Recreation Area, also part of Mackinaw State Forest, is the granddaddy of these trail systems, with about 35 miles of paths.

Although one ride near Midland is listed, the real heart of northeastern Michigan lies much farther north. To experience the quiet sunrise side of the state, set your sights on the secluded northeastern corner and get ready for a solitary ride through a pristine landscape.

Pine Haven Singletrack

Notes on the trail: The hum of U.S. 10 follows riders on this small trail system. The first mile, new singletrack developed in the fall of 2000, forces all but the strongest cyclists off their bikes as the trail runs on the banks of a gully with off-cambered climbs, log hops, and tight, twisting singletrack. The trail crosses a creek over wooden bridges and finally merges with the original singletrack. The rest of the ride mellows out as it twists its way through the woods and crosses dry creekbeds several times. Built and maintained by the Northeast Chapter of the Michigan Mountain Biking Association, the trail is marked with mountain bike signs and is conveniently accessed right off the highway. For more mileage, cycle the wide ski trails intersecting the singletrack.

The Ride

0.0 Trail is located on the west end of the parking lot, near the large trailhead sign.

0.2 Turn right onto the newest and most technical segment of the trail. Get ready for a challenge as the trail climbs in and out of a gully.

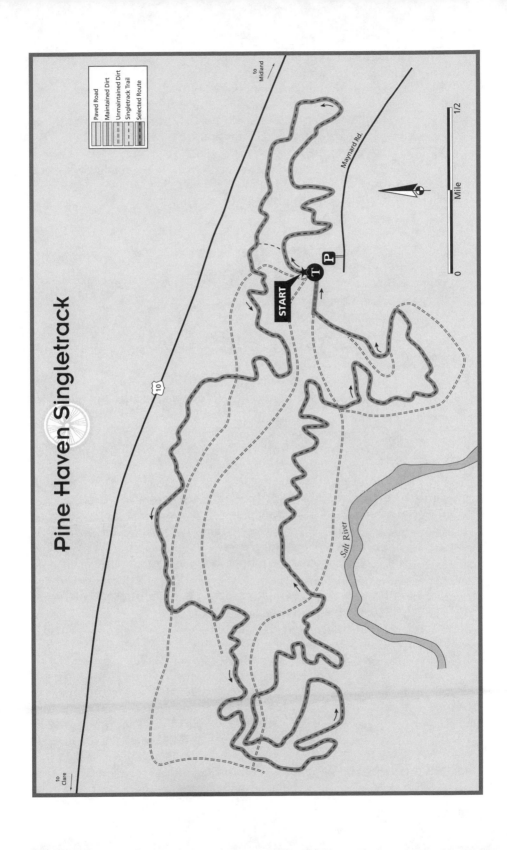

Pine Haven Singletrack

START

to Midland

Maynard Rd.

to Clare

Salt River

10

Paved Road
Maintained Dirt
Unmaintained Dirt
Singletrack Trail
Selected Route

0   Mile   1/2

Continuing straight at the intersection skips this portion and cuts the mileage by almost a mile.

1.1 Stay right as the newer trail merges with the older trail.

2.1 Cross a ski trail and take the singletrack to the left.

3.0 Reach a T intersection with a ski trail. Turn right and then immediately left back onto the singletrack.

4.1 Cross a grassy, open field and get ready for a hilly section.

4.3 Reach the top of a hill and turn left onto a wide singletrack. Pedal back toward the grassy field.

4.5 Back at the trailhead, gear up for another loop!

Hanson Hills Loop

Location:	3 miles southwest of Grayling.
Distance:	6.1-mile loop.
Time:	1 hour.
Tread:	2.75 miles of doubletrack, 3.35 miles of singletrack.
Aerobic level:	Moderate.
Technical difficulty:	2+; mostly smooth singletrack with steep downhills.
Hill factor:	Hilly with one long, sustained climb.
Highlights:	New and old provide big views and fun downhills at an up-and-coming mountain biking area.
Land status:	Hanson State Game Refuge, Hanson Hills Recreation Area.
Maps:	USGS Grayling; map available at Chamber of Commerce (see Appendix A).
Access:	From the intersection of Michigan 93 and Michigan 72, drive west on M–72/M–93 for 1.5 miles. Turn south onto M–93 toward Camp Grayling, and continue for about 0.6 mile. Turn east onto Old Lake Road; in a short distance take the first right into the entrance for the Hanson Hills Recreation Area. Park in front of the cross-country ski lodge at the east end of the parking lot.

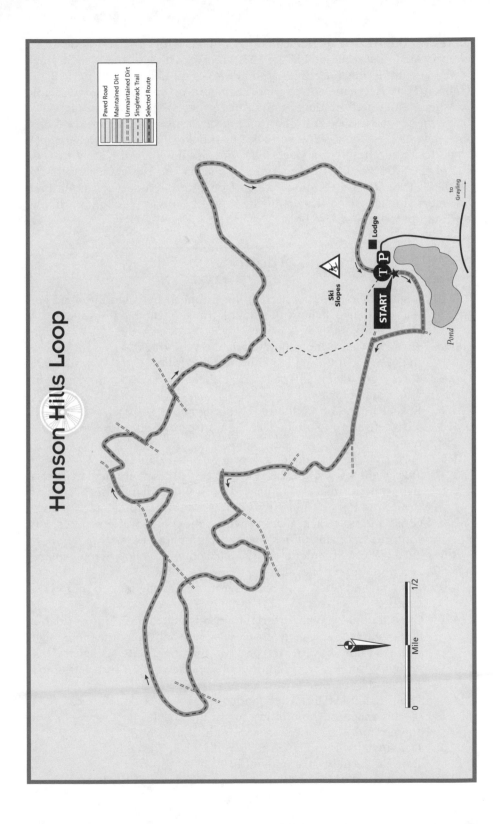

Hanson Hills Loop

Paved Road
Maintained Dirt
Unmaintained Dirt
Singletrack Trail
Selected Route

Ski Slopes

Lodge

START

T P

Pond

to Grayling

0   Mile   1/2

Notes on the trail: This ride combines the old with the new: Wide cross-country ski trails developed in the 1930s merge with late 1990s singletrack trails. The trails meander over a small downhill skiing area, part of the Hanson Hills Recreation Area, and farther into the Hanson State Game Refuge. Maintained by a local community group, the trails have big views from the top of the ski hill and exciting downhills. The route described here begins on a sandy doubletrack but quickly turns off onto a singletrack trail and climbs to a ridge. The trail becomes more clearly marked the farther you pedal with mountain bike signs and red arrows. With the National Trail Day Celebration taking place here the first weekend in June and new singletrack in development, Hanson Hills is a mountain biking destination to keep an eye on.

The Ride

0.0 Begin at the cross-country skiing trailhead between the pond and the ski lodge. Follow the doubletrack, signed with yellow and white markers.

0.3 Turn right onto the yellow-marked doubletrack.

0.5 Arrive back at the ski hill. Turn left and follow the yellow markers.

0.9 Turn right at an intersection with a singletrack, marked with white diamonds.

1.1 Reach the top of a hill after climbing about 100 feet.

1.3 Turn left at a mountain bike sign, also marked with a white diamond.

1.55 Turn right onto a singletrack trail and head uphill.

1.75 Turn right back onto the doubletrack. Almost immediately turn right onto a singletrack, marked with white diamonds.

1.9 Reach the top of a hill after climbing another 100 feet.

2.0 Cross a doubletrack, marked with yellow and white squares, and continue on a singletrack marked with paper plates.

3.5 Turn left onto the doubletrack, marked with yellow/white squares and a mountain bike sign.

3.9 After a sandy downhill, turn right onto a singletrack and climb gently.

4.1 Cross a doubletrack. Turn right almost immediately onto a doubletrack, marked with a white/yellow square and a mountain bike sign, and head uphill. At the top of a hill turn right onto a singletrack.

4.3 A slight drop-off merges into a doubletrack. Soon turn left onto a singletrack, marked with a mountain bike sign.

4.6 The singletrack turns left and dumps into a doubletrack. Soon reach the top of the hill and turn right, back into the woods and down a hill. Fun switchback downhills are coming up!

5.0 The singletrack heads left for a rolling ride through the woods. Be alert for a sandy, steep downhill.

6.4 Reach the parking area after cruising in back of the lodge.

Hartwick Pines Loop

Location:	7.5 miles northeast of Grayling.
Distance:	7.7-mile loop.
Time:	1–2 hours.
Tread:	7.7 miles of doubletrack.
Aerobic level:	Easy to moderate. Hills are more challenging at the end of the loop.
Technical difficulty:	1; sand slows the pace in a few spots.
Hill factor:	Rolling.
Highlights:	Visit an old logging camp as you cycle through hardwoods and along rolling hills.
Land status:	Hartwick Pines State Park.
Maps:	USGS Grayling, Big Bradford Lake; maps available at the visitor center.
Access:	From the north intersection of Michigan 72 and Business 75/Old Michigan 27 in Grayling, drive 2.7 miles north on Business 75. Turn east onto Michigan 93 and go another 3.8 miles to the park entrance. Turn north into the park and pass the contact station. Continue for another 0.3 mile and turn right at the signs to the visitor center. The parking area is another 0.4 mile.

Notes on the trail: A historic logging camp, old-growth pines, and a spectacular visitor center make this ride a standout among the cross-country ski trails turned mountain bike trails that northern Michigan offers. The largest state park in the Lower Peninsula, Hartwick Pines was established in the late 1920s in memory of Major Edward Hartwick, who died during WWI. History can also be found as you pedal along the wide trails and pass by the Logging Museum and Camp, commemorating Grayling's lumber industry. After leaving the camp turnoff, the rolling hills get progressively steeper and sandier. When you return to the visitor center, stroll along the short Old Growth Forest Foot Trail, winding through a forty-nine-acre white pine grove. The visitor center, nestled between the trees, also offers interpretive forest exhibits, a gift store, and guided bike tours. All of this comes with the $4.00-per-vehicle entrance fee.

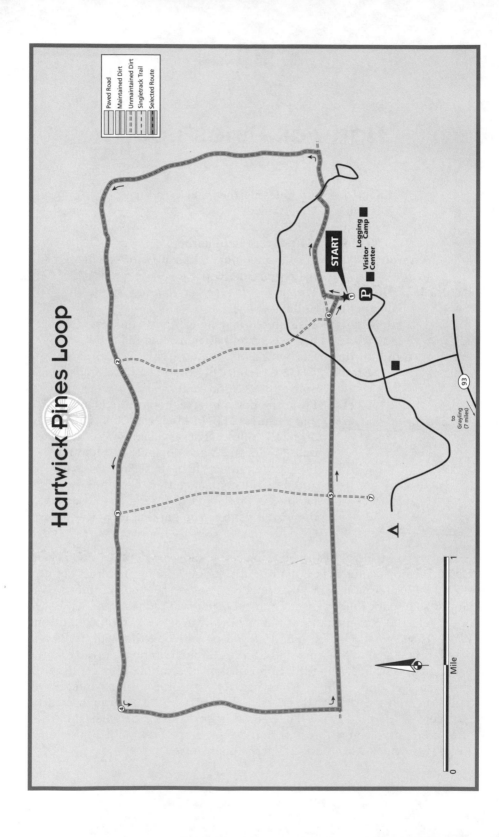

Hartwick Pines Loop

Legend:
- Paved Road
- Maintained Dirt
- Unmaintained Dirt
- Singletrack Trail
- Selected Route

START

Visitor Center

Logging Camp

P

93

to Grayling (7 miles)

Mile

Hartwick Pines' wide trails are family-friendly.

The Ride

0.0 Pedal to the trail map, marked with a "1," on the north side of the visitor center parking area. Continue cycling past the sign. Turn right at the first intersection and follow the arrows.

0.4 Pass the logging camp on the right. Drop your bike and explore.

0.7 Turn right onto a paved road then immediately left back onto the doubletrack.

2.6 Reach Marker 2; continue straight to Marker 3.

3.4 Arrive at Marker 3; continue cycling to Marker 4. From this point on, the hills get steeper and sandier.

4.35 From Marker 4 turn left toward Marker 5. Watch for sand.

6.7 Reach Marker 5 and continue straight to Marker 6.

7.25 Cross a paved road.

7.5 Turn right at Marker 6, and cycle toward the parking area.

7.7 End of ride.

Rifle River Recreation Area

Location:	4.5 miles east of Rose City.
Distance:	14.2-mile loop.
Time:	2–3 hours.
Tread:	12.9 miles of singletrack, 0.7 mile of dirt road, 0.6 mile of paved road.
Aerobic level:	Moderate.
Technical difficulty:	2 to 2+.
Hill factor:	Flat to hilly.
Highlights:	Lung-busting short, steep hills rolling between inland lakes contrast with flat, buffed single-track meandering next to mellow Rifle River.
Land status:	Rifle River Recreation Area.
Maps:	USGS Rose City; maps available at park head-quarters (see Appendix B).
Access:	From Rose City, drive 4.5 miles east on Rose City Road and turn south into the park entrance. Stay right at all paved intersections and continue for 0.5 mile to the visitor parking area, across from the Grousehaven Campground entrance.

Notes on the trail: This outstanding singletrack is a study in contrasts. The trail begins with a series of steep, forest-shrouded hills overlooking Devoe, Grousehaven, and Lodge Lakes. The trail narrows between the lakes and plunges steeply; if enough speed is gained, riders are propelled to the top of the next hill. The second half of the ride follows the bucolic Rifle River, popular with fishermen, on an almost completely flat, well-used singletrack. The adventurous will enjoy fording a flooded area (as of summer 2001), but in general the trails are in good condition and fairly well marked, with signage disappearing in only a few areas. The route here follows the perimeter of the trail in a counterclockwise direction, but other loops are possible. This popular recreation area also offers camp-grounds and water-related activities. A $4.00-per-vehicle entrance fee is charged.

Rifle River Recreation Area

to Rose City

Rose City Rd.

F28

Ridge   Rd.

START

Ranch Rd.

Ranch Rd.

P

Legend:
- Paved Road
- Maintained Dirt
- Unmaintained Dirt
- Singletrack Trail
- Selected Route

Grousehaven
Lake

2

3

5

6

8

7

Grebe
Lake

Devoe
Lake

9

Lodge
Lake

10

11

Scaup
Lake

12

13

Jewett Lake

24

25

14

23

15

22

Rifle River

Rifle River Rd.

16

Lost
Lake

17

18

21

19

20

Clear Creek River

0   Mile   1

The Ride

0.0 Cycle across the road and stay to the left toward the upper campground, sites 40–80. Pedal toward the outhouse and scoot between the toilets. Pick up the trail here and stay left.

0.4 Cross over a paved road and reach Post 2; continue straight to Post 3.

0.7 Reach a picnic area and Post 3. Cycle to the right and through the parking lot to a cul-de-sac. Turn right onto the singletrack and up a short hill. Shortly reach an unmarked intersection and continue straight toward Post 5.

1.1 After crossing a dirt road, reach Post 5 and continue straight.

1.6 At Post 6 pedal straight ahead.

2.2 After a gentle downhill through a young forest, reach Post 7 and turn right toward Post 8.

2.5 After a short, steep climb, cross the road and arrive at Post 8. Continue straight and almost immediately turn right onto a doubletrack then left onto a dirt road. The trail ahead is the return route. Follow the road between Grousehaven and Lodge Lakes; cycle around the gate and pedal up the dirt road.

2.8 At Post 9 turn left and continue up the singletrack. Get ready for steep ascents and descents as the trail follows a ridge between the lakes.

3.4 Turn right at Post 10.

3.7 Turn right at an unmarked intersection and follow the twisting singletrack. Cycling straight spits you out at a dirt road.

4.2 Reach Post 11 and turn right toward Post 12.

4.6 Arrive at Post 12 at Devoe Lake Campground. Turn left down the campground road and then right onto the paved road.

4.8 Turn left back onto the singletrack at Post 25. Cruise by Post 24 and cross over Ranch Road.

5.4 Turn right and cross a wide wooden bridge over the Rifle River. Stay left with the worn trail.

6.0 Cruise by Post 22.

7.5 Pass Post 21 and cross Cedar Creek on a small wooden bridge.

8.0 Walk your bike over the Rifle River on a swinging bridge at Post 20.

8.5 Reach Post 19 on a bridge at a flooded area (in summer of 2001). The trail, resembling a creekbed, turns left off the bridge; carry your bike around the flooded area. Don't despair—you'll soon reach higher ground.

9.5 Stay left at Post 17. A right turn leads to Lost Lake.

10.0 At a trail intersection continue straight and follow the signs to Devoe Lake and Scaup Lake Campgrounds.

10.8 Reach Post 15 and continue straight.

Erin crosses a suspension bridge at the Rifle River Recreation Area.

11.2 Cruise by Post 14.

11.9 Reach Post 13 in an open area and cross a sandy road. Continue straight and parallel Scaup Lake.

12.3 Arrive at Post 10 and turn right up a hill. The next section should look familiar.

12.9 Back at Post 9, turn right onto the dirt road. Cycle around the gate and turn left onto a dirt road and up a hill.

13.2 Reach a fork in the road and turn left onto the singletrack.

13.4 After a short, steep, slippery climb, turn left and cycle back toward the picnic area parking lot. Retrace your tracks back to the parking area.

14.2 End of ride.

Chippewa Hills Pathway

Location:	11.5 miles west of Ossineke.
Distance:	6.6-mile loop.
Time:	1 hour.
Tread:	6.6 miles of singletrack.
Aerobic level:	Moderately easy.
Technical difficulty:	2.
Hill factor:	Rolling to hilly.
Highlights:	Singletrack romp on one of the area's best cross-country pathways.
Land status:	Mackinaw State Forest, Atlanta Forest Unit.
Maps:	USGS Evans Creek and Hubbard Lake West; maps available from DNR offices (see Appendix B).
Access:	From U.S. 23 and Nicholson Hill Road in Ossineke, drive 11 miles west on Nicholson Hill Road. Turn south onto Kissau Road and continue for about 0.5 mile to the trailhead parking on the west side of the road.

Notes on the trail: Chippewa Hills Pathway is popular with locals, and it is easy to see why. By far one of the best cross-country ski trails open to mountain biking in northeastern Michigan, it follows a roller-coaster route through cedar swamp and dense trees. For the most part it is high and dry

Chippewa Hills Pathway

Private Land

START

to Alpena
[23]

Nicholson Hill Rd.

Kissau Rd.

Paved Road
Maintained Dirt
Unmaintained Dirt
Singletrack Trail
Selected Route

0   Mile   1/2

and, best of all, mostly singletrack. The path, like most other Michigan cross-country pathways, is amply marked and relatively hazard-free, except for a few sandy patches.

The Ride

0.0   Cycle to the west corner of the parking lot. Stay to the right and pedal uphill to Post 1, following the trail in a counterclockwise direction.

0.1   Reach Post 1. Continue straight to Post 2 and get ready for a couple of fast downhills. Soon reach Post 2 and turn right toward Post 3.

Hilly Chippewa Hills is a fast cruise.

1.25 From Post 3 turn right toward Post 4. The next section rolls a little more steeply.

1.9 Reach Post 4 and cycle straight toward Post 5. A right turn will cut the ride short.

2.5 Stay left at a primitive campsite and cycle back into the woods. Cruise by Post 5 and continue to Post 6.

2.9 Arrive at Post 6 and continue straight to Post 7. A right turn takes you to the south parking area.

3.5 Cross a doubletrack and reach Post 7. Continue to Post 8.

4.0 Reach Post 8 and continue straight to Post 9. Test your sand aptitude by navigating the sandbar.

4.3 Cruise by Post 9 and continue up a wide, steep hill toward Post 10.

4.8 Cross a doubletrack and arrive at Post 10. Continue straight to Post 11.

6.1 Reach Post 11 and turn right toward Post 12.

6.4 From Post 12 stay right toward Post 1.

6.6 Arrive back at parking area.

High Country Pathway

Location:	10 miles east of Vanderbilt.
Distance:	80.6-mile loop.
Time:	2 or more days; shorter out-and-back segments are possible.
Tread:	2.3 miles of doubletrack, 2.5 miles of dirt road, 75.8 miles of singletrack. (Tread mileage is an estimate.)
Aerobic level:	Strenuous.
Technical difficulty:	2 to 3+.
Hill factor:	Flat to highlands.
Highlights:	Epic loop that offers the best of Michigan—from old-growth forests to grazing elk.
Land status:	Mackinaw State Forest, Pigeon River Unit.
Maps:	USGS Hardwood, Green Timbers, Atlanta, Lake Geneva, Clear Lake; guidebook and maps available from Pigeon River Country Association (see Appendix C).

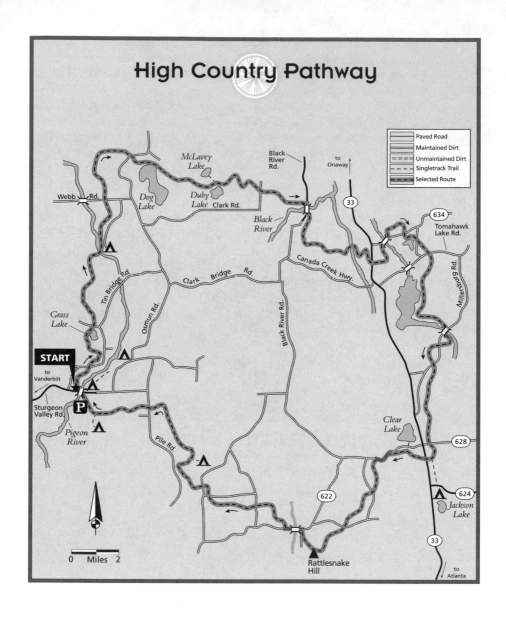

High Country Pathway

Legend:
- Paved Road
- Maintained Dirt
- Unmaintained Dirt
- Singletrack Trail
- Selected Route

McLavey Lake

Black River Rd.

to Onaway

Webb Rd.

Dog Lake

Duby Lake   Clark Rd.

Black River

33

634

Tomahawk Lake Rd.

Canada Creek Hwy.

Clark   Bridge   Rd.

Tin Bridge Rd.

Osmun Rd.

Black River Rd.

Millersburg Rd.

Grass Lake

START

to Vanderbilt

Sturgeon Valley Rd.

P

Pigeon River

Pile Rd.

Clear Lake

628

622

624

Jackson Lake

33

Rattlesnake Hill

to Atlanta

0   Miles   2

Access: From the intersection of Interstate 75 and Old Michigan 27 in Vanderbilt, drive 0.7 mile south on Old 27 to the blinking light. Turn east onto Sturgeon Valley Road. Drive 10.3 miles, just beyond the Pigeon River, to the signed pathway parking area on the south side of the road.

Notes on the trail: This ride offers the best of Michigan, wrapped in an awesome 80-mile, mostly singletrack loop. The trail sees little use and sections can be quite brushy, but don't let that deter you. The rewards on this unique ride are overwhelming, ranging from secluded wilderness lakes to grueling Rattlesnake Hill, the most difficult portion of the ride. Cyclists looking for a multiple-day ride will find several public campgrounds along the route; those looking for a shorter challenge can tackle any portion as an out-and-back ride. Marked with High Country Pathway signage and blue paint, the trail rolls through several historic areas like the Valentine Branch of the Detroit/Mackinaw Railroad. A guidebook, developed by the Pigeon River Country Association, is well worth the $4.95 price for its maps and area descriptions. Two shorter loops, Jackson Lake/Clear Lake Pathway (Mile 51.0) and Shingle Mill Pathway (Mile 0.0), connect to the High Country Pathway and are easy-to-follow alternatives.

The Ride

0.0   Turn left out of the parking area onto Sturgeon Valley Road. After crossing the bridge, turn right onto the trail. (Shingle Mill Pathway ends here. Its trailhead is located in the campground across from the parking area.)

2.4   Turn left at a trail intersection and head toward Post 10.

4.5   Reach Post 11 after a steep climb. Turn left and follow the signs for the High Country Pathway.

5.7   Arrive at a brushy doubletrack on the edge of a field, and turn left.

6.1   Turn right onto a sandy road. Soon turn right onto a narrow singletrack.

8.2   Turn left at a T intersection with a doubletrack. In a short while turn right onto another doubletrack that narrows into a singletrack.

9.2   Reach a series of boardwalks.

9.9   Cross over the Pigeon River on a wooden bridge. Soon reach Pine Grove Campground. Cycle through the campground, following the blue markers, and turn left toward Dog Lake.

12.5   Cross over dirt Webb Road. The next section, although flat, is rooty and bumpy.

15.8   Reach dirt Osmun Road and turn left. In a short distance turn right onto the singletrack.

17.0   Stay left at a primitive campsite and ride out to a doubletrack. Turn right onto a doubletrack.

17.2   Singletrack continues to the right and into the woods. Soon pass Post 11 and Dog Lake Flooding on the right.

18.1   Singletrack dumps into a doubletrack; follow the blue markers.

18.5   Turn right back onto a narrow singletrack.

20.7   Duby Lake Pathway takes off to the right and McLavey Lake Pathway heads left. Continue straight for the High Country Pathway. Soon cross Milligan Creek on a long boardwalk. Boardwalks dot the next section as the trail begins to roll more.

21.6   After a short boardwalk, turn right up a hill.

22.1 Reach a brushy field with route-finding challenges. Follow the worn path and look for blue on stumps and trees.

23.4 Reach a trail intersection in an open area and turn left onto a wide brushy trail. Blue soon reappears on the trees.

24.9 Watch for an easy-to-miss left turn back into the woods.

27.0 Reach dirt Black River Road and turn right. Cross the Black River on a bridge and almost immediately turn left. Cycle diagonally across a dirt parking area and pick up the singletrack at a blue post. The next section features narrow boardwalks crossing lush, rooty terrain.

31.0 Cycle along the top of a hill overlooking a clearcut. Cruise down the hill, cross a sandy road, and climb back up into the roads.

31.4 At the bottom of a steep downhill, cross two sandy roads and look for the blue markings on the trees next to the clearcut.

31.8 Cruise by a rustic cabin and soon cross Canada Creek on a wooden bridge. A steep, sandy hill is ahead. After climbing the hill on switchbacks, turn right and follow the ridge.

33.2 Cross M–33.

34.1 Reach a rough, bumpy clearcut area and follow the blue markers as the worn trail disappears.

34.4 Turn right at County Road 634 and cross Tomahawk Creek on a bridge. Turn left after the creek. Trail climbs back up and crosses CR 634 again in less than 2 miles.

37.5 After paralleling Shoepac Lake on a sandy trail, dump out at a parking area. Turn right onto Shoepac Lake Highway and ride south. As you pass the Shoepac Lake Campground entrance on the right, look for a post with blue paint on the left and turn onto the singletrack disappearing into the woods.

38.1 Cycle straight across a clearing, and look for the blue dots on the trees.

38.4 Cross dirt Tomahawk Lake Highway. Shortly reach Marker 17 and a turnoff to Tomahawk Lake Campground. Continue following the singletrack as it skirts around the campground and boat launch.

39.6 Cross a sandy road.

41.6 Reach a doubletrack and turn left. Cycle through a clearcut.

42.4 Turn right onto a dirt road at a T intersection marked with a blue post. Soon turn left up a sandy doubletrack, and follow the edge of the clearcut.

43.0 Just before a steep gravel hill, turn right with the blue markers into the woods on a singletrack.

43.8 Turn right onto dirt Millersburg Road. After crossing a creek and a swampy area, turn left back onto the trail.

44.3 The trail seems to disappear in an open area. Continue riding diagonally across a field to the right; the trail picks up again in a short distance. The next 3 or so miles cover rough, bumpy, low-lying terrain.

Keith crosses a bridge on the High Country Pathway.

44.5   Pass Post 21.

45.0   Cross Millersburg Road.

46.2   Soon after crossing a grassy doubletrack, come to a low-lying area with a narrow boardwalk.

46.6   Cross Millersburg Road again. Trail begins to follow the historic Valentine Branch railroad grade.

47.2   Reach another section of narrow boardwalks.

47.5   Arrive at a clearing after a swampy area, and stay to the left. Soon cruise past Post 23 and come to a sandy doubletrack. Stay to the left, cycling in the direction of the tall antenna. Look for the blue post.

48.2   Cross a sandy road.

48.6   Cross the sandy road that leads to the tall antenna. Continue on the brushy, tight singletrack.

49.1   Cross a dirt road.

50.5   Cross a sandy road. The trail becomes a doubletrack for a short distance.

50.9   Cross underneath power lines and over a sandy road.

51.0   Turn left at the intersection with Clear Lake Pathway at Post 26.

51.5 Turn left as the trail dumps out onto a sandy road. Cycle underneath the power lines and almost immediately turn right at the stop sign. In less than 0.1-mile turn left at another stop sign; cross the road and follow the singletrack, marked with blue paint, disappearing into the woods.

52.0 Turn right at this easy-to-miss turn toward M–33. The Jackson Lake Pathway continues straight.

52.3 After a fun downhill, reach M–33, watch for traffic, and carefully cross the road.

52.7 Stay right at a trail intersection and follow the blue markers.

53.4 At a T intersection with a doubletrack, turn left and then almost immediately right back onto the singletrack.

53.6 After crossing the CCC Ball Diamond, reach Post 28. Turn left when the trail splits. Staying right will take you to Clear Lake State Park.

54.0 Turn left onto dirt County Road 622.

54.9 After climbing a hill, turn left at the High Country Pathway sign onto a sandy doubletrack.

55.3 Turn left onto the singletrack as the doubletrack continues straight.

56.2 Turn right onto a doubletrack, then almost immediately left back onto the singletrack. Soon cross a rickety bridge over a creek and reach a leaning giant among a small patch of old-growth trees.

57.6 After cruising through a clearcut, cross a dirt road.

58.5 Dump out onto a doubletrack. Shortly cross Rouse Road and continue on the doubletrack. Follow the blue markers and turn right around a berm onto the singletrack.

62.3 After a long, steady climb, reach the first of two overlooks.

62.6 Arrive at the second overlook. The expansive views take in unbroken forest. There are two options for the descent. Cycling straight follows a sandy, steep ORV trail. For the less steep route, turn left down a rocky, sandy hill; about two-thirds of the way down, turn right. Follow the blue markers onto a singletrack. Continue following the blue markers down a fast, fun downhill. Cross over a doubletrack at the bottom of the hill and make a tight, easy-to-miss right turn.

63.8 Reach Rattle Snake Creek Road and County Road 622 and turn left. Cross over a creek on a bridge.

64.4 Turn right at the High Country Pathway signage onto a tight singletrack.

66.2 Reach a field and turn left onto a doubletrack. Shortly see a post on a hill to the right. Circle around the post; the singletrack picks up again on the left as the doubletrack stays right into the woods.

66.8 Cross over Camp 30 Road.

68.8 Watch for an easy-to-miss right turn into the woods.

69.8 Cross over County Road 495.

70.4 Cross over Black River Road. In a short distance, reach a swampy area that stretches for about 0.7 mile with several narrow boardwalks and bridges.

72.1 Cross over a creek on a rustic, highly arched bridge; almost immediately reach another short boardwalk followed by a short, steep climb.

72.5 Cross over a road that leads to the Town Corner Campground.

72.9 Reach a trail that also leads to the Town Corner Campground and stay left with the main trail.

73.3 Reach a turnoff for a scenic overlook on the left.

73.8 Reach a primitive campground with a doubletrack heading down a hill. Look for the blue on the trees, and follow the singletrack.

74.6 Cross the Midland to Mackinac Trail.

76.4 Cross dirt Tin Shanty Road.

78.8 Cross dirt Round Lake Road.

79.4 Continue straight at an intersection with Round Lake Campground.

80.6 Dump out onto Shingle Mill Pathway parking area.

Norway Ridge Pathway

Location:	3.5 miles southwest of Alpena.
Distance:	7.7-mile loop.
Time:	1 hour.
Tread:	7.7 miles of wide ski trail and singletrack.
Aerobic level:	Moderately easy.
Technical difficulty:	1.
Hill factor:	Rolling.
Highlights:	Singletrack side loops roll through hardwood forest.
Land status:	Mackinaw State Forest, Atlanta Forest Unit.
Maps:	USGS Alpena; maps available from DNR offices (see Appendix B).
Access:	From the intersection of U.S. 23 and Michigan 32 in Alpena, drive 2.5 miles south on U.S. 23. Turn west onto Werth Road and drive 3 miles to the trailhead on the north side of the road.

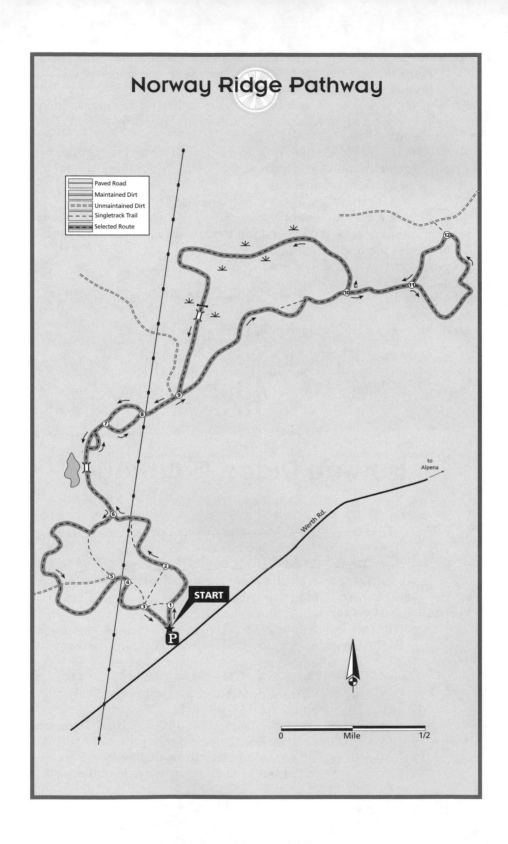

Notes on the trail: Norway pines tower over cyclists as they meander along the wide ski trails and singletrack side loops on this popular trail system. Like most other Michigan pathways, the main trail is marked with numbered posts, but be sure to steer onto the more interesting unmarked singletrack. Snaking through dense woods, these additional loops always merge back with the main trail. Another highlight is the singletrack between Posts 10 and 9 on the return route. This potentially marshy area twists delightfully through a cedar swamp. The route described here follows the perimeter of the pathway in a counterclockwise direction.

The Ride

0.0 Cycle up a small hill to Post 1 and stay right. Cycle into the trees and head toward Post 2.

0.3 Cruise by Post 2 and stay right toward Post 6.

0.5 Reach power lines and look to the right for the first of many unmarked singletracks. For a short but fun alternative, cycle up the hill and cruise through the woods until the trail dumps back onto the main trail.

0.6 Arrive at Post 6 and continue straight to Post 7 and up a sandy hill.

1.0 After a boardwalk crossing, reach another fork in the trail. The trails rejoin in a short distance, but the more interesting route is on the right and climbs a hill.

1.1 The trails rejoin.

1.15 Stay to the right toward Post 8. The trail on the left is the return route.

1.3 Reach Post 8 and turn right toward Post 9.

1.8 From Post 9 turn right and continue toward Post 10. The trail on the left is the return route.

2.2 Reach another fork in the trail. Both trails rejoin a little farther down the route.

2.5 Reach Post 10 and turn right toward Post 11. A left turn takes you back to Post 9.

2.7 At Post 11 stay right to Post 12. Route on the left is the return trail.

3.1 Arrive at Post 12. Stay left and loop back to Post 11 via a swampy area. Cycling straight dumps you out at a snowmobile trail/fire lane.

3.4 Climb back to the intersection with Post 11, and turn right toward Post 10.

3.6 Turn right at Post 10 toward Post 9. The next section rambles through a swampy area and narrows to tight singletrack.

4.8 Cross through a gate and over a boardwalk.

5.1 Reach Post 9 and turn right toward Post 8.

5.6 From Post 8 cycle straight ahead to Post 7.

5.8   From Post 7 turn right, back onto the wide trail, and continue to Post 6.

6.2   Reach Post 6 and turn right toward Post 5.

6.4   Make a hard right onto an unmarked singletrack, just after a curve in the trail. Although short, this relatively new singletrack is a highlight that climbs and dips through the woods.

7.3   The singletrack dumps out onto the wide ski trail. Turn right and ride under the power lines. Shortly reach Post 4 and turn right again toward Post 3.

7.5   Reach Post 3 at the bottom of a short hill and continue straight.

7.7   End of ride.

Rogers City Tour

Location:	Rogers City.
Distance:	6.5-mile loop.
Time:	1 hour.
Tread:	3.8 miles of singletrack and wide trail, 0.7 mile of paved road, 2 miles of paved pathway.
Aerobic level:	Easy.
Technical difficulty:	1+.
Hill factor:	Flat to rolling.
Highlights:	Norman Rockwell town hosts uncrowded, picturesque parks with Lake Huron views.
Land status:	City of Rogers City, Herman Vogler Conservation Area, Seagull Point Nature Area.
Maps:	USGS Roger City, Moltke; maps available at Rogers City Chamber of Commerce.
Access:	From the intersection of Michigan 68 and Business U.S. 23 in downtown Rogers City (at the only traffic light in Presque Isle County), head north on Business 23 for 0.6 mile. Turn northeast onto State Street, just past the Driftwood Motel. Continue straight into the North Shore Park and park here.

Notes on the trail: Rogers City seems like it came straight from a Norman Rockwell painting. An old-fashioned movie theater is downtown's

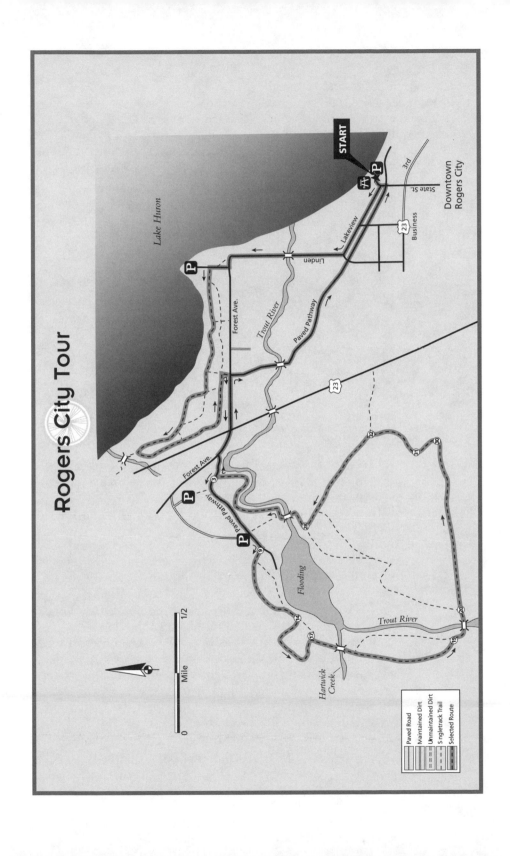

Rogers City Tour

Erin crosses a wooden bridge in the Herman Vogler Conservation Area.

focal point, and clean, whitewashed bungalows look out to Lake Huron. The town is also home to pleasant parks that take cyclists from the beaches of Lake Huron to the dense hardwoods of northern Michigan. The route is a pleasant ramble for all abilities and perfect for a lazy beach picnic.

The Ride

0.0 Pedal out of the parking lot and turn right onto Lakeview Road.

0.3 Turn right at a stop sign onto Linden Road. Follow Linden around to Seagull Park.

0.7 Turn right into the entrance for Seagull Park. Just before reaching the lake, turn left onto a singletrack trail between two posts.

1.6 Just before reaching a bridge, turn left onto a narrow, sandy singletrack heading into the woods.

2.0 Reach a T intersection with a wide trail and turn right. Cross Forest Avenue and turn right onto the bike path that parallels the road. Soon cross over U.S. 23 and follow the bike path into the Herman Vogler Conservation Area.

2.5	Turn right at Post 9 up a steep dirt hill toward Post 10.
2.9	Reach Post 14 and turn right up a hill. Cruise by Post 15.
3.0	Turn right at Post 17. Soon cruise past Post 18 and continue straight.
3.6	Reach Post 19 and stay right. Soon cross over a bridge. Shortly climb a steep hill and reach Post 20. Continue straight to Post 21.
4.2	Arrive at Post 30 and turn left toward Post 31. Soon reach Post 31 and turn right toward Post 32.
4.6	Reach Post 32. Turn left and head to Post 28.
4.9	From Post 28 stay right and soon cross over the Trout River on a bridge. Almost immediately turn right onto a trail following the river. Continue on that trail to Post 3.
5.0	Turn right onto the paved trail and pedal over U.S. 23. Follow the paved path back to North Shore Park.
6.5	Arrive back at the parking area.

Ocqueoc Falls Pathway

Location:	11.5 miles east of Onaway.
Distance:	6.6-mile loop.
Time:	1–2 hours.
Tread:	6.3 miles of doubletrack, 0.3 mile of single-track.
Aerobic level:	Easy.
Technical difficulty:	2.
Hill factor:	Rolling.
Highlights:	Pleasant pathway rolls through pockets of old growth and next to the Ocqueoc River.
Land status:	Mackinaw State Forest, Atlanta Forest Unit.
Maps:	USGS Ocqueoc; maps available at trailhead.
Access:	From the intersection of Michigan 68 and Michigan 33 in Onaway, drive 11.5 miles east on M–68. Turn west (hard left) onto Ocqueoc Falls Road, just before the Ocqueoc Cemetery, and continue for 0.3 mile. Turn north into the Ocqueoc Falls Pathway parking lot.

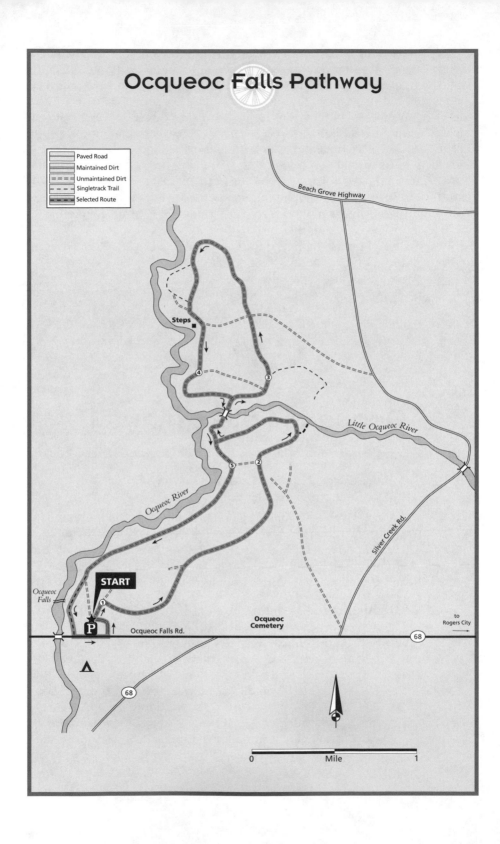

Notes on the trail: This ride gives you a wilderness feel, yet it is close to civilization. Following a ridge through dense trees, the Ocqueoc Falls Pathway dips down to the Ocqueoc River. After crossing the river, the trail passes through pockets of old-growth trees. The last half of the ride follows the Ocqueoc River, with several inviting overlooks offering peaceful picnic areas. The ride ends with views of the Ocqueoc Falls, the largest waterfall in the Lower Peninsula. Hazards include sand and cars at the end of the ride when the trail dumps out onto Ocqueoc Falls Road. There are also many intersecting doubletracks and adventurous singletracks to explore. Navigation is sometimes confusing, but the pathway is fairly well marked with blue triangles and posts.

The Ride

0.0 Ride begins at the large map located at the northeast end of the parking lot. Cycle toward Post 1.

0.05 Reach Post 1 and turn right toward Post 2.

0.6 Reach a T intersection with a doubletrack, and turn right.

1.3 Reach a fork. Stay left and continue along the ridge.

1.6 Arrive at Post 2. Continue cycling the ridge to Post 3.

1.85 Turn left and then left again with the blue markers. Do not head downhill.

2.25 Reach a doubletrack T intersection and turn right with the arrow. Cycle down a short hill and turn right at the bottom.

2.5 Reach a bridge and cycle over the Little Ocqueoc River. Pedal up a steep, sandy hill, and turn right at the top.

2.65 Reach an intersection and continue straight to Post 3. Shortly arrive at Post 3 and turn left toward Post 4.

3.5 Cross a doubletrack. Follow the blue triangles as the trail bends to the left.

3.7 There's an adventurous singletrack on your right. The main trail continues straight.

4.0 Reach a T intersection with a doubletrack. Turn left and follow the blue triangles.

4.2 Arrive at an overlook with steps leading down to the Ocqueoc River. Continue a short distance on the wide doubletrack then turn right with the river.

4.4 Reach Post 4; continue straight.

4.6 Back at the T intersection above Little Ocqueoc River Bridge. Turn right, cycling downhill, and retrace your tracks over the bridge.

4.9 Reach an intersection and continue straight toward Post 5.

5.1 Arrive at Post 5. Continue straight toward Post 1.

6.1 The trail splits. A left turn takes you to the parking lot. Cycle straight up the hill toward the Ocqueoc Falls picnic area. Listen for the falls.

A tricky creek crossing on adventurous singletrack near the Ocqueoc Falls Pathway.

6.2 Arrive at the picnic area, and enjoy the views. Continue cycling next to the river. The trail ends with a steep, short climb to Ocqueoc Falls Road. Watch for cars!

6.4 Turn left onto Ocqueoc Falls Road. Soon turn left at the sign for Ocqueoc Falls.

6.6 Arrive back at parking area.

Black Mountain Ramble

Location:	12 miles southeast of Cheboygan.
Distance:	15.4-mile loop.
Time:	2–4 hours.
Tread:	15.4 miles of doubletrack.
Aerobic level:	Moderate.
Technical difficulty:	1+; a few sandy patches are the only obstacles.
Hill factor:	Hilly. Steepest climbs come at the end.
Highlights:	A roller-coaster ride through the Black Mountain Recreation Area with Lake Huron views.
Land status:	Mackinaw State Forest, Atlanta Forest Unit.
Maps:	USGS Black Lake Bluffs; maps available at Mackinaw Forest offices (see Appendix B).
Access:	From the intersection of U.S. 23 and Michigan 27 in downtown Cheboygan, drive 2 miles south on U.S. 23 toward Alpena. Turn south (right) onto Cheboygan County Road F05/Butler Road and continue for 10 miles as it becomes Black River Road. Turn east onto Twin Lakes Road and drive for 3.5 miles to the Black River Recreation Area. Park in the large parking area.

Notes on the trail: The "mountain" in Black Mountain Recreation Area is an exaggeration; but in an otherwise flat landscape, these hills are welcome relief to cross-country skiers, hikers, and bikers. With about 35 miles of trails, Black Mountain offers many different loops of varying length. This ride takes you around the perimeter of the area, up and over Black Mountain twice. On the way you pass two inviting wooden shelters and many black-diamond side loops and catch a glimpse of Lake Huron on the

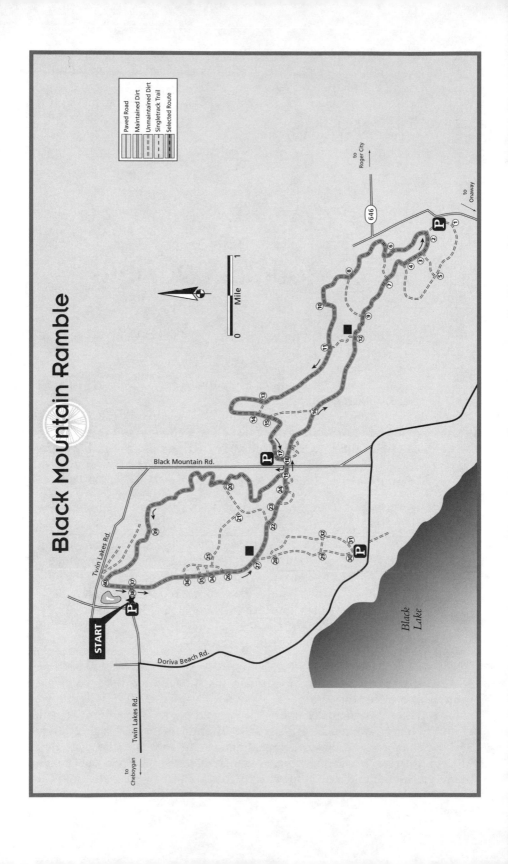

Black Mountain Ramble

Numbered posts and maps make it virtually impossible to get lost on the Black Mountain Recreation Area trail system.

north side of the trail. The route ends on a series of challenging hills that will lure you back with your cross-country skis when the trails are blanketed in white.

The Ride

You will not get lost if you follow this sequence: 38, 37, 36, 35, 34, 26, 27, 22, 23, 24, 19, 18, 16, 12, 9, 7, 4, 3, 2, 6, 8, 10, 11, 13, 14, 15, 17, 18, 19, 20, 39, 40, 37, 38. These are the numbers posted at each intersection and in the order in which you will encounter them. The trail system is so well marked that if you just follow this sequence of numbers, you will cycle the loop described below.

0.0 Pedal past the large trail map. Turn right at Post 38. Stay on this gently rolling trail, cycling past Posts 37, 36, 35, 34, and 26. Cross the ORV trails several times.

1.5 Reach a wooden shelter on your left at Post 27. Soon after leaving the shelter, climb a steep, sandy hill, shared with an ORV trail.

2.0	The route leaves the ORV trail at Post 22 and bears right. Cycle past Posts 23 and 24.
2.7	Reach Post 19 and continue straight. Cross Black Mountain Road and cycle toward Post 12, passing Posts 18 and 16 on the way. Look to your right for views of Black Lake.
4.4	Arrive at Post 12 and another wooden shelter. Cruise past Posts 9, 7, 4, and 3.
6.0	Reach Post 2 and continue toward Post 6, climbing steadily. Cycling downhill will take you to the southeast parking area for the Black Mountain Recreation Area.
6.6	Arrive at Post 6. Follow the ridge past Posts 8, 10, and 11. Look to your right for glimpses of Lake Huron. At Post 10 there is a fenced-off gravesite for a Black Forest Recreation Area supervisor.
8.5	Reach Post 13, turn right, and follow the sign for Post 14. Pedal by Post 14 and continue on to Post 17.
11.0	Cycle across a parking area and then to the left toward Post 17. Turn right at Post 18 and cross the Black Mountain Road once again. Turn right at Post 19 and head toward 20. Some of the steepest climbs are still to come.
12.1	Reach Post 20 and turn right toward 39. Get ready for a fast roller-coaster ride. Pass a small lake on your right, and continue past Posts 40 and 37.
15.4	Arrive at Post 38 and cycle out of the forest to your vehicle.

Eastern Upper Peninsula:
Sandstone Cliffs and Island Trails

The rides in the eastern Upper Peninsula (UP) combine local charm with pristine wilderness for a folksy mix. Primitive Grand Island exemplifies this unique flavor. Located in Lake Superior and only a half mile from Munising, Grand Island is home to perhaps the best mountain bike ride in Michigan. Offering clifftop views of massive Lake Superior, the island embodies what is magical about the eastern Upper Peninsula: sandy beaches, dense woods, rocky lakeshore, and rugged individuals.

Split from the western UP by the natural division made by the Au Train Basin—waterways that run between Au Train Bay near Munising to Little Bay de Noc near Escanaba—the eastern UP is dominated by Hiawatha National Forest and Pictured Rocks National Lakeshore. Hiawatha National Forest is home to Bruno's Run, a popular singletrack loop, and numerous forest pathways.

Touching the shores of three of the Great Lakes, the eastern UP stretches past Sault Ste. Marie and into Lake Huron with Drummond Island. This rustic getaway retains an unspoiled charm where mountain bikers find miles of doubletracks to explore. A different island experience is found on Mackinac Island. Where Drummond Island is relatively new to the tourist experience, Mackinac Island has fully embraced tourism. Home to the famous Grand Hotel, featured in the movie *Somewhere in Time*, Mackinac Island is motor vehicle–free and welcomes mountain bikers to its singletracks, located in the middle of the island.

Back on the mainland, Seney Wildlife Refuge sits in the middle of the eastern UP. Offering cyclists a maze of old roads, the refuge rolls past numerous ponds teeming with migrating birds, from sandhill cranes to eagles. With so much terrain to explore, the eastern UP unfolds like a juicy novel, boasting a new adventure on every page.

Mackinac Island Trails

Location:	Mackinac Island State Park.
Distance:	9.3-mile loop.
Time:	1–2 hours. Allow time to explore other trails and island amenities.
Tread:	0.7 mile of dirt road, 2.3 miles of paved road, 6.3 miles of singletrack.
Aerobic level:	Moderate.
Technical difficulty:	2–3 for most trails; 5 for first 1.2 miles of Tranquil Bluff Trail.
Hill factor:	Rolling to hilly.
Highlights:	Motor vehicle–free resort island boasts miles of singletrack trails—and rich, delicious fudge.
Land status:	Mackinac Island State Park.
Maps:	USGS Round Island; excellent map available for $1.00 at Mackinac Island State Park Visitor Center (see Appendix B).
Access:	Three ferry companies offer seasonal service to Mackinac Island from St. Ignace or Mackinaw City. The ride runs about $20 per person, including the bicycle fee—steep but well worth it. Once on the island, exit the ferry landing and turn right onto Huron Street and look for the Mackinac Island State Park Visitor Center on the right in a few blocks. Stop and purchase a map. The ride begins here.

Notes on the trail: Who would have guessed that one of Michigan's most popular tourist attractions was also home to Michigan's most difficult section of singletrack? The first 1.2 miles of the Tranquil Bluff Trail will leave you anything but tranquil. Following a steep, rooty route along a cliff, the trail provides peek-a-boo glimpses of Lake Huron. It is also possible to skip this difficult portion of the trail and pick up Tranquil Bluff a little farther along the route. The rest of the ride follows well-marked interconnecting singletracks that crisscross the middle of the island. In short, it is a spectacular place to bike, where motorized vehicles are not allowed and horses are the only other traffic on the streets. Horses are also common on the trails, so never submit to your need for speed. End your ride by cycling the

Mackinac Island Trails

Lake Huron

Tranquil Bluff Trail

Porter Hanks

Croghan Water

Swamp Trail

Lydia

Nicki

Partridge

State Rd.

British Landing Rd.

Scott Rd.

Crack-in-the-Island

Leslie Ave.

Crooked Tree Rd.

Annex Rd.

Garrison Rd.

Coffee Trail

Murray Trail

Tranquil Bluff Trail

Park Ave.

Rifle Range Rd.

Lake View Blvd.

Annex Rd.

Grand Hotel

West Bluff Rd.

Cadotte Ave.

Market St.

Huron St.

Fort St.

S. Bicycle Trail

START

?
State Park Info Center

185

0   Mile   1/2

paved road around the island, and take in the views of late-1800s Victorian homes. As you wait for your ferry ride home, sample the delicious fudge for which the island is famous.

The Ride

0.0   Turn left onto Fort Street and cycle up the steep hill as the road becomes a paved path.

0.2   Turn right at the top of the hill and cycle along a paved road. The fort is on the right.

0.4   Reach the paved South Bicycle Trail and continue straight into the woods.

1.0   Reach Arch Rock. Check out the views and then continue on the paved path. Cross Rifle Range Road and continue on the paved path as it turns into Leslie Avenue. Soon meet unmarked Tranquil Bluff Trail on the right and cycle onto the wide singletrack. The next 1.2 miles are very difficult. To skip this section, continue on Leslie Avenue then turn right onto Murray Trail, which leads to Tranquil Bluff (see description at Mile 2.5).

2.1   The trail dumps out onto Leslie Avenue. Look to the right and cycle back onto the singletrack.

2.5   Continue straight at the intersection with Murray Trail. Soon cruise by Soldiers Garden Trail on the left.

2.9   Cross dirt Scott's Road and soon cruise past Swamp Trail on the left.

4.3   Porter Hank's Trail comes in on the left; continue straight. Soon pass the British Landing Nature Trail.

4.5   Cross British Landing Road and begin the Croghan Water Trail.

4.9   Reach a maze of trails. Stay to the right and follow unmarked Lydia Trail.

5.1   Cross State Road. Pick up Straits Trail and *walk* your bike. This trail is a horse-jumping trail, and cycling is discouraged.

5.2   Turn left onto Nicki Trail and start riding again. Turn left onto Partridge Trail at the 5.3-mile mark.

5.8   At an unmarked four-way intersection, turn right onto the wide trail. Almost immediately turn left onto Crack-in-the-Island Trail. Follow the trail as it curves to the left away from the airport.

6.2   Reach State Road and turn right.

6.5   Turn right onto British Landing Road.

6.7   Turn left onto Garrison Road, then almost immediately turn right onto Coffee Trail. Follow the trail as it crosses Huron Road and twists its way to Annex Road.

7.6   Reach Annex Road and continue straight onto Park Avenue. At a T intersection turn left onto Lake View Boulevard.

Keith climbs Pontiac Trail on Mackinac Island.

8.0 Soon after the road becomes paved, look to your right for Pontiac Trail, between two homes and across from a large blue house with a wraparound porch. Cruise along this tiny trail, sandwiched between stately Victorians and a cliff.

8.2 The trail ends at a turnstile on paved West Bluff Road. Cycle down the hill and in front of the Grand Hotel. Stay right onto Cadotte Avenue.

8.9 Turn left onto Market Street, which ends at Fort Street. Turn right onto Fort Street.

9.3 Arrive back at visitor center.

Resort Ramble

Location:	Drummond Island Resort and Conference Center.
Distance:	6.4-mile loop; other possible loop combinations.
Time:	1 hour.
Tread:	2.4 miles of paved road, 1.4 miles of dirt road, 1.5 miles of doubletrack, 1.1 miles of singletrack.
Aerobic level:	Easy.
Technical difficulty:	1–1+.
Hill factor:	Flat to rolling.
Highlights:	Luxurious resort hosts island views, gracious dining, and secluded nature preserve.
Land status:	Private. Landowners graciously permit mountain bikers to use trails; please respect property and stay on established trails.
Maps:	USGS Drummond; maps available at the resort.
Access:	Catch the Drummond Island Ferry from Detour. From the ferry landing on Drummond Island, drive 7.9 miles east on Michigan 134. Turn north onto Townline Road and continue for 1.5 miles. Turn east onto Maxton Road for 3

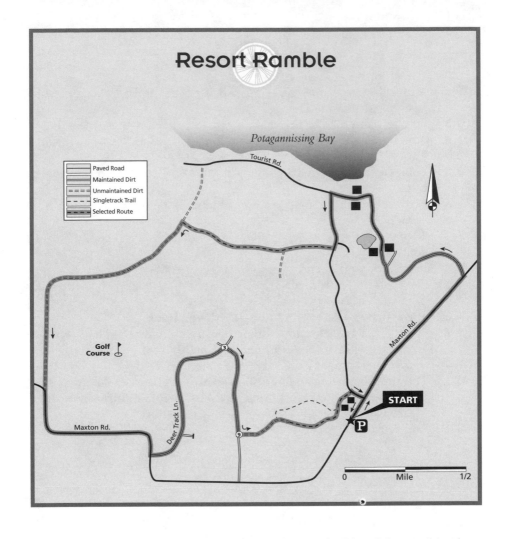

Resort Ramble

Potagannissing Bay

Tourist Rd.

Paved Road
Maintained Dirt
Unmaintained Dirt
Singletrack Trail
Selected Route

Golf
Course

Maxton Rd.

Deer Track Ln.

Maxton Rd.

START

P

0   Mile   1/2

miles. Park on the south side of the road in the large dirt parking lot across from the resort.

Notes on the trail: This ride rolls along gentle doubletracks through lovely resort grounds and deep woods and past the perfectly landscaped The Rock golf course. The route is sporadically marked but still easy to follow. Families will find it a pleasant ride but watch for traffic on the paved roads. Cyclists should keep in mind that this is only a small taste of the mountain biking that Drummond Island has to offer. Dan Harrison, Michigan Mountain Biking Association board member, is working with local officials to secure more trails for mountain bikers. His hard work can be found in a trails guidebook to Drummond Island, available at the Drummond Island Resort.

The Ride

0.0   Cycle northeast along paved Maxton Road.

1.0   Turn left onto a dirt road, marked with a sign for Potagannissing Lodge and Bayside Dining.

1.5   Stay left at a fork in the road. Road soon becomes pavement.

1.9   Stay left as the road merges into Tourist Road at Bayside Dining.

2.1   Turn left onto a paved road and pedal up a hill.

2.3   Look for a trail sign on your right, and turn right onto the singletrack.

2.8   Cruise by a trail map and doubletrack on the left. Continue straight.

3.2   Turn left onto a rocky doubletrack. Cruise past The Rock golf course.

3.6   Watch for traffic, and turn left onto paved Maxton Road.

4.5   Turn left onto dirt Deer Track Lane and pass several lots for sale. The road narrows as it curves to the right.

5.2   Turn right at Post 3 onto a brushy doubletrack.

5.7   Turn left at Post 9 onto another brushy doubletrack. Stay right at all intersections as the trail narrows and becomes quite rooty and rocky.

6.3   The trail dumps out behind the resort. Pedal across the grass and cycle through the resort back to Maxton Road. Turn right onto Maxton Road.

6.4   End of ride.

McNearney Ski Trail

Location:	4 miles northeast of Strongs.
Distance:	6.3-mile loop.
Time:	1–2 hours.
Tread:	5.2 miles of doubletrack, 1.1 miles of dirt road.
Aerobic level:	Moderate.
Technical difficulty:	1+.
Highlights:	Rugged doubletrack leads to solitary exploration.
Land status:	Hiawatha National Forest, Sault Ste. Marie Ranger District.
Maps:	USGS McNearney Lake; maps available from forest offices (see Appendix B).
Access:	From the intersection of Michigan 28 and Salt Point Road (Forest Road 3159), drive 4 miles north on Salt Point Road (road curves east). Parking area is on the north side of the road.

Notes on the trail: If you are looking for buffed singletrack, then skip this ride; but if solitude and adventure are your goal, read on. This rugged pathway rolls endlessly on a slow often-spongy trail. Mixing doubletracks with dirt roads, the pathway rambles through areas of selective logging and over many downed trees. The often-steep hills plunge through two clearings with an old-orchard feeling, perfect for a picnic. Although marked with numbered posts and maps, the trail has some confusing sections, possibly the result of logging. The North Country Trail crosses nearby, and a log cabin—a skiers' warming hut in the winter—gives the area a rustic feel.

The Ride

0.0 Pick up the wide trail on the north end of the parking lot, past the log cabin. Soon turn right at a posted map onto Camp 4 Loop; follow the arrows.

0.6 Turn left onto a dirt road and follow the arrow. Shortly, turn right onto Big Pine Loop at a marked trail intersection.

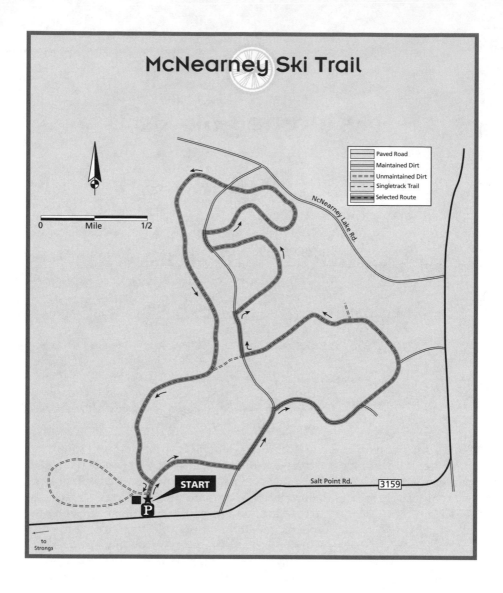

McNearney Ski Trail

Paved Road
Maintained Dirt
Unmaintained Dirt
Singletrack Trail
Selected Route

0   Mile   1/2

NcNearney Lake Rd.

START

Salt Point Rd.   3159

P

to
Strongs

1.3 Continue straight at the top of a hill and follow the arrow down a doubletrack.

1.6 Continue straight at an unmarked intersection with a road coming in from the right.

1.9 Turn left onto a marked doubletrack.

2.5 At a marked intersection, turn right onto dirt Forester/Forestry Loop.

2.7 Turn right onto a marked doubletrack.

3.0 At a doubletrack intersection, turn left and follow the signs.

3.4 Turn right at a road intersection. Almost immediately turn right onto a brushy doubletrack and follow the blue diamonds.

4.8 Cross a dirt road to a map, and continue straight up the hill.

5.4 After a fast downhill and substantial climb, reach an unmarked sandy road and turn left. Soon reach an intersection with a marked doubletrack going back into the woods. Turn right back onto Camp 4 Loop and follow the markers.

6.3 Arrive back at the parking area.

Canada Lakes Pathway

Location:	6 miles southeast of Newberry.
Distance:	8.9-mile loop.
Time:	1–1.5 hours.
Tread:	8.9 miles of doubletrack (shorter loops available).
Aerobic level:	Moderately easy.
Technical difficulty:	1.
Highlights:	Web of doubletracks offers spring wildflowers and hours of exploration.
Land status:	Lake Superior State Forest, Newberry District.
Maps:	USGS Roberts Corner; maps available at forest offices (see Appendix B).
Access:	From the intersection of Michigan 28 and Michigan 123, drive 1 mile east on M–28. Turn south onto Luce County Road 403. Continue 1.8 miles to the parking lot at the end of the road.

Notes on the trail: During spring, delicate white wildflowers blanket the forest surrounding this doubletrack maze. Hosting skiers in winter and hikers and mountain bikers in summer, the hard-packed trail is a fast, rolling ride that crosses an inviting ORV singletrack and rambles through dense forest with trees sprouting huge, gnarled growths like crouching gargoyles. The trail is fairly well marked with the typical pathway posts, arrows, and maps, but it does become a bit of a puzzle between Posts 6 and 8. Vandalized signs with missing maps leave riders confused, but there are so many other doubletracks to explore that being lost might be a welcome diversion. Riders shouldn't be surprised if they cycle at least a half mile without seeing signage.

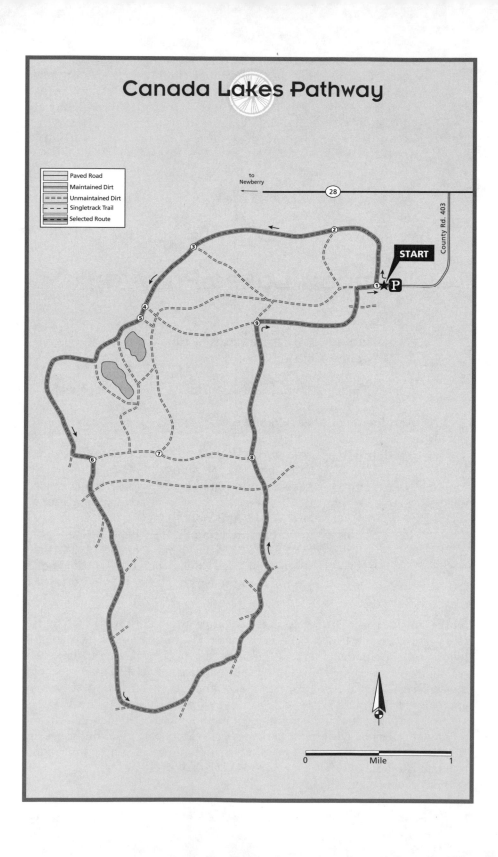

The Ride

0.0 Pedal to the west end of the parking lot. Turn right at Post 1 and head to Post 2.

0.5 Cruise past Post 2.

1.1 Arrive at Post 3 and continue to Post 4. Soon reach an intersection with a doubletrack and continue straight.

1.5 Cruise past Post 4 and almost immediately reach Post 5.

2.7 At a fork in the trail, stay left up a steep hill. Soon reach Post 6 and turn right to Post 8.

3.3 Stay left at another fork.

3.8 Turn right and follow the arrow pointing toward Post 8.

4.2 A doubletrack comes in from the left; continue straight.

4.7 Reach a T intersection with a vandalized post. Turn left and follow the blue markers on the trees.

5.2 Turn left at a T intersection with another vandalized marker.

5.5 Turn left at another T intersection.

6.0 Reach a T intersection with a map and turn right. Soon turn right onto a brushier doubletrack, marked with blue pathway signs and a large arrow. Almost immediately turn left up a steep, short hill.

6.4 Reach a signed post and continue straight.

6.8 Cruise through a sandy intersection at the bottom of a fast downhill.

7.1 Arrive at Post 8 and turn right to Post 9.

8.2 Reach Post 9 at a Y intersection and stay right to Post 1.

8.7 Cross over an unmarked sandy doubletrack and continue into the pines. Soon turn right onto a marked, wide doubletrack.

8.9 End of ride.

Seney Wildlife Refuge

Location:	1.5 miles southwest of Germfask.
Distance:	22.4-mile loop.
Time:	2–4 hours. Allow time for bird-watching.
Tread:	22.4 miles of dirt road.
Aerobic level:	Easy.
Technical difficulty:	1.
Hill factor:	Flat.
Highlights:	Birds, birds, and more birds!
Land status:	Seney National Wildlife Refuge.
Maps:	USGS Seney and Germfask; maps available at Refuge Visitor Center (see Appendix B).
Access:	From Germfask, drive 1 mile south on Michigan 77. Turn west onto Robinson Road toward the Northern Hardwoods Cross Country Ski Area, and continue 0.5 mile to the parking area.

Notes on the trail: This is a ride where the scenery surpasses the thrill of the trail. Numerous protected birds call this 95,000-acre refuge home. It is common to cruise by one of the twenty-six pools and see trumpeter swans, loons, sandhill cranes, and eagles relaxing in their protected environment. About 35 miles of clearly signed dirt roads, closed to motor vehicles, are open to bicycles. All the potential routes pass bird-inhabited pools and through red pine forests and clearings. It is the perfect area for cyclists of all ages to enjoy a relaxing ramble and picnic. Don't forget the binoculars. If you leave them at home, the visitor center—open May 15 through October 15 from 9:00 A.M. to 5:00 P.M. daily—loans binoculars free of charge.

The Ride

0.0 Cycle around the gate and continue on the flat, wide dirt road.

0.3 Pass the Northern Hardwoods Cross Country Ski Area and steer clear—no bikes allowed. The road climbs gently into the woods.

1.9 After a pleasant downhill, turn left toward T–2 Pool and Chicago Farm. Follow Pine Creek for the next few miles as the road rolls in and out of trees.

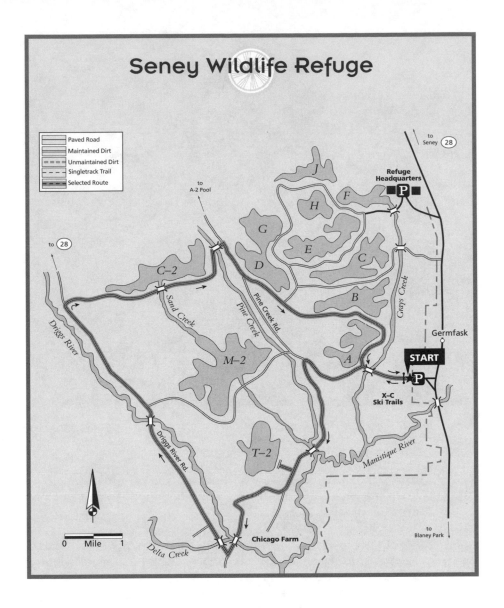

Seney Wildlife Refuge

Paved Road
Maintained Dirt
Unmaintained Dirt
Singletrack Trail
Selected Route

to
Seney (28)

Refuge
Headquarters

to
A-2 Pool

to (28)

J

F

H

G

E

C

D

B

Grays Creek

Germfask

Pine Creek Rd.

Sand Creek

Pine Creek

C–2

M–2

A

START

P

X–C
Ski Trails

Driggs River

T–2

Manistique River

Driggs River Rd.

0   Mile   1

Delta Creek

Chicago Farm

to
Blaney Park

4.3   Turn right toward the T–2 Pool.

4.55 At the pool look for loons, trumpeter swans, and sandhill cranes. Retrace your tracks back to the intersection and turn right onto the main road.

5.2   Stay right when you reach an intersection with the Chicago Farm side loop, a dead end.

6.4   Reach another intersection with the T–2 Pool. Continue straight.

7.0   Cross over the Driggs River Bridge.

7.2   Reach an intersection with Driggs River Road. Turn right and parallel the river.

Easy-to-follow signs, wide roads, and many interesting bird species make the Seney Wildlife Refuge a perfect family destination.

7.5   Pass by the Delta Creek Pool access road and continue straight.

10.5   Reach intersection with M–2 Pool and continue straight. A right turn cuts the ride short.

13.2   Turn right at an intersection with C–2 Pool.

14.5   C–2 Pool is to the left. Trumpeter swans frequent this pool, and eagles nest to the south. On the right, M–2 Pool stretches watery fingers to the road.

16.6   Turn right at Pine Creek Road intersection and follow the creek.

16.9   Reach an intersection with a dirt road and stay left. A right turn takes you to a dead end.

17.3   Turn left at another dirt road intersection toward the Marshland Wildlife Drive.

18.5   Reach an intersection with D Pool, popular with loons. Turn right, heading toward A and B Pools, and follow the raised road as it rolls between the bodies of water.

21.5   Turn left at a T intersection with a dirt road and retrace your tracks back to the parking area.

22.4   End of ride.

Rapid River National Trail

Location:	6 miles north of Rapid River.
Distance:	8.6-mile loop.
Time:	1.5–2 hours.
Tread:	8 miles of singletrack and wide ski trail, 0.6 mile of doubletrack.
Aerobic level:	Moderate.
Technical difficulty:	2+; sand, overgrown trails, and hoof-pocked steep hills.
Hill factor:	Rolling to hilly.
Highlights:	Thrilling descents and a ridge ride surrounded by a sea of trees.
Land status:	Hiawatha National Forest, Rapid River Ranger District.
Maps:	USGS Rapid River; maps available at forest offices (see Appendix B).
Access:	From the intersection of U.S. 2 and U.S. 41 in Rapid River, drive north on U.S. 41 for 5.5 miles, then follow SKI AREA signs west onto an unsigned dirt road. The parking area is located about 0.25 mile down the road.

Notes on the trail: Immense pines guard this 20-mile trail system, designed for cross-country skiing. Taking cyclists from flat wide trails to thrilling descents, the route described here follows narrow, classic skiing trails, occasionally merging with wide skating lanes. The trail dips into a few marshy areas that require bike walking, but for the most part riders stay high and dry along a ridge with sweeping views of the surrounding forest. Although fairly well marked, it is still a rugged experience, with brushy terrain and hills chewed up by horse's hooves. The beginning and end of the ride, however, are relaxing cruisers.

The Ride

0.0 Head toward the trailhead in the northwest corner of the parking lot. Almost immediately turn right and follow the sign to Loop A and Tot Loop onto a brushy singletrack heading into the woods.

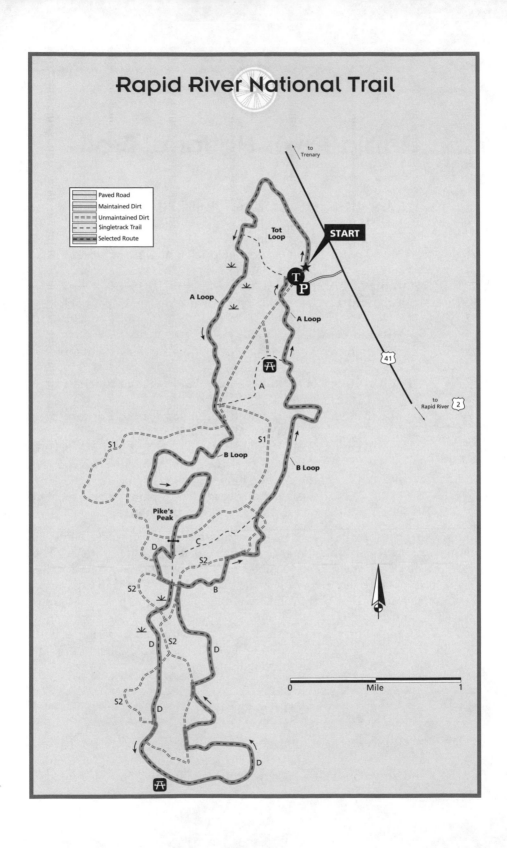

Rapid River National Trail

Rapid River's tough, sandy hills eventually push everyone off their bikes (as Keith discovered).

0.3   Turn left and follow the well-worn path.

0.5   Turn left again, away from the gas line and into the woods.

0.7   Reach an intersection with a doubletrack and continue straight on brushy Loop A. Cycle through Pine Haven, past red pines and through a cedar swamp.

1.5   Turn right onto a wide trail, S1/B Loop.

1.65 Veer to the left onto the narrower B Loop as S1 goes to the right. Cruise along gently rolling Pine Ridge.

3.2   Reach Pike's Peak. Cruise down a sandy hill and cross a wide trail. Cycle back uphill and around a gate.

3.35 Reach an intersection with Loops B, C, and D. Turn right onto Loop D.

3.5   Turn left at the top of a hill and head downhill on S2/Loop D. Get ready for a series of steep descents and ascents, all appropriately named.

3.6   Turn left at a T intersection with another trail, and continue on Loop D. Ride along a ridge.

3.7 Turn right down steep Purgatory. Shortly hit a marshy area and *walk* your bike.

4.1 Rejoin S2 and turn right. Cycle up a short hill, turn left, and follow Loop D.

4.3 Trail merges with S2. Cycle up and down a sandy hill.

4.5 Continue straight on Loop D along a picturesque ridge when S2 makes a hard left.

4.8 Cycle past a map and bench.

5.2 Cross an old doubletrack.

5.5 Reach a T intersection with S2 and turn right. Immediately head up a steep, sandy hill. Get ready to walk. Turn right at the top of the hill and continue climbing.

5.8 Merge with S2. Turn right and head up another sandy hill. Prepare to walk. S2 splits to the left at the top of the hill. Stay right with Loop D and continue uphill.

6.0 Cross a doubletrack and continue straight on Loop D. Walk your bike through a marshy area.

6.4 Arrive back at S2. Turn right and up the hill. Turn right onto Loop B at the top of the hill.

6.8 The trail merges with S2. Turn right.

7.0 The trail splits. Stay with Loop B.

7.2 Reach intersection with Loop C and continue straight on Loop B.

7.5 Continue straight at an unmarked intersection with doubletrack.

8.3 At a four-way intersection, marked on the left with a bench and trail markers, turn right onto unmarked singletrack Loop A. This is easy to miss!

8.6 Arrive back at the parking area.

Bruno's Run

Location:	13 miles southeast of Munising.
Distance:	10.1-mile loop.
Time:	1.5–2 hours.
Tread:	10.1 miles of singletrack.
Aerobic level:	Moderate.
Technical difficulty:	2 + –3.
Hill factor:	Rolling to hilly.
Highlights:	A lake at every turn and challenging switchbacks grace this Upper Peninsula roller coaster.
Land status:	Hiawatha National Forest, Munising Ranger District.
Maps:	USGS Corner Lake; maps available at trailhead.
Access:	From the intersection of Michigan 94 and Michigan 28 just south of Munising, drive 1.5 miles east on M–28. Turn south onto Alger County Road H–13, and drive 11 miles to the Moccasin Roadside Rest Area. Park here.

Notes on the trail: Reminding you of why Michigan is called "Water Wonderland," Bruno's Run offers endless inland lake views. Bouncing over exposed roots, the trail dumps you out at Pete's Lake Campground. During lazy summer afternoons, kayakers and small sailboats drift on Pete's Lake, and the delighted screams of playing children follow cyclists back into the forest. The trail continues on a roller-coaster ride through dense trees and crosses over forest roads, the Indian River, and the McKeever Cross County Trail System. Roots offer challenges throughout the ride, but the most difficult sections come at the end with a series of switchback climbs and two challenging downhills. The trail, marked with small bear signs and blue diamonds, is also popular with hikers.

The Ride

0.0 Pick up the trail on the other side of County Road H–13 and cycle toward Pete's Lake.

0.25 Cross paved Forest Road 2173.

Bruno's Run

START

to Munising

P

Moccasin Lake

Town Lake

Fish Lake

Irwin Lake

Indian River

Pete's Lake

Grassy Lake

Kimble Lake

H–13

2163

2163A

McKeever Lake

2173

Wedge Lake

2258

Dipper Lake

0 Mile 1

to Nahma Junction

Paved Road
Maintained Dirt
Unmaintained Dirt
Singletrack Trail
Selected Route

1.0 Cruise by the boat launch at Pete's Lake. Get prepared for a rooty ride over the next mile.

1.1 Reach Pete's Lake picnic grounds. Follow the paved path past the rest rooms and next to the lake. The trail picks up to the right and follows the lakeshore.

1.6 Watch for easy-to-miss blue diamonds, and follow the trail as it turns left away from the lake. If you end up in a campsite, you've gone too far.

2.0 Cross FR 2173 again. Grassy Lake is on the left.

2.3 Dump out onto a paved turnout. The trail continues almost immediately on the left.

3.1 Cross FR 2173 again. McKeever Lake is on the right.

4.7 Reach an intersection with McKeever Hills Ski Trail and continue straight.

4.9 The trail splits; cycle either way.

5.0 Stay left and climb a steep hill.

6.4 Cross over FR 2258.

Lakes dot Bruno's Run.

6.7 After a short, sandy hill, reach paved County Road H–13. Lift your bike over the guardrail, turn left, and cross a bridge over the Indian River. The trail picks up on the right at the end of the guardrail.

8.2 Cycle over a wooden bridge crossing the Indian River. To the left is Fish Lake. Soon cross a dirt road and tackle the first steep switchback. This section includes the most difficult ascents and descents.

8.8 Reach a T intersection with another trail and turn left onto the wider trail.

8.9 Look for a blue arrow pointing to the right, and follow it back onto tight singletrack.

10.1 Arrive back at Moccasin Lake, end of ride.

Pine Marten Run

Location:	17 miles south of Munising.
Distance:	17.6-mile loop.
Time:	2–3 hours.
Tread:	2.5 miles of doubletrack, 15.1 miles of single-track and wide ski trail.
Aerobic level:	Moderate.
Technical difficulty:	3; hoof-pocked trails are the biggest challenge.
Hill factor:	Rolling to hilly.
Highlights:	Mostly singletrack cruiser that rolls past secluded lakes and Adirondack shelters.
Land status:	Hiawatha National Forest, Manistique Ranger District.
Maps:	USGS Corner Lake; maps available at the trailhead.
Access:	From the intersection of Michigan 28 and H–13/Forest Highway 13 in Munising, drive 17 miles south on H–13. Turn east onto Forest Road 2258 and continue southeast for 2.5 miles. Cross a bridge over the Indian River and look for the trailhead on the east side of the road. The parking area and pit toilet are on the west side of the road.

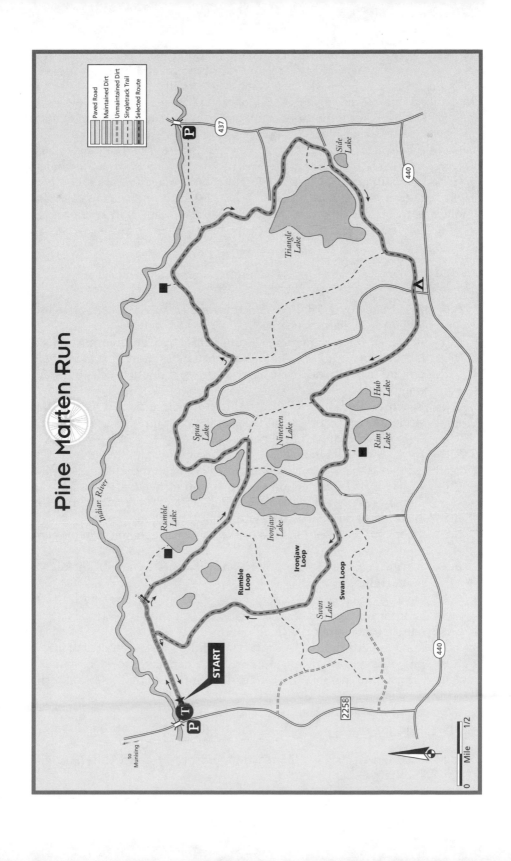

Notes on the trail: Adirondack shelters dot this secluded Hiawatha National Forest trail, which twists and rolls past several inland lakes. The 26-mile, mostly singletrack trail system is actually five interconnecting loops (Rumble, Swan, Ironjaw, Spud, and Triangle Lakes). The route described here takes in portions of all these loops, but those looking for a shorter ride will find plenty of options. The first half of the route is the most difficult; the second half allows cyclists to sit back and cruise through the forest. The most picturesque section of the trail meanders next to the southern end of Triangle Lake, where anglers are a common sight. The trail is well marked with maps posted at intersections and diamonds on trees. The only drawback of this outstanding trail system is the occasionally rough, hoof-pocked sections of trail.

The Ride

0.0 Cycle back over FR 2258 and continue on the doubletrack, paralleling the Indian River.

1.0 Reach an intersection with a singletrack trail on the right. This is the return route. Continue straight; in a short distance, cycle around a barricade. Trail narrows from a doubletrack to a wide trail.

1.5 Reach an intersection; turn right and cycle up a hill. Continuing straight leads to an Adirondack shelter on Rumble Lake. Trail will soon narrow into a singletrack.

2.6 At a marked intersection, turn left onto a tight singletrack. The next section twists through trees and over numerous roots.

3.0 Cruise by an intersection with a trail that heads down to a lake. Shortly reach another mapped intersection and continue straight.

3.8 Turn left at an intersection with Spud Lake Loop.

5.6 Reach a T intersection and turn left toward a shelter. Mud is common on the next section.

6.5 A trail peels off to the left toward the shelter. Stay right on the main trail.

7.0 Turn right at a trail intersection. Continuing straight leads to another trailhead and Forest Road 437. Upcoming section includes one of route's more difficult climbs.

7.7 Make a hard right up a short, steep hill at a road intersection.

7.8 As you approach Triangle Lake and a campsite, look to your left for a white diamond on a tree. Turn left here and follow the singletrack along the shoreline.

9.2 Cross a road and continue on the singletrack.

10.9 Trail crosses through a campground and picks up on the other side.

12.3 Turn left at a signed intersection and head toward Hub Lake and another shelter.

Keith cruises through heavy foliage on the Pine Marten Run.

13.0	Cruise past the turnoff to the Rim Lake shelter.
13.4	Cycle over a road that leads to Nineteen Lake.
14.1	Reach a T intersection and turn right onto Ironjaw Loop.
14.9	Reach a trail intersection and continue straight on Rumble Loop.
16.6	Turn left at a T intersection with the ride's first doubletrack, and retrace your tracks back to the parking area.
17.6	End of ride.

Grand Island Loop

Location:	0.5 mile north of Munising in Lake Superior.
Distance:	21.7-mile loop.
Time:	3–5 hours. Allow time for sight-seeing and sunbathing.
Tread:	17.15 miles of singletrack, 0.2 mile of doubletrack, 4.35 miles of dirt road.
Aerobic level:	Moderate.
Technical difficulty:	2–2 + .
Hill factor:	Rolling, with a few longer climbs.
Highlights:	Cliff-hugging singletrack on primitive island.
Land status:	Grand Island National Recreation Area, Hiawatha National Forest.
Maps:	USGS Munising and Wood Island; maps available at ferry landing and National Forest Visitor Center (see Appendix B).
Access:	From the blinking light in downtown Munising, drive 2.5 miles west on Michigan 28. Turn north into the Grand Island ferry landing parking lot. Park here and board the ferry.

Notes on the trail: This is simply the most spectacular ride in Michigan. A pontoon ferryboat whisks visitors 0.5 mile across Lake Superior to rugged Grand Island. The route follows the perimeter of the island and offers views of sandstone cliffs, sea caves, and 1,000-foot freighters. Alert riders will catch glimpses of nearby Pictured Rocks National Lakeshore as the trail turns south after the 12-mile point. At times the well-marked trail passes sugar-sand beaches that look more like Hawaii than rocky Lake Superior shoreline. Purchased by Hiawatha National Forest in 1990 from

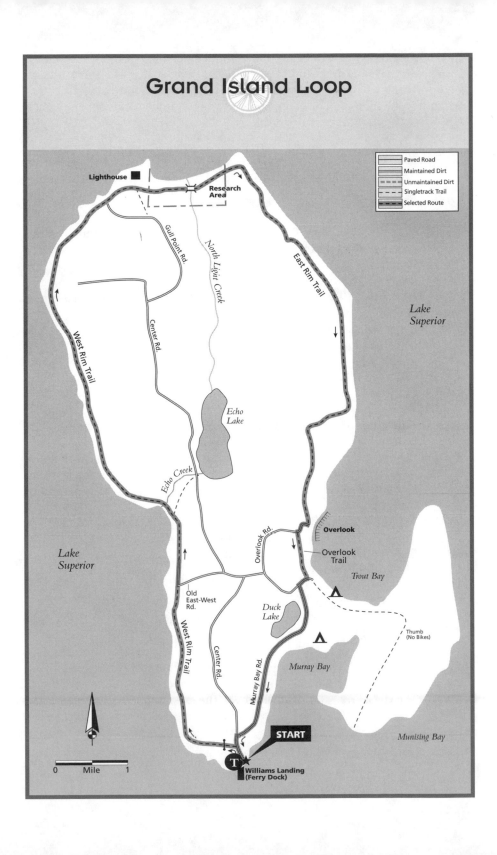

the Cleveland Cliffs Iron Company, the island also provides primitive campsites, particularly popular with sea kayakers. The $17 ferry charge, including entrance fee to Grand Island, might make you balk—but it's a ride not to be missed. The ferry schedule is limited, so contact the visitor center for the most recent timetable.

The Ride

0.0 From William's Landing, cycle straight on the dirt road (the only road).

0.15 Turn left onto West Rim Trail. Cycle around the gate and continue on wide singletrack. Soon the trail parallels Lake Superior.

3.1 Reach an intersection with Old East-West Road and continue straight. The trail widens into a dirt road.

4.0 Next to a gate, the trail turns right and back onto wide singletrack.

4.3 Follow the lakeshore for the next 3 miles, passing Mather Beach Steps and Echo Lake Creek, with continuous views of islands and colorful sandstone cliffs.

7.0 Reach a high point. Take your time and enjoy the views over the next few miles.

10.4 Continue straight at the intersection with doubletrack Gull Point Road.

10.6 Continue straight at an intersection with a private road. The CLOSED sign refers to motorized vehicles.

11.0 Reach North Light Creek Bridge. Cross with care. A short distance past the bridge is a sandy beach, perfect for picnics. Look back for a view of the North Point Lighthouse at one of the upcoming turnouts.

11.3 Arrive at a brushy trail intersection near Northeast Point. Continue straight and follow the lakeshore.

16.5 Reach a trail intersection and turn left.

17.6 The trail becomes a dirt road.

18.0 Turn left onto the Overlook Trail.

18.8 Turn right onto a dirt road.

19.0 Stay left at the fork onto Murray Bay Road. Cycle past Duck Lake on the right.

19.7 Pedal past Murray Bay campground and day-use area on the left. A historical cemetery soon appears on the right.

21.4 Turn left onto Center Road.

21.7 Arrive back at the ferry landing.

55

Days River Pathway

Location:	5 miles northwest of Gladstone.
Distance:	9-mile loop.
Time:	1–2 hours.
Tread:	9 miles of singletrack.
Aerobic level:	Moderate.
Technical difficulty:	2; watch for roots and sand.
Hill factor:	Rolling.
Highlights:	Cruise next to Days River for views of tree-dotted hills.
Land status:	Escanaba River State Forest, Escanaba Unit.
Maps:	USGS Gladstone. Maps available at trailhead.
Access:	From the intersection of Michigan 35 and U.S. 2/U.S. 41 in Gladstone, drive north on U.S. 2/U.S. 41 for 3 miles. Turn west onto Days River Road and continue west for 2 miles to the parking area on the north side of the road.

Notes on the trail: Rolling next to the Days River, this popular trail follows a ridgeline with views of tree-covered hills. There are just enough roots and sandy sections to keep riders alert, but the trail is really a cruiser. Mats cover the sandiest sections and the buffed, well-marked singletrack makes confusing intersections easy to decipher. Sections of the trail touch private land, and cyclists should always stay on the main path. It is rare to have the trail to yourself; expect to see other people, from the high school cross-country team to hikers with dogs. However, this is the Upper Peninsula, and even popular trails seem deserted compared with other parts of Michigan.

The Ride

0.0 Cycle to the north end of the parking area. Follow the worn trail and cycle over the Day's River on a wooden bridge.

0.2 Reach Post 1 and turn right toward Post 2. The trail rolls along the river and next to a golf course.

1.05 Reach Post 2 and turn right toward Post 3. Follow the river and pass through a clearcut.

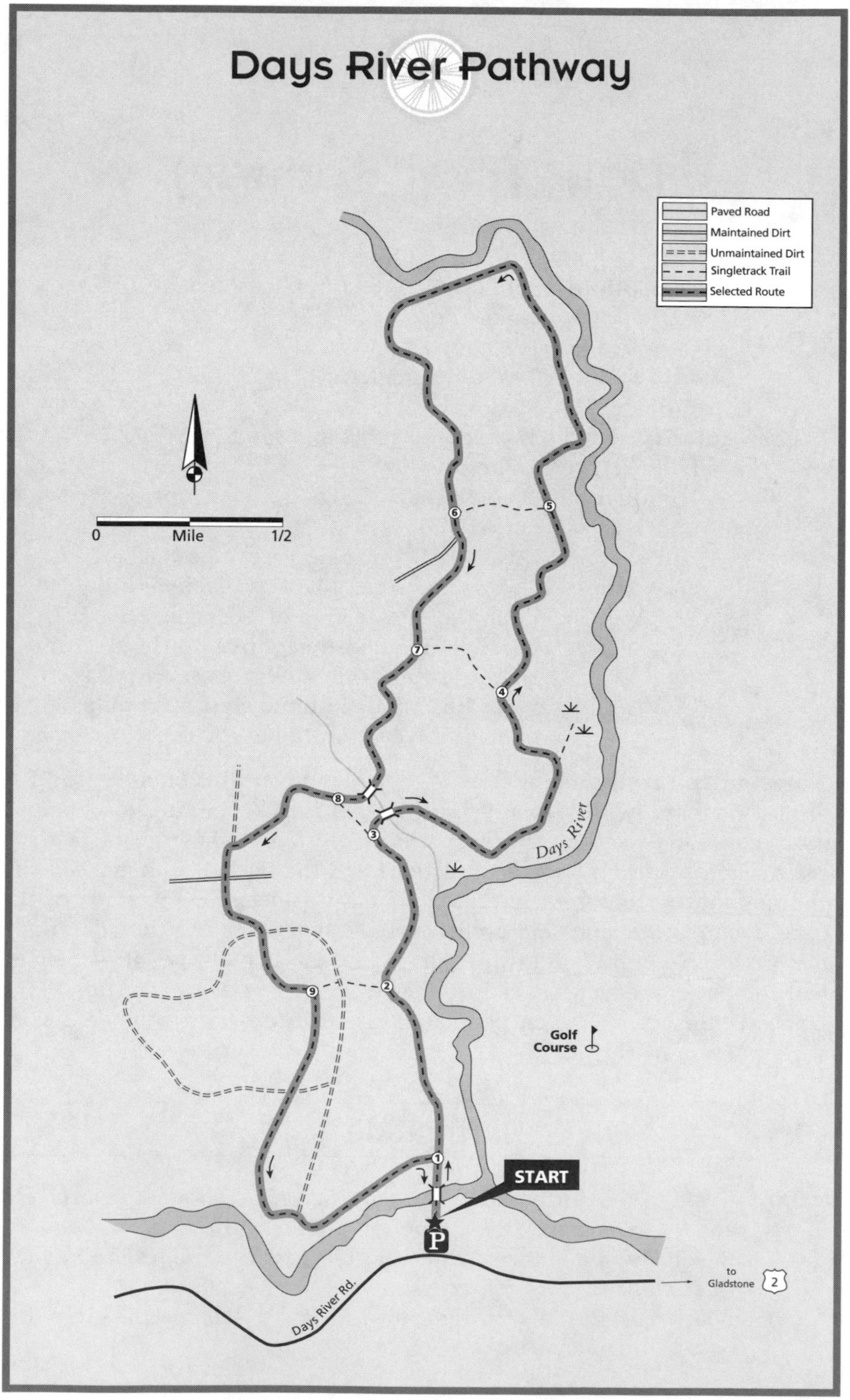

Days River Pathway

Legend
- Paved Road
- Maintained Dirt
- Unmaintained Dirt
- Singletrack Trail
- Selected Route

0 Mile 1/2

START

P

Days River

Golf Course

to Gladstone — 2

Days River Rd.

1.8	Arrive at Post 3 and turn right toward Post 4. Soon cross the river on a wooden bridge and continue cycling next to the river.
2.8	After a fast downhill, veer left with the worn path and up a hill. Cycling straight leads to a swampy area.
3.4	Turn right toward Post 5 at Post 4.
3.8	Reach Post 5 and continue straight. A left turn shortens the ride and eliminates the prettiest scenery.
5.8	Arrive at Post 6 and continue straight to Post 7. Shortly reach a Y intersection with a dirt road and veer left onto the singletrack.
6.3	Reach Post 7 after a fun downhill. Turn right, toward Post 8.
7.1	Arrive at Post 8 just after crossing a bridge. Turn right and follow the edge of a clearcut.
7.5	Doubletrack comes in from the right and continue straight. The trail widens after crossing a dirt road.
7.8	Cross a doubletrack and cycle uphill.
8.2	Reach Post 9 and turn right toward Post 1. The trail rolls steadily downhill and follows the river.
8.8	Turn right at Post 1 and cross over the river on the wooden bridge.
9.0	Arrive back at parking area.

Western Upper Peninsula:
Rocky Forests and Rugged North Woods

Once mountains taller than the Rockies existed in the western Upper Peninsula (UP). Today, rocky cliffs, steep hills, and dense forest are all that is left of this ancient mountain range. Boasting the highest point in Michigan, 1,979-foot Mt. Arvon, the western UP's rugged terrain is also home to Michigan's most challenging trails.

From the most northern point of the UP in the Keweenaw Peninsula to the most southern in Menominee and stretching a little past the UP's largest city, Marquette, the western UP offers mountain bikers a variety of trails and sights. The almost million-acre Ottawa National Forest has opened its doors to mountain bikers, allowing mountain biking on all its trails except the North Country Trail and designated wilderness areas. Near the forest headquarters in Ironwood, the Tuesday Night Fat Tire Club (see Appendix C), a grassroots mountain bike club, is developing challenging singletrack at the Wolverine Ski Trail.

Steeper climbing can be found at the Porcupine Mountains near Ontonagon and Mount Lookout in the Keweenaw Peninsula, which offers unparalleled views of Lake Superior. On a clear day Mount Lookout provides a glimpse of Isle Royale National Park, the remote 44-mile-long island 50 miles from the mainland. The Keweenaw Peninsula is also home to the Copper Harbor Mountain Bike Trail System, another grassroots effort headquartered at the Keweenaw Adventure Company (see Appendix A), and the annual Copper Harbor Fat Tire Festival in September. Riddled with doubletracks and logging roads, the Keweenaw is a dynamic area with new singletrack in development as old routes disappear due to logging operations.

The trails around Marquette—home to Northern Michigan University and the only U.S. Olympic training site connected to a university—become a tangled web of singletracks in summer. Close to town, Marquette's singletrack has gained a reputation for steep climbing and rocky descents. Unfortunately, many of the best singletrack trails in the area are unmarked and only known to locals, so visitors are advised to hook up with riders on a bike store–sponsored weekly ride (see Appendix A). The adventurous will want to sign up for Marquette Mountain Ski Area's annual Mountain Chase Mountain Bike Race or the 40-mile Ore to Shore Mountain Bike Race (see Appendix C).

It will make your head spin thinking of all the recreational opportunities possible in the western UP, so sit back, grab a hot pasty—a tasty UP specialty—and select any of the following rides. You can't go wrong.

Fumee Lake Loop

Location:	5 miles northeast of Iron Mountain.
Distance:	9-mile loop.
Time:	1–2 hours.
Tread:	9 miles of doubletrack.
Aerobic level:	Moderately strenuous. Two long climbs push the endurance meter.
Technical difficulty:	2.
Hill factor:	Flat to highlands.
Highlights:	Thrilling mile-long descents and equally long climbs.
Land status:	Fumee Lake Natural Area
Map:	USGS Norway.
Access:	From the intersection of U.S. 141 and U.S. 2 in Iron Mountain, drive 4 miles east on U.S. 2. Turn north onto Upper Pine Creek Road and go 1 mile to the entrance on the west. Continue driving back to the large parking area.

Notes on the trail: This area is a study in contrasts. Sustained 1-mile ascents and descents combine with flat, mellow doubletrack that circumnavigates two pristine inland lakes. This popular recreation area, however, is not without controversy. Some locals want the Fumee Lakes, once the water sources for nearby Norway, completely closed to people; others desire more recreation-oriented development. During the summer of 2000, a twisting 2-mile singletrack was finished, giving riders on the South Ridge Trail an alternate route. More singletrack near the bottom of the Fumee Mountain Trail is also in development. The well-marked trail has few technical difficulties, but watch for rocks and rutted areas when flying down the hills.

The Ride

0.0 Cycle back to the dirt road. Continue pedaling northwest and slip around the gate.

0.25 Pass the power lines and an old structure. Turn right and follow the east shore of Little Fumee Lake. Ignore all unmarked singletracks on the right.

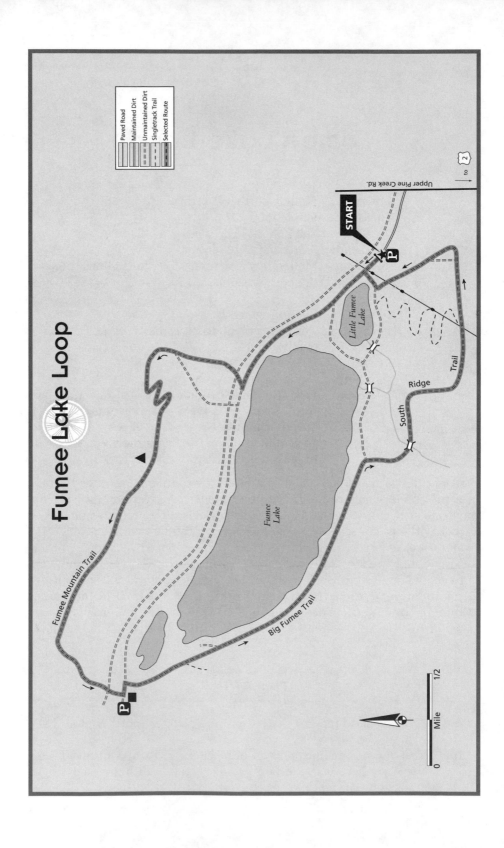

Cruising down the Fumee Mountain Trail.

0.6	Reach an unmarked doubletrack intersection and stay right. A left turn leads to a short loop around Little Fumee Lake.
1.4	Arrive at the intersection with the Fumee Mountain Trail. Turn right and cross a doubletrack. Let the climbing begin!
1.9	Ignore the trail coming in from the left, and continue straight.
2.05	Follow the arrow and turn left. The climbing gets serious for the next mile with a few peek-a-boo views.
3.0	Top out and get ready for a 1.5-mile thrilling descent.
4.5	Cross over a doubletrack. Soon reach a T intersection in front of an outhouse. The right takes you to the west parking area. Turn left and veer right onto the South Fumee Lake Trail, a flat tree-tunnel.
5.0	Ignore the singletrack, passing through boulders on the right.
5.2	The trail merges with another doubletrack.
6.5	Turn right onto South Ridge Trail. Prepare for a mile of climbing.
7.6	Just after crossing under the power lines, look for the singletrack on the left and head downhill. You can continue on the wide ski trail or take the singletrack down. The route described here follows the wider trail.
8.1	Stay left when the trail splits near the bottom of the hill. Continue the fast descent.
8.6	Just after passing under the power lines, reach an intersection with Little Fumee Lake and turn right.
8.7	Turn right at a Y intersection with an old cabin on the left, and follow the sign to the parking area.
9.0	Arrive back at parking area.

Lake Mary Plains Pathway

Location:	5 miles southeast of Crystal Falls.
Distance:	7.7-mile loop.
Time:	1–2 hours.
Tread:	7.45 miles of singletrack, 0.25 mile of dirt road.
Aerobic level:	Moderate.
Technical difficulty:	2+.
Hill factor:	Hilly.
Highlights:	Secluded trail with brushy singletrack and picturesque boardwalk.
Land status:	Copper Country State Forest, Crystal Falls Unit.
Map:	USGS Lake Mary.
Access:	From the intersection of U.S. 2/U.S. 141 and Michigan 69 in Crystal Falls, drive 4 miles east on M–69. Turn south onto Lake Mary Plains Road; continue for 1 mile to the trailhead parking on the north side of the entrance road, next to Lake Glidden.

Notes on the trail: Cyclists should expect to share this brushy, secluded trail with porcupines and white-tailed deer. Rolling through a forest fire recovery area, the trail frequently gives riders a choice between hilly and flat sections. The route described here always follows the hillier option, but both options merge later in the trail. The middle segment passes by secluded inland lakes and rolls along hills overlooking the Lake Mary plains. The end of the ride rambles over a long boardwalk next to Lake Glidden and an interpretive trail, marking maple, oak, and tamarack trees. Sand will slow you down a bit, but overall the path is consistently marked with blue paint, numbered posts, and trail maps at major intersections.

The Ride

0.0 Cycle south on the dirt road and through the campground.

0.25 Reach the trailhead and continue straight to Post 1 on a wide singletrack.

0.5 Stay left at Post 1 and head toward Post 2 on a narrower trail.

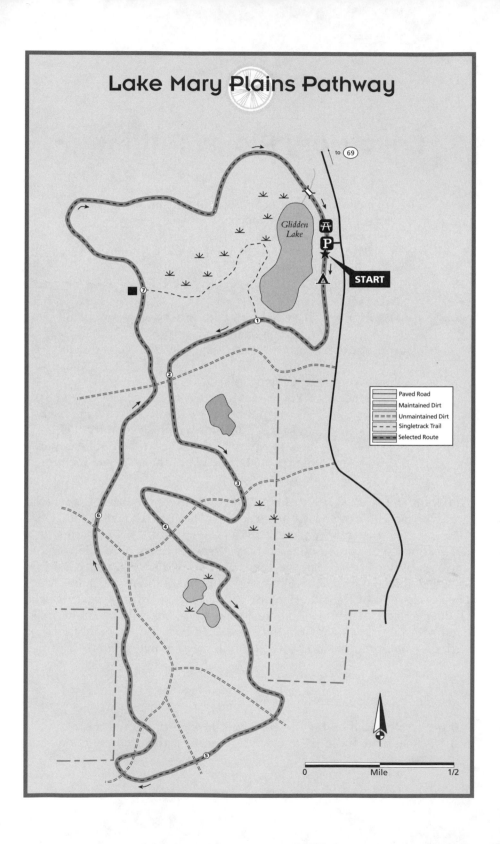

0.8	Stay left at a split in the trail, and follow the singletrack.
1.0	Reach Post 2 just before a dirt road crossing, and then continue to Post 3.
1.2	Reach another split in the trail. The option to the left is flatter; the right trail is hillier. Both meet up in a short distance.
1.6	Arrive at Post 3 and continue straight on the singletrack to Post 4.
2.3	Reach Post 4 after a short climb and continue straight to Post 5. A right turn shortens the loop.
2.6	Reach another intersection with a hilly or flat option. The hilly option is brushy, with views of two lakes.
3.1	Cross a grassy doubletrack after rolling by the lakes, and continue straight on the singletrack down an open hill.
3.5	Reach Post 5 just before crossing a doubletrack, and continue straight on the brushy singletrack. The trail gets progressively brushier from lack of use. Look for the blue paint on trees and you won't get lost.
3.8	Cross a doubletrack after a steep climb and continue on the singletrack.
4.3	Another hill or flat option. The hill option runs straight down a steep hill, climbs back up the hill, and rejoins the flat option.
4.9	Reach Post 6 after crossing another doubletrack and continue straight to Post 7. Trail tread improves from here on.
5.9	Reach Post 7 at an Appalachian-style cabin. Stay left and follow the RETURN sign. An interpretive trail begins on this flat and fast trail.
7.2	Cycle over a boardwalk and pass a Tamarack grove.
7.5	Pedal over a longer boardwalk with Glidden Lake on the right.
7.7	End of ride.

A long boardwalk next to Glidden Lake on the Lake Mary Plains Pathway.

58

Agonikak/Land O' Lakes Loop

Location:	Intersection of U.S. 2 and U.S. 45 in Watersmeet.
Distance:	21.6-mile loop.
Time:	3–5 hours.
Tread:	17.6 miles of doubletrack, 2.8 miles of paved road, 1.2 miles of gravel road.
Aerobic level:	Moderate.
Technical difficulty:	2; challenges include mud, rocks, and route finding.
Hill factor:	Flat to hilly.
Highlights:	Rolling, forest-shrouded doubletrack leads to Wisconsin.
Land status:	Ottawa National Forest, Watersmeet Ranger District.
Maps:	USGS Land O' Lakes and Watersmeet.
Access:	Trailhead is located near the Ottawa National Forest Visitor Center at the southeast corner of the intersection of U.S. 2 and U.S. 45 in Watersmeet. Park in the visitor center parking lot.

Notes on the trail: Watersmeet and Land O' Lakes, the two towns this ride touches, are famous for their recreation. In winter the forest hums with the sound of snowmobiles; in summer those trails become mountain bike routes. Marked sporadically with blue-and-white mountain bike signs, the 12-mile Agonikak Trail wanders through dense forest and past inland lakes. The rugged doubletrack is quintessential Upper Peninsula riding. The route crosses into the quaint village of Land O' Lakes, Wisconsin—a good lunch stop—and the return route follows the flat Land O' Lakes Rail-Trail.

The Ride

0.0   Pedal out of the parking lot the way you drove in. Turn right at the first intersection onto the service road and cycle uphill toward U.S. 45.

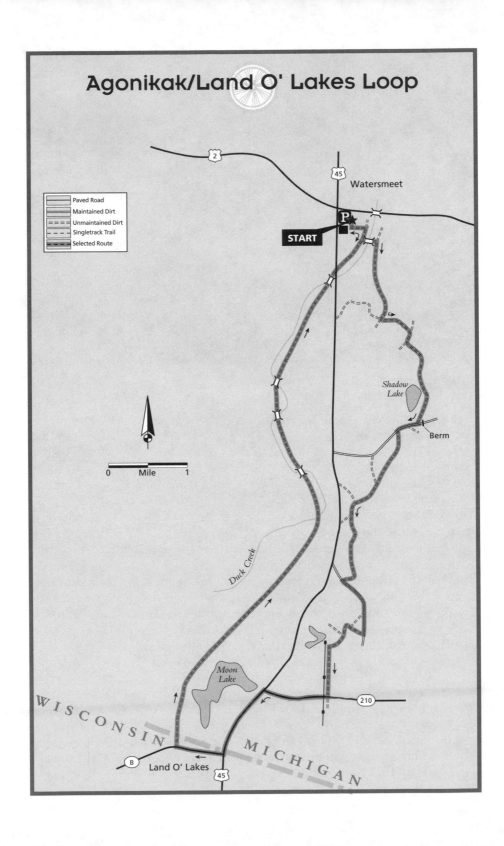

Keith relaxes on the flat Land O' Lakes Rail-Trail.

0.2   Turn left at an unmarked doubletrack that leads toward an antenna tower.

0.5   Turn right onto a rail-trail at the Ottawa National Forest Visitor Center sign.

0.7   Turn left at the blue-and-white mountain bike sign and cross a bridge over Duck Creek.

0.9   Turn right at a mountain bike sign and head into the woods.

1.5   Ignore the road on the left.

2.1   Turn left at a four-way intersection marked with a mountain bike sign.

2.6   Reach another intersection. Turn right and follow the mountain bike sign.

2.7   Watch out! Turn left at the first unmarked doubletrack. You have missed the turn if you reach Basso Road.

4.0   Shadow Lake is on the right.

4.8   Doubletrack ends at a road with a berm on the left. Turn right onto the dirt road.

5.2   Turn left at the narrow doubletrack trail marked by a mountain bike sign. Continue following the mountain bike signs as you roll and twist through the forest.

7.5   Turn left and follow the orange and black arrow.

8.1   Turn left and follow a mountain bike sign onto a wide dirt road. A right turn here leads to U.S. 45 in about 0.5 mile.

8.9	Turn right and follow the mountain bike sign onto a doubletrack.
9.6	Turn left at the unmarked intersection next to the power lines. Continue pedaling next to the power lines until you reach paved Gogebic County Road 210/ Indian Village Road.
10.3	Turn right onto Gogebic CR 210 and follow it to U.S. 45.
11.2	Watch for traffic and turn left onto U.S. 45. Ride on the wide shoulder.
12.0	Turn right at Vilas County Road B and enter Land O' Lakes Village. Welcome to Wisconsin.
12.7	Turn right at the Land O' Lakes Rail-Trail, marked by a large snowmobile sign. The trail is easy to follow as it meanders through the countryside and crosses Duck Creek numerous times on bridges.
20.2	Cross U.S. 45.
20.9	Retrace your tracks back to the parking lot.
21.1	Turn left at the VISITOR CENTER sign and pedal uphill.
21.4	Turn right onto the paved service road and head toward the parking lot.
21.6	Turn left into the parking lot.

Wolverine Singletrack

Location:	2 miles east of Ironwood.
Distance:	9.1-mile loop. Shorter loops are possible.
Time:	1–2 hours.
Tread:	3.7 miles of singletrack, 5.1 miles of wide, grassy trail.
Aerobic level:	Moderate.
Technical difficulty:	2–4; rocks, roots, steep descents, and logs to jump.
Hill factor:	Hilly to highlands.
Highlights:	Handcrafted singletrack built by local fat-tire enthusiasts and views of the greater Ironwood area from the top of Big Powderhorn Ski Area.
Land status:	Private. Landowners graciously permit mountain bikers to use trails; please respect property and stay on established trails.

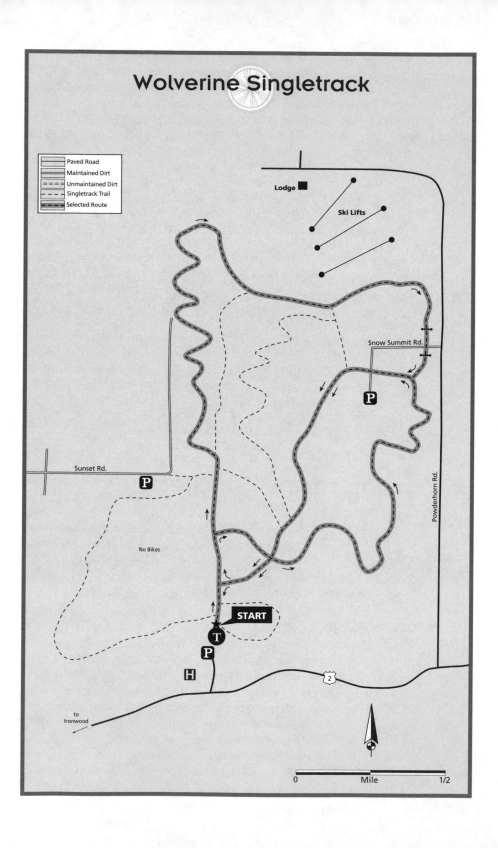

Maps: USGS Bessemer; maps available at Trek & Trail outdoor store (see Appendix A).

Access: Drive about 2 miles east of Ironwood on U.S. 2 and turn north at the entrance to Grandview Hospital. Continue to the hospital's rear parking lot. A large trail map will be on the right as you drive into the parking area.

Notes on the trail: Nestled a few miles outside the old mining community of Ironwood is a stretch of singletrack that will leave you dazzled by its difficulty. Twisting around young maple trees on trails so tight that hooking a handlebar is a real fear, the Rock and a Hard Place Singletrack has every obstacle imaginable. Developed during the summer of 1999, the trail is part of the Wolverine Nordic Trails and maintained by the Wolverine Ski Club and Tuesday Night Fat Tire Club. The Schnake Trail, the other singletrack trail in this route, is a roller coaster ride with challenges of its own, but the well-marked Wolverine Nordic Trails are not just about getting pounded by singletrack. Views of forest, brightly colored with splashes of red and orange during autumn, greet you as you climb up the ski slopes of the Big Powderhorn Ski Area. *Note:* Do not be tempted by the 3-mile Wolverine Loop; it is closed to mountain bikes. More singletrack is in development and can be explored with the gang from Trek & Trail outdoor store on Tuesday-night rides from June through September.

The Ride

0.0 Pedal past the trailhead map and continue on the rolling hills. Soon pass a trail on the right (this is the return route).

0.4 Just below the crest of a hill, look for the Schnake Singletrack Trail, descending steeply on the right. The singletrack is marked with orange and blue diamonds and blue-and-white mountain bikes.

0.6 Cross the ski trail and continue on the singletrack.

0.8 Cross a shallow creek followed by a steep, short climb.

2.3 Singletrack ends; turn left back onto the ski trail.

2.5 Cross Snow Summit Road and continue on the ski trail.

2.7 Reach the junction with Powderhorn Cutoff and stay left.

3.3 Continue straight at an intersection with a trail on the right.

3.4 Schnake Singletrack Trail crosses the ski trail and continues climbing.

3.6 Back at the main ski trail, turn right to continue the ride and retrace your tracks past Schnake Singletrack. Turn left for a shorter ride (3.9 miles) and return to the trailhead.

4.1 Continue straight at the trail intersection.

4.3 Look to the left for a sign with a black arrow on a yellow diamond. This signage is used throughout the next portion of singletrack.

Ride up a steep short hill to begin the Rock and a Hard Place Singletrack. If you would rather test your skills another day, continue straight on the well-marked ski trail and rejoin the directions at Mile 6.1.

4.5   Stay left at an intersection with a faint trail, and follow the yellow arrow.

4.9   Reach a clearing and turn left down a hill.

5.0   The trail turns right into the woods.

5.2   Cross another clearing and head back into the woods.

5.7   Stay left onto a dirt road at an intersection with another trail. Turn right and find the trail at the end of a cul-de-sac; climb steeply.

5.9   Turn right up Shotgun Ski Run, part of Big Powderhorn Mountain Ski Area. Reach the top and look to the left for a view of Copper Peak Ski Flying Hill (Ride 60).

6.1   Singletrack trail rejoins cross-country skiing trail. Continue uphill with the chairlifts on the left.

6.3   Head back into the woods. Soon reach a trail intersection and follow the arrows to the left.

6.6   Stay left at an intersection with Powderhorn Cutoff and ride by a pond to the top of the chairlifts. To shorten the ride, turn right and pick up the trail description at Mile 7.9.

6.8   At the top of Alpen Ski Run, with chairlifts on the left, turn right; head down the ski run and follow the doubletrack.

7.0   Turn right, away from the downhill ski area, and cruise back into the woods. Cycle around a gate.

7.2   Cross Snow Summit Road and pedal around another gate.

7.5   Schnake Singletrack rejoins the ski trail on the left. Stay on the wide trail back to the main ski trail.

7.9   Stay left at an intersection with Powderhorn Cutoff on the right.

8.8   This intersection should look familiar. Stay left to return to the trailhead.

9.1   Arrive back at the parking area. Don't forget to make a donation—a donation box is located a short distance up the hill from the trail map.

Copper Peak Loop

Location:	10 miles north of Bessemer and Ironwood.
Distance:	5.7-mile loop.
Time:	1–2 hours.
Tread:	1.1 miles of singletrack, 3.8 miles of double-track, 0.8 mile of paved road.
Aerobic level:	Moderate to strenuous.
Technical difficulty:	3–3+; steep, slippery descents and ascents, rocks, unmarked trails, and mud.
Hill factor:	Highlands. Total elevation gain of about 600 feet over a short distance.
Highlights:	Cycle to the top of the world's largest ski-flying hill; enjoy 360-degree views, a singletrack wooded descent, and a short ramble along the Black River.
Map:	USGS Copper Peak.
Land status:	Private. Landowners graciously permit mountain bikers to use trails; please respect property and stay on established trails.
Access:	Driving west from Bessemer on U.S. 2, drive 1.1 miles from the traffic light and turn north onto Powderhorn Road. Continue for almost 3 miles, then turn west onto Gogebic County Road 513. Drive another 8 miles and bear right at the COPPER PEAK sign. Park in the main parking area near the chairlift and ski shop/chalet.

Notes on the trail: Built in 1970, the Copper Peak Ski Flying Hill hosted the first international ski jumping competition in the Western Hemisphere. As equipment and techniques improved, the ski jumpers began landing too far down the hill for safety, and the ski-flying hill was closed to competition. Today the lift whisks tourists up the mountain, where an elevator continues the journey to the top of the flying hill. The route described here climbs the ski-flying hill, descends on a twisting singletrack, and continues along the Black River. The trails are inconsistently marked with blue-and-white mountain bike signs and orange arrows; however, you can spend many aerobic hours climbing up and down the twisting trails without getting lost. If you are not in an energetic mood, you and

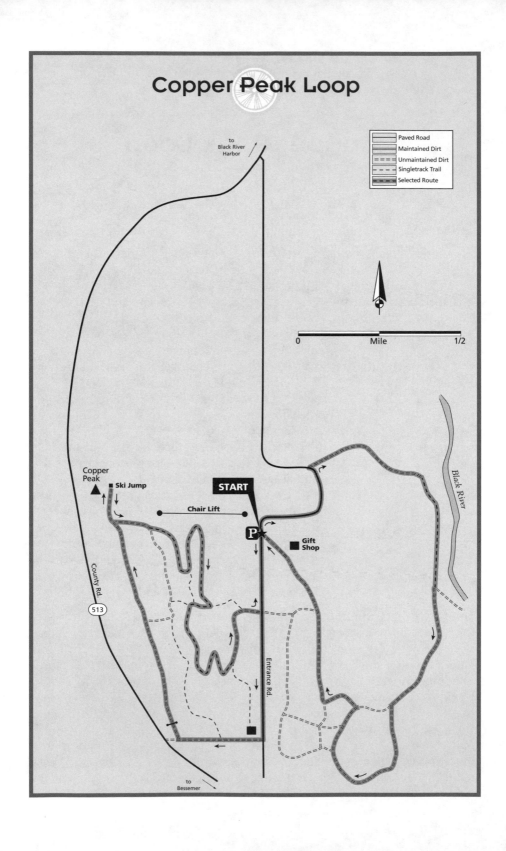

your mountain bike can take the chairlift to the top for a fast singletrack descent. Tickets for the chairlift and elevator can be purchased at the ski shop/chalet near the parking area.

The Ride

0.0 Ride back down the entrance road to the little brown booth on the right, marked with a blue-and-white mountain bike sign.

0.8 Turn right at the booth, pedal over a berm, and continue uphill. Ignore the two trails on the right.

1.1 Turn right at the mountain bike sign and cycle around a gate. Continuing straight takes you to County Road 513.

1.4 Pass a trail on the right and continue up the hill.

1.7 Pass another trail on the right, this is the return route. Continue straight.

1.9 Reach the top of Copper Peak after gaining 350 feet in elevation. From the lip of the jump, three ski resorts come into view and Lake Superior stretches out behind you. Pedal back down the hill.

2.1 Turn left at the first trail on the left.

2.3 Reach a fork and stay left. Climb a short distance, then begin a twisting, challenging descent. Trail to the right descends back to the brown booth.

Copper Peak's ski flying hill.

2.7 Turn right at a T intersection. Climb steeply and pass another trail on the right. The trail you have just turned off descends steeply and shortens the ride.

2.8 Turn left and begin the descent back to the road. Continuing straight leads back uphill. Soon pass a dead-end trail on the left and cycle down two switchbacks.

3.1 Pass a quarry on the left and pedal straight out to the road. The trail on the right leads back to the brown booth.

3.4 Cross the road and follow the trail to the left.

3.6 Stay left at a trail intersection and pass the chalet/gift shop. Cycle through the parking lot and around the ski jump landing area.

3.9 Turn right at a trail marked with a faded mountain bike sign on a pole. Descend toward the Black River and lose almost 200 feet in elevation.

4.1 Make a hard right at the mountain bike sign and cycle along the Black River on a delightful singletrack.

4.4 Continue straight. The trail on the left ends at the river.

4.8 Turn left at the unmarked intersection. Descend a short distance, then climb once again to the right and pedal into the woods. Bear right and pass two trails on the left. Continue back into the woods.

5.2 Turn left at the third trail, marked by a berm and a mountain bike sign. Shortly turn to the left and continue over a second berm. Watch for the pothole on the other side. Stay right and parallel the edge of the woods.

5.3 Turn right onto a cross-country ski trail and follow it back to the parking lot.

5.7 Cycle by the chalet and back to the parking area.

Gogebic Ridge Trail

Location:	4 miles northeast of Bergland on Old Michigan 64.
Distance:	18.5-mile loop.
Time:	3–6 hours.
Tread:	9 miles of singletrack, 5.3 miles of paved road, 4.2 miles of gravel road.
Aerobic level:	Strenuous.
Technical difficulty:	3–4; roots, rocks, logs, downed trees, and steep ascents and descents.
Hill factor:	Hilly to highlands. Several 100- to 200-foot climbs.
Highlights:	Primitive trail that rewards riders with breathtaking forest views.
Land status:	Ottawa National Forest, Bergland Ranger District.
Maps:	USGS Bergland, Bergland NE, Merriweather.
Access:	From the intersection of Michigan 28 and Michigan 64 in Bergland, turn north onto M–64. Drive 2 miles then, as M–64 curves to the left, turn east onto Old Michigan 64. This turn is easy to miss, and the small brown wooden sign is visible only after making the turn. Continue on the dirt road for 3 miles. Veer left after 1 mile and head north. Look for the GOGEBIC RIDGE TRAIL sign to the east. Park at the side of the road or at the turnout about 0.25 mile farther down the road.

Notes on the trail: If you are looking for a rugged Upper Peninsula adventure, the Gogebic Ridge Trail is for you. Built in 1977 by the Youth Conservation Corps, the trail follows a portion of the Lake Gogebic–Iron River Indian Trail used in the 1800s. Offering difficult descents and ascents, rocks, many downed trees, and route-finding challenges, the trail also has its rewards. Most of the route rambles through pristine, dense forest with views of Lake Gogebic, the largest lake in the Upper Peninsula, and the unspoiled Ottawa National Forest. The trail is so little used that it would be a surprise to see another person, but wildlife is abundant.

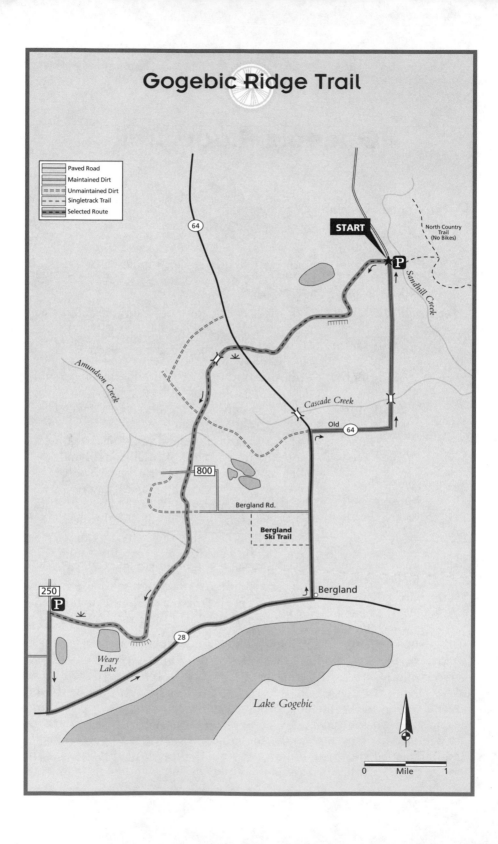

Gogebic Ridge Trail

Legend:
- Paved Road
- Maintained Dirt
- Unmaintained Dirt
- Singletrack Trail
- Selected Route

64

START

P

North Country Trail (No Bikes)

Sandhill Creek

Amundson Creek

Cascade Creek

Old 64

800

Bergland Rd.

Bergland Ski Trail

250

P

Bergland

Weary Lake

28

Lake Gogebic

0 Mile 1

Marked with white and blue diamonds, the loop allows riders to cut the ride short at 5.6 miles. The last portion of the ride is on state highways with wide shoulders and minimal traffic and Old M–64, where you cycle beneath a canopy of trees.

The Ride

0.0 Head west, steeply up the trail, and follow the white diamonds. The trail to the east ends in about 0.5 mile at the North Country Trail and is not open to mountain bikes.

0.4 After climbing about 100 feet, reach a clearing and follow the trail back into the woods.

1.1 Cross a creek.

1.3 Reach Cookout Mountain summit and begin a steep descent (walking might be necessary).

1.5 Dump your bike and follow the trail on the left to views of the Ottawa National Forest and Lake Gogebic. Retrace your tracks and continue downhill as the trail curves to the right.

1.8 Cross a creek after a long descent and continue on the flat trail through hardwood forest.

2.5 The trail joins a doubletrack and heads downhill. Soon the trail turns to the left, back into woods and away from the doubletrack.

2.8 Cross M–64. After descending a short hill, the trail follows a narrow boardwalk and crosses a marshy area for about 0.25 mile. Soon reach a technical rocky section.

3.5 This is the only point on the trail where logging has made the diamonds hard to find. Continue on a straight line with the last visible diamond directly behind you. Look back as you cycle, and locate the diamonds posted for trail users going in the opposite direction. The diamonds are once again easily visible within 0.1 mile.

4.0 Turn right and cross a dirt road. The trail heads slightly to the left; look for the diamond.

4.2 Cross Forest Road 800.

4.4 Walk your bike over a log bridge and continue steeply uphill.

5.2 Cross another creek.

5.6 Reach Bergland Road doubletrack, marked by a yellow metal land survey sign. Continue straight to follow the full loop. To shorten the ride turn left, cycle uphill, and follow Bergland Road for 1.5 miles. Watch for dogs! Turn left onto M–64 and follow the ride directions beginning at Mile 15.4.

6.0, 6.2, and **6.6** Make three more creek crossings.

7.4 Reach a clearing with many downed trees. Soon arrive at the Lake Gogebic overlook. Proceed with caution as the trail closely follows a cliff.

Erin looks out over the Ottawa National Forest from the Gogebic Ridge Trail.

7.6 Cross pipeline clearing.

7.8 Enjoy a second view of Lake Gogebic. The trail descends steeply down the fall line and parallels the cliff.

8.0 View Weary Lake on the left.

8.2 Cross a marshy area on two wooden bridges.

9.0 Reach the west trailhead and turn left onto Forest Road 250.

10.1 Turn left onto M–28.

13.4 Turn left onto M–64 at the blinking light in Bergland.

15.4 Turn right onto Old M–64.

18.5 The ride ends.

Porcupine Mountain Loop

Location:	15 miles west of Ontonagon.
Distance:	13.8-mile loop. Total of 25 miles of trails to explore.
Time:	2–4 hours.
Tread:	13.8 miles of wide ski trails.
Aerobic level:	Moderate to moderately strenuous.
Technical difficulty:	1+–2.
Hill factor:	Hilly to highlands. The total elevation gain for the loop is about 900 feet.
Highlights:	Cycle along a road built in the 1800s and climb to views of Lake Superior and the largest state park in Michigan.
Land status:	Porcupine Mountains Wilderness State Park.
Maps:	USGS White Pine and Government Peak; maps available at the visitor center (see Appendix B).
Access:	From Ontonogan drive 13 miles west on Michigan 64, then 4 miles west on Michigan 107 through Silver City. Turn south at the PORCUPINE MOUNTAINS SKI AREA sign. Park at the east end of the third level parking lot.

Notes on the trail: A trip to the Upper Peninsula is not complete without a visit to the Porcupine Mountains Wilderness, the largest state park in Michigan. Crouched along the shore of Lake Superior, the park offers waterfalls, Lake Superior views, and 90 miles of hiking trails. Mountain

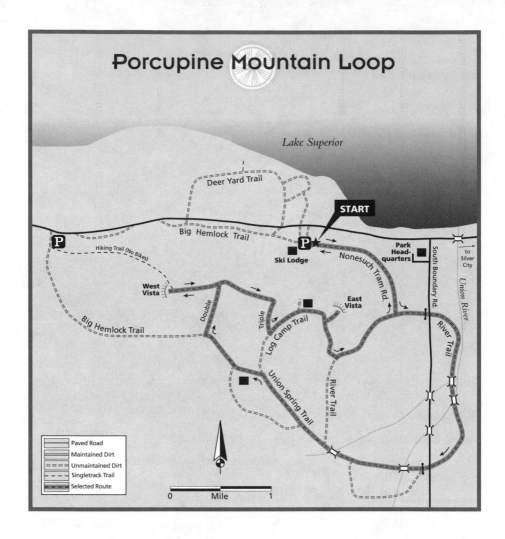

Porcupine Mountain Loop

Lake Superior

Deer Yard Trail

START

Big Hemlock Trail

P

Hiking Trail (No Bikes)

Ski Lodge

Nonesuch Tram Rd.

Park Head-quarters

South Boundary Rd.

to Silver City

Union River

West Vista

Double

Triple

Log Camp Trail

East Vista

Big Hemlock Trail

Union Spring Trail

River Trail

River Trail

Paved Road
Maintained Dirt
Unmaintained Dirt
Singletrack Trail
Selected Route

0   Mile   1

bikes are not allowed on the hiking trails—except for two short sections where the hiking and cross-country skiing trails merge. Instead, the 25 miles of cross-country skiing trails become mountain biking trails in the summer. This ride begins by cycling along a road built in the 1800s, then climbs to the top of the downhill ski area for breathtaking views of Lake Superior. Many of the trails are near creeks or rivers in low-lying areas, so mud and soft soil are problems. Branches, rocks, and brush are common; however, the trails are wide enough that cyclists can skirt around most obstacles. Like all Michigan state parks, there is a $4.00-per-vehicle entrance fee.

Huge trees punctuate the Porcupine Mountain trails.

The Ride

0.0 Pedal to the eastern end of the parking lot. Cycle onto a trail marked with a mountain bike sign.

0.8 Turn right onto the Nonesuch Tram Road, built in 1881.

1.3 The Nature Trail merges from the left.

1.4 Stay left at the trail intersection and onto the River Trail.

1.8 Pass through a gate and pedal across South Boundary Road. Follow the Union River and cross many boggy sections.

2.7 Come to a road. Turn left and cross over a bridge. Turn left after the bridge and cycle through a campground. Look for the cross-country skier sign on the right as the trail continues steeply uphill.

3.6 Cross South Boundary Road and continue straight.

3.7 Pass a trail map and cycle around a gate onto Union Spring Trail.

4.1 Stay right at the fork in the trail and follow the sign. Shortly after the intersection, pass the trail to the Union River Cabin on the right.

4.7 Continue straight at the intersection with River Trail.

5.0 Union Spring Trail is on the left and is not recommended because of perpetual mud.

5.7 Continue straight past Log Camp Trail.

5.9 Pass a warming shelter on the left. Soon pass a trail on the left.

6.3 Stay right on Double Trail and climb steeply. Big Hemlock veers to the left through low-lying, muddy terrain.

7.0 Reach the top and turn left toward West Vista.

7.6 Arrive at West Vista and enjoy the panoramic views of the park's interior and Lake Superior. Hiking trails branch off from the top; remember that mountain bikes are not allowed on these trails. Retrace your tracks back to the top of Double Trail.

8.2 Continue past the entrance to Double Trail and head downhill.

8.9 Turn right onto Triple Trail and coast downhill.

9.5 Slow down and make a hard left onto Log Camp Trail.

10.1 Cycle past the trail and warming hut on the left, and continue straight.

10.3 Turn left onto East Vista Trail.

10.5 Reach East Vista. Lake Superior stretches to the east. The White Pines Mine breaks through the trees to the south. Retrace your tracks to Log Camp Trail.

10.7 Turn left onto Log Camp Trail.

11.4 Turn left at the intersection with River Trail.

12.4 Turn left at the intersection with Nonesuch Tram Road/Trail and continue back to the parking lot.

13.8 End of ride.

Maasto Hiihto/ Churning Rapids Loop

Location: Hancock.

Distance: 14.2-mile loop.

Time: 2–3 hours.

Tread: 2 miles of singletrack, 1.3 miles of gravel road, 10.9 miles of doubletrack.

Aerobic level: Moderate. Steepest climbs come at the end of the ride.

Technical difficulty: 1 + –3; steep descents and ascents, mud, and loose rocks.

Hill factor: Hilly.

Highlights: Cycle through gorges with exciting descents and views of the Portage Canal; pedal by huge oak trees and shimmering aspens on a serpentine singletrack.

Land status: City of Hancock and private. Landowner graciously permits mountain bikers to use trails; please respect property and stay on established trails.

Maps: USGS Hancock; Massto Hiihto maps available at visitor center in Houghton (see Appendix A); Churning Rapids maps are posted at intersections.

Access: From downtown Hancock, take U.S. 41 north. Turn north onto Ethel Avenue. After a few blocks turn west onto Ingot Street. Turn north into the Houghton County Arena parking lot.

Notes on the trail: Hancock is proud of its Finnish roots—from the only Finnish-American college in the United States, Suomi College, to its world-class cross-country skiing area, Maasto Hiihto, meaning "cross-country" in Finnish. Not only are the trails expertly groomed in winter, but local fat-tire enthusiasts continue trail maintenance in the summer. Located on the hilly sides of Portage Canal, opposite Hancock's city sister of Houghton, the trails wind through a small gorge. About halfway through the Maasto

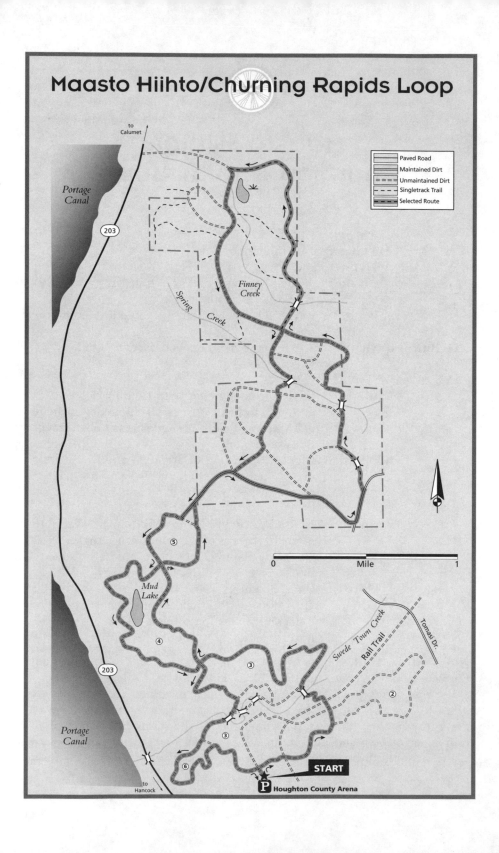

Hiihto Trails, the ride crosses onto Churning Rapids, a private nature preserve of about 900 acres and open to nonmotorized users. Churning Rapids begins on a clearcut that is beginning to grow back, and within a few miles you are twisting along a tight singletrack past oaks and aspens and through four challenging gorges. Cyclists need to remember that this beautiful piece of land is open to the public because of the generosity of the owners. Treat it with respect.

The Ride

0.0 Begin at the large trail map and turn right onto St. Urho's Loop.

0.2 Cross the Hancock/Calumet Rail-Trail

0.4 The trail forks; stay right with the green trail marker. Soon take a right at the T intersection at the power lines, and continue into the woods.

0.6 Turn left back out to the power lines and follow the TRAIL 1 sign. Head toward Railroad Ravine and ignore the other intersecting trails. Quincy Loop, on the right, adds another 2 miles to the route.

0.7 Cross the rail-trail again. Get ready for the Railroad Ravine, a sweeping downhill with many loose rocks and logs at the bottom.

0.9 Cross the Swedetown Creek on a wide bridge and turn right onto Trail 3. This section can sometimes be a mud bath. A left turn shortens the ride and follows the picturesque River Trail.

1.2 Prepare to climb the steep Dam Hill out of the gorge. Reach the top and continue following the TRAIL 3 signs to the left.

1.5 Continue right and ignore the trail on the left.

1.8 Continue straight at the four-way intersection.

2.2 At an unmarked intersection; continue straight. A trail map will be on the right in a short distance.

2.3 Turn right onto Trail 4, the Australia Loop.

2.7 Turn right again at a sign for Trail 4.

3.1 Turn right onto Trail 5, Yooper Looper, and continue uphill. This loop has many intersecting trails. Follow the blue square signs marked with a "5" and you won't get lost.

3.5 Turn right onto the connector trail to Churning Rapids. Climb steadily toward the Sunset Trail. The Yooper Looper continues downhill to the left.

3.9 At the top of a hill, turn right at a four-way intersection onto a wide gravel road, the Sunset Trail. Stay to the right, following the perimeter of Churning Rapids. Ignore all other roads.

4.6 Turn left at a T intersection onto an unsigned road.

4.8 Turn left onto a rough doubletrack that turns almost immediately into a singletrack. The road you are currently on curves to the right. Soon cross a long wooden bridge over a marsh.

A grassy meadow opens up the views at Churning Rapids.

5.3 Turn right and almost immediately right again. Cycle around a gate. In less than 0.5 mile, pass Lookout Landing, an observation tower with Lake Superior views.

5.9 Turn left and cycle downhill into the woods on the Thoroughfare Trail.

6.4 Turn right at a four-way intersection and onto an unsigned single-track trail, Cross Cut II. Enter the John Christiansen Wildlife Sanctuary, named after the former owner.

6.75 Turn left at the trail intersection onto Finney Creek Trail and then an immediate right onto Crosscut I. Picturesque Finney Creek dumps back out onto Thoroughfare. This is an easier route. If in doubt of your skills, turn here, and pick up the route description at about Mile 9.0.

6.9 Watch out! Steep hill ahead.

7.0 Turn left at the trail intersection with Lake Annie Trail and then right immediately onto the Great Oaks Trail. Only three more gullies to go. Take Lake Annie Trail back to Thoroughfare if you have had enough.

7.9 Intersection with Thoroughfare Trail; turn left and begin climbing. A right turn dumps out to Michigan 203.

9.0 Turn right onto Crosscut III. Head slightly downhill along Spring Creek and then back out to the clearcut.

9.5 Stay left at an intersection onto Crosscut IV.

9.8	Continue straight onto Crosscut V.
10.0	Make a soft right, heading slightly downhill, back onto the Hiito Highway. A hard right leads to Grassy Lane. You are now heading back to the Maasto Hiihto Trails.
10.4	Rejoin the Yooper Looper and coast downhill.
10.6	Trail turns into the woods on the left. Look for the blue sign with a "5."
10.8	Yooper Looper ends. Turn right back onto the Australia Loop, Trail 4.
12.1	Stay right and look for the blue Trail 4 markers.
12.3	Turn right onto the Gorge Trail, Trail 3.
12.5	Stay left at an intersection.
12.7	You are about to descend Anaerobic Gulch, a steep hill with many loose rocks. Sidewinder Pass, on the left, bypasses the Gulch for a gentler descent.
12.9	Stay right at the bottom of Anaerobic Gulch. Cross the creek and climb Sisu Hill out of the gorge.
13.2	Turn right at the top of the hill onto Mieto Loop, Trail 6. Follow the ridge downhill, always bearing right.
13.4	Make a hard left and cycle steeply uphill.
13.7	Turn right at an intersection with the Gorge Trail, Trail 3.
13.9	Turn right and head back to the Houghton County Arena.
14.2	Back at the parking lot, don't forget to leave a donation if you enjoyed the ride.

Mount Lookout

Location:	Eagle Harbor.
Distance:	7.6 miles out and back.
Time:	1–2 hours; allow time to enjoy the views.
Tread:	0.8 mile of paved road, 6.8 miles of double-track.
Aerobic level:	Moderately strenuous; 800-foot gain in 3.4 miles.
Technical difficulty:	2 +; loose rock and sand.
Hill factor:	Highlands.
Highlights:	Amazing views of the entire Keweenaw Peninsula, including Isle Royale.
Land status:	Lake Superior Land Company (Commercial Forest Act land). Landowner graciously permits mountain bikers to use trails; please respect property and stay on established roads.
Maps:	USGS Eagle Harbor, Delaware.
Access:	In the village of Eagle Harbor, park along the sandy beach on Michigan 26, just west of the Shoreline Motel.

Notes on the trail: This ride has the feel of a Western-style trail: a steep climb ending with spectacular views. The climbing begins almost as soon as you turn off the main road onto a rough snowmobile trail. A sand trap at the beginning of the ride forces most cyclists off their bikes, and the obstacles increase the higher you go. The doubletrack, however, is wide enough to allow riders to cycle around most of the rocks. Views begin at about 2.8 miles; 1 mile later you have arrived at the top of Mount Lookout. On a clear day Isle Royale National Park is visible to the north. Lake Bailey looms below you, while the forest wraps around Mount Lookout like a sea. Consider cycling past your car after your fast descent off the mountain and follow the signs to the Eagle Harbor Museum and Lighthouse.

The Ride

0.0 Cycle east out of town on M–26. Continue south on the Eagle Harbor Cutoff Road when M–26 turns east and head uphill toward Delaware.

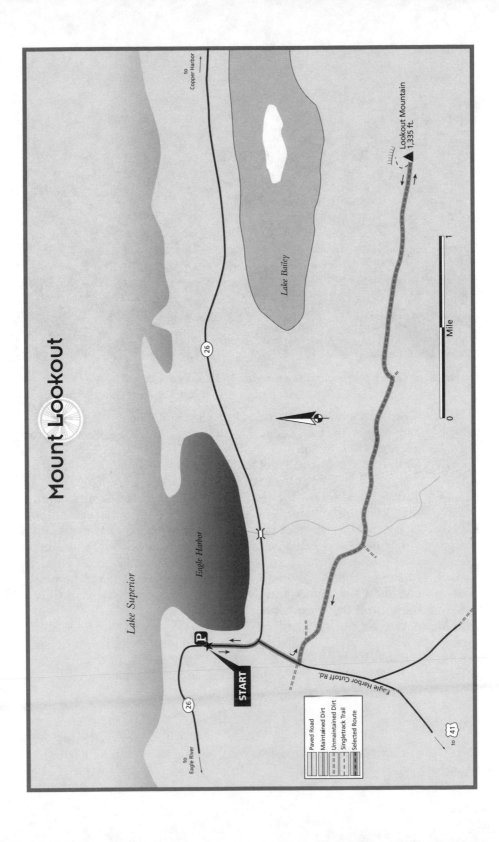

Lake Superior views are endless from the top of Mount Lookout.

0.4 Turn left onto a doubletrack after a snowmobile crossing sign.
0.6 Stay right at the fork and follow the snowmobile signs. Prepare for a steep, sandy uphill.
1.2 Leave the snowmobile trail and turn left onto a doubletrack. Head downhill to a creek crossing.
2.4 Turn left and follow the well-worn path. The doubletrack continues steeply uphill.
2.8 Enjoy the first views of the ride, a preview of more to come.
3.1 Cycle out to a clearing. Your destination is now in sight; continue the uphill grind.
3.8 At the summit, enjoy the Lake Superior views. Follow the twisting, short singletrack to different viewpoints. Retrace your tracks back down the mountain.
7.6 Arrive back at your car.

Copper Harbor Mountain Bike Trail System

Location:	Copper Harbor.
Distance:	11.8-mile loop.
Time:	1–3 hours.
Tread:	1.2 miles of paved road, 3.3 miles of dirt road, 2.0 miles of doubletrack, 5.3 miles of single-track.
Aerobic level:	Moderately strenuous.
Technical difficulty:	2–4; rocks, roots, mud, innovative bridges, and treacherous downhills.
Hill factor:	Hilly to highlands.
Highlights:	Soaring singletrack rambles through dense forest with views of the Keweenaw Peninsula and historical side trips.
Land status:	Fort Wilkins State Park, Keweenaw County, and Commercial Forest Act land. Landowner graciously allows mountain bikers to use trails; please respect property and stay on existing trails.
Maps:	USGS Fort Wilkins, Lake Medora; maps available at Keweenaw Adventure Company (see Appendix A).
Access:	From downtown Copper Harbor, turn east at the blinking light onto U.S. 41. Turn south again onto Second Street. Park to the west, just before Lake Fanny Hooe Resort.

Notes on the trail: This trail system is a ride through Copper Country history. Starting at the Lake Fanny Hooe Resort, the original site of the Fort Wilkin's Garden, the trail leads to the 377-acre Estivant Pines Sanctuary, a stand of old-growth Eastern white pine. Mechanized vehicles of any type are strictly prohibited here, so drop your bike before strolling through the forest. Later the Red Trail climbs steeply past the Keweenaw Mountain Lodge and continues along an old hiking trail, both 1930s WPA projects. Cyclists need to thank local fat-tire enthusiasts for grooming the excellent singletrack trails. For a thorough introduction to the Copper Harbor trails,

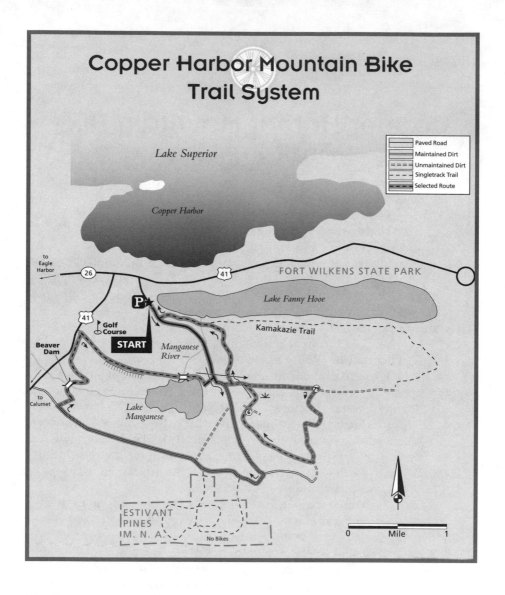

Copper Harbor Mountain Bike Trail System

Lake Superior

Copper Harbor

	Paved Road
	Maintained Dirt
	Unmaintained Dirt
	Singletrack Trail
	Selected Route

to
Eagle
Harbor

FORT WILKENS STATE PARK

Lake Fanny Hooe

Golf
Course

START

Beaver
Dam

Manganese
River

Kamakazie Trail

to
Calumet

Lake
Manganese

79

6

ESTIVANT
PINES
IM. N. A.

No Bikes

0   Mile   1

join Sam Raymond at the Keweenaw Adventure Company for Thursday-night group rides during summer.

The Ride

0.0   From the parking area, continue riding up Second Street and pass Lake Fanny Hooe on the left.

0.9   After a steady climb, reach an intersection with a lake access road and turn left. The pavement soon ends and becomes a dirt road. Stay on the main road and ignore the doubletracks bombarding you from all sides. Follow the E. PINES (Estivant Pines) signs.

1.9 Turn right at the sign pointing toward E. Pines.

2.4 Reach the entrance to the Estivant Pines Wilderness Sanctuary. Remember that mountain bikes are not allowed. After leaving the Estivant Pines, continue pedaling on the dirt road and ignore all other doubletracks and roads.

4.2 Turn right onto a doubletrack, marked with red and blue triangles painted onto surrounding trees. This is the beginning of the Red Trail Loop. If you reach U.S. 41, you have missed the turn.

4.6 Turn left at the red and blue triangles.

4.65 Stay left with the red and blue triangles as the doubletrack narrows into a singletrack.

4.7 Cross a small pond on a bridge of sticks and logs over a beaver dam. Slip into your low gear for a series of steep climbs.

5.4 Turn right onto a brushy trail.

5.6 Turn right again. Stay in low gear for an extended climb. A left turn here leads to U.S. 41.

5.8 The Keweenaw Mountain Lodge Golf Course is on the left. Continue pedaling up the service road that runs parallel to the fourth-hole fairway.

6.0 Look for a red triangle painted on a tree; turn right onto a bypass, created by the lodge for mountain bikers, behind the fifth-hole tee-off. Do not cut across the tee-off or fairway. The trail soon becomes a singletrack, which hugs the ridgeline and dips up and down for the next mile.

6.7 Pass a sign on the right warning about a steep hill. This is not a joke; proceed with caution.

7.0 Cross a boggy area on a series of rickety bridges.

7.4 Cross a stable but narrow bridge at the mouth of Manganese Creek. After the bridge, climb steeply to the left.

7.6 The singletrack temporarily becomes a doubletrack. Look for the red and blue markings on a tree to the right, and continue on the singletrack as it parallels the lake. After another short but spooky downhill, the singletrack ends at the Lake Manganese public access road. Continue riding up the paved access road.

7.8 Arrive back at the same intersection you reached at Mile 0.9. Turn right off the paved road. This section should look familiar. Turn left up a doubletrack in less than 0.1 mile. Cut the ride short by taking the paved road back to your vehicle.

8.3 Cycle past Black Bear Trail on the right, and continue climbing.

8.6 Turn right onto Surprise Valley at the ski trail sign marked with a "7" and a "9."

9.2 Come to an open area and look to the right for the blue triangles painted on trees. Follow the faint trail as it rolls through a brushy area.

9.8 Dump out at a road with another ski trail sign, marked with a "6." Turn right onto the road and immediately turn left at the

Keith cruises over rough boardwalk on the Copper Harbor Mountain Bike Trail System.

blue triangle painted on a tree. Continue on the rough trail. Soon cross over a marshy area on a bridge. Continue up a steep, soft hill.

10.2 The trail ends by merging with an earlier trail. Continue downhill. Soon turn right onto the Swaney Singletrack, marked by a blue triangle.

10.8 Reach a boggy area and push your bike over the planks.

10.9 Paul's Plunge, the upcoming descent, is for those with nerves of steel; the rest of us walk our bikes.

11.1 Reach the end of the hill. Turn left onto the Kamakazie Ski Trail at an intersection,

11.2 Cross the bridge over Manganese Creek. Enjoy the view of cascading waters. Reach a trail intersection soon after the bridge; stay right and continue downhill.

11.4 Turn left and follow the ski trail arrow.

11.6 Turn right at the paved road.

11.8 Reach the parking area.

66

Harlow Lake Sampler

Location:	6.5 miles north of Marquette.
Distance:	9.8-mile loop.
Time:	2–3 hours. Allow time to soak in the views.
Tread:	7.8 miles of narrow and wide singletrack, 1.3 miles of doubletrack, 0.7 mile of dirt road.
Aerobic level:	Moderately strenuous.
Technical difficulty:	3 to 3+.
Hill factor:	Hilly to highlands.
Highlights:	Cycle along rocky Lake Superior shoreline and climb to a forest overlook.
Land status:	Escanaba River State Forest, Gwinn Unit.
Maps:	USGS Harlow Lake; maps available at area bike stores (see Appendix A).
Access:	From the intersection of Wright Street and Marquette County Road 550/Sugar Loaf Avenue in Marquette, turn north onto CR 550. Continue for about 6.5 miles and turn east into the Little Presque Isle/Song Bird Trail parking area. If you cross the Harlow Creek Bridge, you have gone too far. Park in the Song Bird parking lot (first on the left).

Notes on the trail: If you have time for only one ride in the Marquette area, this is the one. Although Marquette County is riddled with unmarked singletrack, most of the trails are confusing to the uninitiated. This popular trail system welcomes both newcomers and seasoned locals with its fairly well-marked trails. Combining sections of the North Country Trail, Harlow Lake Trails, and Song Bird Trail, the route boasts some of the best views in the Marquette area. Jumping in and out of forest, up to a rocky lookout, and then back down to Lake Superior, the trail challenges riders with sandy sections and an extremely rocky, rooty 1-mile portion toward the end near Wetmore Landing. The occasional frustration, however, is worth it for the awesome views of Lake Superior and Little Presque Isle. More exhilarating singletrack is scattered throughout Marquette and is best discovered through one of the many bike store–sponsored group rides (see Appendix A).

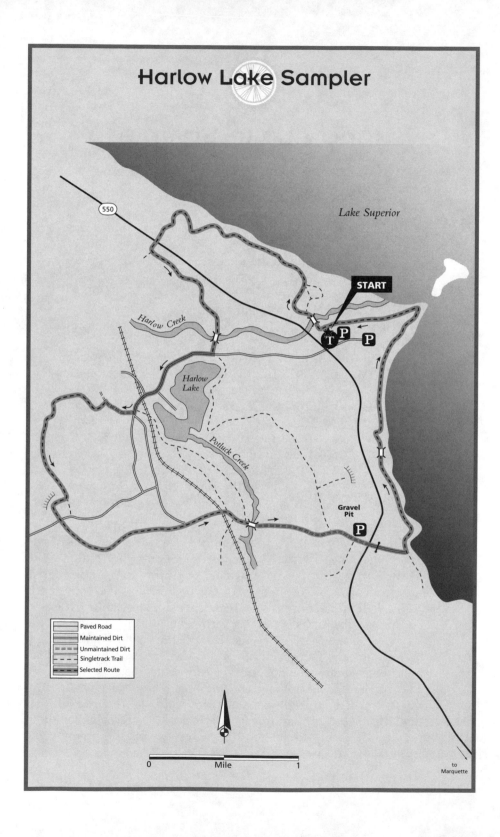

Harlow Lake Sampler

Lake Superior

550

Harlow Creek

Harlow Lake

Potluck Creek

START

T P   P

Gravel
Pit

P

Paved Road
Maintained Dirt
Unmaintained Dirt
Singletrack Trail
Selected Route

0   Mile   1

to
Marquette

The Ride

0.0 From the parking area pick up the singletrack Song Bird Trail. Soon hit a trail intersection and continue straight. Cross over Harlow Creek on a bridge and pass several other trail intersections. Continue straight and follow the signs for the North Country Trail.

0.3 Stay left with the North Country Trail. Lake Superior is on the right. Continuing straight leads back to the parking area. The next section twists and turns, becoming quite sandy next to Lake Superior before heading back into the woods. Follow the blue triangles/paint at unmarked intersections.

1.9 Cross County Road 550 and continue on the singletrack. Soon reach a signed intersection. Stay left and follow the arrow for Harlow Lake.

2.5 Cruise past an intersection and follow the blue triangles/paint on the trees.

2.7 Cross Harlow Creek on a bridge. Soon reach a dirt road and turn right. Harlow Lake is in front of you.

3.2 Cruise past a road on the left.

3.3 Turn left onto an unmarked dirt road. The old railroad grade is on the right.

Erin walks her bike through a technical section on the Harlow Lake Sampler.

3.4 Reach a multiple-trail intersection. Stay right, head uphill on a doubletrack, and follow the blue signs. Soon come to a fork; stay right.

3.6 Turn left at another fork and up a hill onto a wide singletrack.

4.7 Reach the top after a steady climb. Look for the singletrack on the right leading to a rocky lookout, and push (ride if you can!) your bike to the top. Enjoy the views of the forest and Lake Superior. Pick up the trail again to the right of the lookout for a fast, technical downhill.

4.9 Cruise over a dirt road at the bottom of the hill and continue on the singletrack.

6.1 Come to an intersection with the railroad grade and continue straight onto a wide trail. Soon reach a sign and follow the arrow for Gravel Pit parking.

6.3 Cross over Potluck Creek on a bridge to the left of the barricade. The trail widens to a doubletrack.

6.9 Reach an intersection with a posted map, and continue straight.

7.2 Reach the Gravel Pit parking and cross County Road 550. Continue straight on the dirt road and pedal around the gate.

7.4 Reach Lake Superior. Cycle next to the fence on a wide trail and follow the blue paint and North Country Trail signs.

7.8 After a rocky, technical section next to the lake, hoist your bike and climb the stairs.

8.1 Cross a gully on a wooden bridge, with Lake Superior on the right.

8.4 Reach another staircase and carry your bike back down to the beach. The most difficult section of the ride is over. Pick up the singletrack and cycle next to Lake Superior. The trail becomes sandier as the route returns to Little Presque Isle Point. Reach Little Presque Isle Point and follow the blue markings away from the lake and into the woods.

9.7 Turn left at a T intersection back toward the parking area.

9.8 End of ride.

Hill Street Trails

Location:	Ishpeming.
Distance:	6.2-mile loop.
Time:	1–2 hours.
Tread:	6.2 miles of wide trails and doubletracks.
Aerobic level:	Moderate.
Technical difficulty:	2 to 2+; route finding is one of the biggest challenges.
Hill factor:	Hilly.
Highlights:	Rugged doubletracks soar and plummet with views of Cleveland Cliffs' Tilden Iron Ore Mine.
Land status:	Cleveland Cliffs Inc. Landowner graciously allows mountain bikes to use designated trails; please respect property and stay on established trails.
Maps:	USGS Ishpeming; maps available at area bike stores (see Appendix A).
Access:	From the intersection of Business 28/Lakeshore Drive and U.S. 41 in Ishpeming, drive 1.4 miles east on Business 28 as it becomes Division Street. Turn south onto Jasper Street and continue until the road splits. Take the right fork on Hill Street and continue to the parking area at the end of the road.

Notes on the trail: The aptly named Hill Street Trails are part of the impressive Range Mountain Bike Trail System, which also includes the nearby Al Quaal Recreation Area and Suicide Bowl Trails. Developed during 1997, the system boasts about 25 miles of trails, mostly cross-country skiing routes, and is currently in a transitory state. With the Cleveland Cliffs mining company reopening operations on its land used for the Suicide Bowls and new, exciting trails in development near the Al Quaal Recreation Area, this trail system will be putting a new face forward in the next year or so.

The Hill Street Trails, however, are firmly rooted in their rugged doubletrack past. The route described here follows the perimeter of the system up and down steep hills and past inland lakes and offers views of the Tilden Mine. This ride is best done during a dry spell, since mud is often

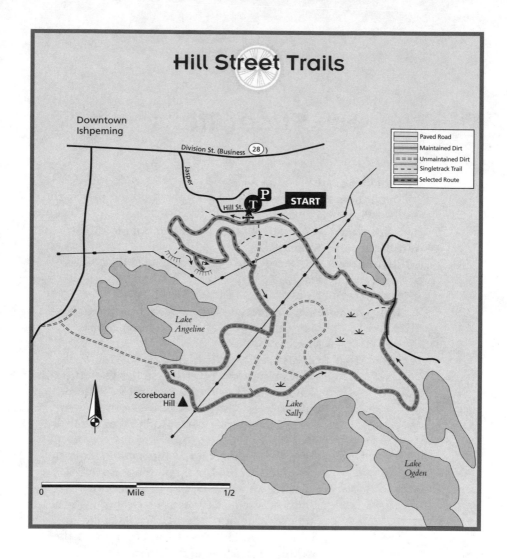

Hill Street Trails

Downtown
Ishpeming

Division St. (Business (28))

Jasper

P

T **START**

Hill St.

Paved Road
Maintained Dirt
Unmaintained Dirt
Singletrack Trail
Selected Route

*Lake
Angeline*

Scoreboard
Hill ▲

*Lake
Sally*

*Lake
Ogden*

0   Mile   1/2

a problem. It is also a route-finding challenge with minimal signage. A few ridiculously steep hills highlight the difficult Sandi's Loop, and trees touch overhead in places for a tunnel effect. Riders looking to explore other sections of the Range Mountain Bike Trail System should hook up with group rides leaving from Maple Lane Sports (see Appendix A) on Wednesday night.

The Ride

0.0 From the southwest corner of the parking lot, cycle beneath the gate and climb the hill. Turn right at the T intersection.

0.3 Stay right at a fork. Soon reach another fork and stay left.

0.7 Reach the turnoff for the first lookout on the right. Soon pass a trail coming in on the left; continue straight.

0.9 Turn right toward the next lookout over Lake Angeline. Enjoy the views and retrace your tracks to the main trail.

1.1 Turn right back onto the trail and continue on the main trail.

1.5 Make a hard right onto a wide trail. This turn is easy to miss! Soon cruise down a hill and come out to the power lines. Turn right onto a possibly muddy doubletrack.

1.9 Come to a fork in the trail just past the second power lines, and stay right up a hill.

2.1 Reach another intersection at the top of the hill, and turn right.

2.4 Ignore the doubletrack coming in on the right, and continue straight. Soon hit the power lines again.

2.8 Reach a T intersection after climbing a hill, and make a hard left. Continue up the extremely steep hill on rough trail.

3.0 Reach the top of Scoreboard Hill. Power lines are in front of you.

3.3 Continue straight as another trail peels off to the left.

3.5 Continue straight again where another trail comes in on the left.

3.7 and **3.9** Ignore trails on the left, and cycle straight.

4.2 Stay straight, with another trail on the left.

5.1 Dump out onto an old paved road, and turn left.

5.2 Soon reach a multiple-trail intersection. Turn left onto the second left-hand trail, heading in a northwesterly direction. Soon bear right at a trail intersection and head up a hill.

5.65 Stay right.

5.8 At another multiple-trail intersection, turn left and cycle underneath the power lines. At a multiple-trail intersection, stay on the most-worn path.

6.1 Reach another trail intersection (you've been here before) and turn right. Cruise underneath the gate.

6.2 Arrive back at parking area.

Appendix A:
Map Sources and Group Rides
Mentioned in the Book

Adrian

Maps for Heritage Park:
Adrian Locksmith and Cyclery
611 North Main Street
Adrian, MI 49221
(517) 263–1415

Copper Harbor

Thursday-night group mountain bike rides and maps for Copper Harbor trails:
Keweenaw Adventure Company
145 Gratiot Street/U.S. 41 (P.O. Box 70)
Copper Harbor, MI 49918
(906) 289–4303
www.keweenawadventure.com

Grayling

Maps for Hanson Hills:
Chamber of Commerce/Visitor Center
213 North James Street (City Park)
Grayling, MI 49738
(989) 348–2921

Houghton

Maps for Maasto/Hiito trails:
Visitor Center/Chamber of Commerce
326 Shelden Avenue
Houghton, MI 49931
(906) 482–5240

Ironwood

Tuesday-night group mountain bike rides and maps for Wolverine:
Trek & Trail
1310 East Cloverland Drive
Ironwood, MI 49938
(906) 932–5858
www.trekandtrail.net

Ishpeming

Wednesday-night group mountain bikes rides meet at nearby Jasper Ridge Brewery and maps for area rides:
Maple Lane Sports
Country Village
1015 Country Lane
Ishpeming, MI 49849
(906) 485-1636
www.exploringthenorth.com/maple/maple.html

Marquette

Thursday-night group mountain bike rides and maps for area rides:
Downwind Sports
514 North Third Street
Marquette, MI 49855
(906) 226-7112
www.downwindsports.com

Quik Stop Bike Shop
Friday-night group mountain bike rides and maps for area rides:
1100 North Third Street
Marquette, MI 49855
(906) 225-1577
www.thequickstop.com

Petoskey

Thursday-night group mountain bike rides and maps for area rides:
Fitness Source & Cycle
100 North Division Road
Petoskey, MI 49770
(231) 347-6877 or (800) 242-4188

Port Huron

Maps for Ruby Campground:
The Bicycle & Fitness Barn
1604 Stone Street
Port Huron, MI 48060
(810) 987-2523

Rogers City

Maps for Roger City trails:
Chamber of Commerce
292 South Bradley Highway
Rogers City, MI 49779
(989) 734-2535

Appendix B: Forests and Parks

Michigan Department of Natural Resources
Parks and Recreation Division
530 West Allegan Street (P.O. Box 30028)
Lansing, MI 48909
(517) 373-9900
www.dnr.state.mi.us

State Forests

Au Sable State Forest
191 South Mt. Tom Road
Mio, MI 48647
(989) 826-3211

Gladwin Unit, Au Sable State Forest
801 North Silver Leaf
Gladwin, MI 48624
(517) 426-9205

Copper Country State Forest
Box 427, U.S. 41 North
Baraga, MI 49908
(906) 353-6651

Crystal Falls Unit, Copper Country State Forest
1420 U.S. 2 West
Crystal Falls, MI 49920
(906) 875-6622

Escanaba River State Forest
6833 U.S. 2
Gladstone, MI 49837
(906) 786-2351

Gwinn Unit, Escanaba River State Forest
410 West Michigan 35
Gwinn MI 49841

(906) 346-9201
Lake Superior State Forest
Route 4, Box 796
Newberry, MI 49868
(906) 293-5131

Sault Ste. Marie District, Lake Superior State Forest
2001 Ashmun Street
Sault Ste. Marie, MI 49783
(906) 635-5281

Mackinaw State Forest, Headquarters
1732 West Michigan 32 (P.O. Box 667)
Gaylord, MI 49735
(989) 732-3541

Atlanta Unit, Mackinaw State Forest
P.O. Box 30
Atlanta, MI 49709-9605
(989) 785-4252

Indian River Unit, Mackinaw State Forest
6984 Michigan 68 (P.O. Box 10)
Indian River, MI 49749
(231) 238-9314

Pigeon River Unit, Mackinaw State Forest
9966 Twin Lakes Rd.
Vanderbilt, MI 49795
(989) 983-4101

Pere Marquette State Forest, Headquarters
8015 South U.S. 131
Cadillac, MI 49601
(616) 775-9727

Cadillac Unit, Pere Marquette
State Forest
8015 Mackinaw Trail
Cadillac, MI 49601
(231) 775-9727

Kalkaska Unit, Pere Marquette
State Forest
2089 North Birch Street
Kalkaska, MI 49646
(231) 732-3541

Traverse City Unit, Pere Marquette
State Forest
404 West Fourteenth Street
Traverse City, MI 49684
(231) 922-5280

State Parks and Recreation Areas

Bald Mountain Recreation Area
1330 East Greenshield Road
Lake Orion, MI 48360-2307
(248) 693-6767

Bass River Recreation Area
104th Avenue
Grand Haven, MI 49417
(616) 798-3711

Brighton Recreation Area
6360 Chilson Road
Howell, MI 48843
(810) 229-6566

Fort Custer Recreation Area
5163 West Fort Custer Drive
Augusta, MI 49012
(616) 731-4200

Hartwick Pines State Park
4216 Ranger Road
Grayling, MI 49012
(989) 348-7068

Highland Recreation Area
5200 East Highland Road
White Lake, MI 48383
(248) 889-3750

Holly Recreation Area
8100 Grange Hall Road
Holly, MI 48442
(248) 634-8811

Ionia Recreation Area
2880 David Highway
Ionia, MI 48846
(616) 527-3750

Island Lake Recreation Area
12950 East Grand River
Brighton, MI 48116
(810) 229-7067

Maybury State Park
20145 Beck Road
Northville, MI 48167
(248) 349-8390

Pontiac Lake Recreation Area
7800 Gale Road
Waterford, MI 48327
(248) 666-1020

Pinckney Recreation Area
8555 Silver Hill Road
Pinckney, MI 48169
(734) 426-4913

Porcupine Mountains Wilderness
State Park
412 South Boundary Road
Ontonagon, MI 49953
(906) 885-5275

Rifle River Recreation Area
2550 East Rose City Road
Lupton, MI 48635
(989) 473-2258

Sleepy Hollow State Park
7835 Price Road
Laingsburg, MI 48848
(517) 651-6217

Yankee Springs Recreation Area
2104 Gun Lake Road
Middleville, MI 49333
(616) 795-9081

Other Parks and Resorts

Boyne Mountain Ski Area
1 Boyne Mountain Road
Boyne Falls, MI 49713
(231) 549-6000
www.boyne.com

Burchfield Park
881 Grovenburg
Holt, MI 48842
(517) 676-2233
www.ingham.org/PK/Burchfield.htm

Cannonsburg Ski Area
6800 Cannonsburg Road (P.O. Box 19)
Cannonsburg, MI 49317
(616) 874-6711
www.cannonsburg.com

Crystal Mountain Resort
12500 Crystal Mountain Drive
Thompsonville, MI 49683
(800) 968-7686
www.crystalmountain.com

Deerfield County Park
2425 West Remus Road
Mt. Pleasant, MI 48858
(989) 772-2879

Dr. T. K. Lawless County Park
15122 Monkey Run Street
Vandalia, MI 49095
(616) 476-2730
www.casscoroad.com/lawless.htm

Ella Sharp Park
3225 Fourth Street
Jackson, MI 49203
(517) 787-2320

Hanson Hills Recreation Area
7601 West Old Lake Road
Grayling, MI 49738
(989) 348-9266
www.hansonhills.org

Pine Haven Recreation Area, Midland County Park
Maynard Street
Midland, MI 48640
(989) 832-6870

National Forest Service

Hiawatha National Forest Headquarters
2727 North Lincoln Road
Escanaba, MI 49829
(906) 786-4062
www.fs.fed.us/r9/hiawatha

Rapid River Ranger District
8181 U.S. 2
Rapid River, MI 49878
(906) 474-6442

Manistique Ranger District
499 East Lake Shore Drive
Manistique, MI 49854
(906) 341-5666

Munising Ranger District
400 East Munising Avenue
Munising, MI 49862
(906) 387-2512

Sault Ste. Marie Ranger District
4000 I-75 Business Spur
Sault St. Marie, MI 49783
(906) 635-5311

St. Ignace Ranger District
1798 West U.S. 2
St. Ignace, MI 49781
(906) 643-7900

Huron-Manistee National Forest Headquarters
1755 South Mitchell Street
Cadillac, MI 49601
(231) 775-2421 or (800) 821-6263
www.fs.fed.us/r9/hmnf

Baldwin/White Cloud Ranger Station
650 North Michigan Avenue
Baldwin, MI 49304
(231) 745-4631

Manistee Ranger Station
412 Red Apple Road
Manistee, MI 49660
(231) 723-2211

Mio Ranger Station
401 Court Street
Mio, MI 48647
(989) 826-3252

Huron Shores Ranger Station
5761 North Skeel Road
Oscoda, MI 48750
(989) 739-0728

Ottawa National Forest Headquarters
6248 U.S. 2
Ironwood, MI 49938
(906) 932-1330
www.fs.fed.us/r9/ottawa

Bessemer Ranger District
500 North Moore Street
Bessemer, MI 49911
(906) 932-1330

Iron River Ranger District
990 Lalley Road
Iron River, MI 49935
(906) 265-5139

Kenton Ranger District
Michigan 28, Box 198
Kenton, MI 49967
(906) 852-3500

Ontonagon Ranger District
1209 Rockland Road
Ontonagon, MI 49953
(906) 884-2085

Watersmeet Ranger District/ Visitor Center/Interpretive Association
Old U.S. 2 (P.O. Box 276)
Watersmeet, MI 49969
(906) 358-4551

Seney Wildlife Refuge
Michigan 77
Seney, MI 49883
(906) 586-9851
midwest.fws.gov/seney

Appendix C: Advocacy Groups, Racing, and Tourism

Advocacy Groups

International Mountain Biking
Association
P.O. Box 7578
Boulder, CO 80306
(303) 545–9011
www.imba.com

League of Michigan Bicyclists
P.O. Box 16201
Lansing, MI 48901
(517) 334–9100 or (888) 642–4537
www.lmb.org

Michigan Mountain Biking
Association
4217 Highland Road #268
Waterford, MI 48327
(248) 288–3753
www.mmba.org

North Country Trail Association
229 East Main Street
Lowell, MI 499331
(888) 454–NCTA
www.northcountrytrail.org

Pigeon River Country Association
P.O. Box 122
Gaylord, MI 49734
(989) 983–4101
www.otsego.org/prca

Rails-to-Trails Conservancy,
Michigan Field Office
416 South Cedar Street, Suite C
Lansing, MI 48912
(517) 485–6022
www.railtrails.org/MI

Top of Michigan Trails Council
445 East Mitchell Street
Petoskey, MI 49770
(616) 348–8280
www.topofmichigantrails.org

Traverse Area Recreation and
Transportation Trails (TART)
P.O. Box 252
Traverse City, MI 49685
(231) 941–4300
www.traversetrails.org

Tuesday Night Fat Tire Club
Trek & Trail
1310 East Cloverland Drive
Ironwood, MI 49938
(906) 932–5858
www.trekandtrail.net

Racing

Fun Promotions
P.O. Box 1383
Grand Rapids, MI 49501
(616) 453–4245
www.funpromotions.com

Iceman Promotions
P.O. Box 3127
Traverse City, MI 49685–3127
(231) 922–5926
www.iceman.com

Mountain Chase
P.O. Box 40
Marquette, MI 49855
(888) 578–5499
www.mountainchase.com

Ore to Shore Mountain Bike Epic
P.O. Box 864
Marquette, MI 49855
(888) 578-6489
www.oretoshore.com

Tailwind Enterprises
5805 Ormond Road
Davisburg, MI 48350
(248) 634-6178
www.tailwind.net

Also see the Michigan Mountain Biking Association under "Advocacy Groups."

Tourism and Travel Information

Metropolitan Detroit
211 West Fort Street, Suite 1000
Detroit, MI 48226
(800) DETROIT
www.vistdetroit.com

Michigan's Sunrise Side Travel Association
1361 Fletcher Street
National City, MI 48748
(800) 424-3022
www.misunriseside.com

Travel Michigan
P.O. Box 3393
Livonia, MI 48151
(888) 78-GREAT
www.michigan.org

Upper Peninsula Travel and Recreation Association
P.O. Box 400
Iron Mountain, MI 49801
(800) 562-7134
www.uptravel.com

Western Michigan Tourist Association
1253 Front Avenue, NW
Grand Rapids, MI 49504
(800) 442-2084
www.wmta.org

Keith Radwanski and Erin Fanning PHOTO BY JOAN RADWANSKI

About the Authors

Keith and Erin quit their jobs in 1998 to travel full-time in their recreational vehicle. This led to numerous adventures—from kayaking in Lake Superior to mountain biking Sedona's red rocks—and culminated with researching and writing this book. Today they split their time between Erin's native Idaho and Keith's home state of Michigan, where Keith is a manufacturer's representative. Erin is a freelance writer and researcher whose articles have appeared in *Silent Sports, Michigan Sports and Fitness, Oregon Outside,* and *RV Life.* Keith and Erin are both members of the Michigan Mountain Biking Association, and Erin is active with the Top of Michigan Trails Council.